Manchester Studies in Religion, Culture and Gender

Literature, theology and feminism

Manchester University Press

edited by Grace M. Jantzen

Already published

Religion and culture
Michel Foucault
selected and edited by Jeremy R. Carrette

Representations of the post/human
Monsters, aliens and others in popular culture
Elaine L. Graham

Becoming divine
Towards a feminist philosophy of religion
Grace M. Jantzen

Divine Love
Luce Irigaray, women, gender, and religion
by Morny Joy

Manchester Studies in Religion, Culture and Gender

Literature, theology and feminism

Heather Walton

Manchester University Press

Manchester and New York

distributed exclusively in the USA by Palgrave

The right of Heather Walton to be identified as the author of this work has been asserted by her in accordance with the Copyright, Designs and Patents Act 1988.

Published by Manchester University Press
Oxford Road, Manchester M13 9NR, UK
and Room 400, 175 Fifth Avenue, New York, NY 10010, USA
www.manchesteruniversitypress.co.uk

Distributed exclusively in the USA by
Palgrave, 175 Fifth Avenue, New York, NY 10010, USA

Distributed exclusively in Canada
UBC Press, University of British Columbia, 2029 West Mall,
Vancouver, BC, Canada V6T 1Z2

British Library Cataloguing-in-Publication Data
A catalogue record for this book is available from the British Library

ISBN 978 0 7190 6090 8 hardback

First published 2007

16 15 14 13 12 11 10 09 08 07   10 9 8 7 6 5 4 3 2 1

Typeset in Joanna with Frutiger display
by Koinonia, Manchester
Printed in Great Britain
by CPI, Bath

For Reinier

CONTENTS

Acknowledgements   *page* ix

Introduction   1

Part I   The uses of literature

1   If literature is a girl   10

2   Visions and revisions   37

3   Beyond the one and the other   60

4   The problems with poststructuralism   77

Part II   Feminist religious reading

5   Julia Kristeva and journeys to the end of night   96

6   Luce Irigaray and the threshold of the divine   125

7   Hélène Cixous and the mysteries that beat in the heart of the world   144

8   An open conclusion   167

Postscript: Reading Elizabeth Smart   174

References   194

Index   209

ACKNOWLEDGEMENTS

I would to like to express love and thanks to my parents and grandparents who filled my life full of books and poems, sermons and stories.

Particular thanks are also due to Reinier Holst, who is my greatest encourager and most radical critic. Also to David Jasper whose own work provided the initial inspiration for this book and whose helpful advice and good humour have sustained me throughout its preparation. Many others have also helped me a great deal along the way. I am indebted to all those friends and colleagues who offered their creative advice, criticism and support as my ideas began to take shape. Amongst these are Elaine Graham, Frankie Ward, Ann Jones, Helen Baston, Erica Burman, Ian Parker, Gennie Georgaca, Pamela Anderson, Yvonne Sherwood, Alison Jasper, Susan Durber, Stuart Robbins, Jane Hodges, Ian Stephens, Alec Mitchell, Linda Balfe, Sian Long, Will Storrar and Angel Gordo-Lopez. Thanks are also due to the editor of this series, Grace Jantzen, and to the staff of Manchester University Press.

An earlier version of parts of Chapter 1 appeared as 'Literature and Theology: Sex in the Relationship' in D. Bird and Y. Sherwood (eds) *Bodies in Question*, Aldershot: Ashgate (2005). I am grateful for permission to make further use of this material.

Introduction

The purpose of this book is to generate a critical framework through which to interrogate the way in which religious feminists have employed women's literature in their texts. This is in order that both the way we read literature and the literature we read might be subject to scrutiny, and that new reading practices be developed.

This process will reveal how conventional understandings of the relation between literature and theology have been reproduced within feminist scholarship in ways that now merit critical attention. It will also expose the lack of engagement with poststructuralist theory which has been so influential in shaping current understandings of the politics of reading and the nature of texts. The reluctance by religious feminists to allow poststructuralism to influence their readings of women's literature is particularly significant given the fact that feminist biblical scholars and philosophers of religion have found it to be such a useful resource in their work.[1] I shall argue that there are key insights found in the work of women poststructuralist thinkers that point towards more creative ways of engaging with women's literature than are currently practised. Underlying my call for new ways of reading is a conviction that feminist theology requires the continual challenge and provocation of women's creative writing. However, we deprive ourselves of the full benefits of this creative resource if we continually employ the energies of literature to serve our own political project – rather than allowing our own visions and aspirations to be challenged by the imaginative power of literary texts.

The uses of literature

Having both a critical and constructive agenda, this is a book in two parts. In Part I I locate my study of the use of women's writing by religious feminists in a much

---

1 The most notable exception to this general rule lies in the way a number of religious feminists have embraced the work of Foucault in their encounter with women's writing. In chapter 3 I consider the reasons why his theories appear more acceptable than those of other post-structuralist thinkers.

wider frame than has previously been attempted. In the past individual religious feminists have been criticised, often publicly and loudly, for the use they have made of particular literary texts.[2] The criticisms made have frequently concerned the legitimacy of appropriating material produced in one context and employing it in another. Critics have typically emphasised the proprietorial rights of female authors in relation to their work and the literary significance of ethnicity, sexual identity and religious belonging. A preoccupation with these immediate political concerns has drawn attention away from academic questions concerning what might be envisioned as an appropriate interdisciplinary relationship between literature and theology. This is a shame, not only because a significant academic debate on this topic has taken place to which feminist scholars have yet to make a distinctive contribution. It is also the case that disputes in this field take us to the heart of the binary and hierarchical symbolic system out of which meaning and order are generated within Western thought. For literature and theology are gendered fields within our culture and deeply inscribed understandings of the 'masculine' and 'feminine' spheres[3] are brought into play whenever the two disciplines are placed in conjunction.

But the fact that strong conventions regulate the relations between literature and theology does not mean that these very conventions cannot be appropriated for progressive ends. It has been the political genius of poststructuralist theory that it has exploited the disruptive potential of the subordinated, feminised term in order to destabilise established discursive regimes. Long before poststructuralism, however, women had taken cultural constructions of femininity and employed them subversively to dispute male-centred understandings of such important social categories as work, citizenship and political action (see, for example, Daggers, 2000: 55). Significantly for the concerns of this book they had also begun using a 'feminine' voice to challenge received understandings of authorship and the nature of the divine.

My concern in the first part of this book is thus not to 'wish away' the gendered conventions that are brought into play when literature and theology are related but rather to make these operations apparent so that they may be subject to scrutiny and their political consequences assessed. Chapter 1, therefore, begins by establishing the ways in which a gendered complementarity is assumed to exist between literature and the logocentric discourses of theology

---

2 See pp. 46 and 61.

3 When referring to masculine and feminine spheres I am not referring to the social location of women and men but rather to the manner in which meaning is generated in Western culture through a process of distinguishing between opposing terms such as light/darkness, soul/body, reason/passion, etc. This binary system is hierarchical in that one term predominates over the other and it is gendered in that the predominant term is associated with the masculine sphere. The origins of these symbolic oppositions lie in antiquity but they continue to exercise a powerful influence today.

and philosophy.[4] The latter disciplines have been held to point with masculine clarity towards the truth about God. Literature has also been deemed worthy to testify to the divine when she stands in harmonious partnership with them. However, within the Western symbolic system true complementarity is rarely achieved and I argue that, in the case of literature and theology, until very recently complementarity has assumed subordination. Yet, in an epoch in which theological discourse has been subjected to the postmodern criticism of all grand narratives, this established hierarchy is becoming unstable. The second part of the chapter demonstrates how contemporary theology is now looking to the feminised resources of literature to sustain it in difficult times. Three contrasting approaches are explored.

Canonical narrative theologians proclaim the distinctiveness of Christian claims to truth and the divergence of the Christian narrative based on scriptural witness from other Western cultural forms. However, they establish their case through the use of literary categories and literary texts, ironically demonstrating the inadequacy of attempts to free theology from its complicity with 'alien' influences: its foreign wives.

Constructive narrative theologians are frank about the interrelationship of theology and culture and even, in the case of Don Cupitt, go as far as lamenting the alienation of theology from the feminised resources of myths, literature and storytelling. Yet in celebrating the 'fecund' nature of literary creativity the gesture they perform is once more to employ the resources of literature as support and sure foundation for their own theological endeavours.

The last approach to literature in contemporary theology explored in chapter 1 is the one I find the most challenging. Theologians who have engaged deeply with poststructuralism, not as an esoteric theoretical discourse but rather as a passionate response to the holocausts of the twentieth century, have also feminised literature and placed 'her' in an antithetical relation to theology. These *religious readers* are not looking to subordinate literature to theology but rather to challenge, deconstruct and even dismantle the machinery of theological power out of fidelity to a divine encounter that literature has pressed upon them.

Chapter 1 thus employs gender as a lens through which to examine the way that literature and theology have been related in contemporary debate. Having explored literature and theology as gendered categories I then return to more familiar territory and consider the relations between women's creative writing and feminist theology. In chapters 2 and 3 I set out two differing approaches to the use of literature by religious feminists which have predominated up till now. It will be evident that both of these draw upon the gendered conventions

---

4   The theological and philosophical disciplines are still assumed to share a fundamental relationship to each other in the work of many scholars. These are here represented by Eliot, Maritain and Cupitt in particular.

previously outlined. However, other concerns also come into play – specifically the relation of the female author to her text.

The first strategy, which is set out in chapter 2, places women's literature in contradiction to the male-centred religious tradition. I illustrate, through the representative work of Carol Christ and Alicia Ostriker, how theological sources are seen as 'male writing' and contrasted with 'women's literature' which articulates women's sacred understandings. The now contested expression 'woman's experience'[5] was of vital importance in the development of feminist theology and early works by religious feminists sought to challenge male-centred theology 'from the viewpoint of feminine experience' (Saiving, 1979: 25). Literature written by women was seen as an authentic expression of this experience. Although both Christ and Ostriker have developed more sophisticated understandings of 'women's experience' than those employed in the first works of feminist theology they continue the convention of characterising women's literature as the voice of wisdom, based on female experience, speaking out in opposition to the 'Word of the Father' articulated through philosophy and theology. Women's writing is imaged as equivalent in status to, and equally capable of representing the divine as, male writing. The gendered assumptions discussed in chapter 1 certainly lend weight to Christ's and Ostriker's representations of literature's female voice. However, these operate in the background and what both women foreground is literature as a privileged place of self-expression and experimentation for women – particularly in their relation to the divine. I argue that the development of feminist theology would not have been possible without such moves to claim women's literature as an alternative source of sacred knowledge. However, problems quickly emerged in conceptualising the new relation between women's writing and feminist theology. The tendency exists in the work of both Christ and Ostriker to blur the distinctions between the two fields, and the effect of this is to repeat the gesture, discussed in chapter 1, of annexing the territory of literature and exploiting the resources found there for theological ends.

A changing political climate in the 1980s and 1990s shifted the feminist agenda beyond differences between men and women towards the significance of differential power relations based on ethnicity, sexual identity, class or the many legacies of colonial exploitation. Within this changed environment literature written by women continued to be seen as a feminine voice raised against the discursive traditions of male authority. However, new ways of characterising

---

5   Black women and lesbians quickly disputed the assumption that female experience could be universalised. Fierce debates took place on this issue and for many years the expression became so contentious that it was difficult to use effectively in scholarly debate (see chapter 4). However, a number of feminist writers have now returned to consider whether some concept of 'women's experience' is essential to the critique of patriarchy. See, for example, Ramazanoglu and Holland (2000).

this female voice now developed. It is now the tendency identified in theology and philosophy towards abstraction and universalism that is characterised as masculine (rather than its roots in male scholarly guilds). Literature is seen as feminine because it resists these totalising powers and is always specific, located, embodied, plural, partial and dialogical. In chapter 3 the works of Katie Cannon and Kathleen Sands are taken as representative of this significant shift in emphasis.

Katie Cannon makes the bold rhetorical gesture of incarnating the specificity of African American women's writing in the ancestral figure of Zorah Neale Hurston.[6] She argues that Hurston, and the generation of women writers who claimed her legacy, transcribe in the most authentic form the spiritual inheritance of African Americans. However, Cannon struggles to find a way of relating a literature that is radically religious but defiantly 'uncanonical' to the theological traditions of the black churches. Kathleen Sands protests against a tendency she identifies within feminist theology to replace men's authority and man's God with women's experience and the female divine. She argues that such gestures are always totalising and always exclude and marginalise the other. Her work is a passionate plea for attentiveness to what literature manifests for us: all that is dissident, deviant or particular in human life. Furthermore, she challenges religious feminists not to exclude the intense pain of existence from their thinking in order to create discourses of wholeness, harmony and closure which will ultimately have the same theological consequences as male thinking. She argues that literature testifies to the real nature of the human condition and she opposes this to the theatrical gestures of *all* current forms of theology. However, herein lies the dilemma within her work. Is she able to articulate the power of literature to embody alterity as well as difference? In refusing concordat between literature and theology has she confined literature to a realm of immanence leaving theology alone to scan the heavens?

The evocative language used by Sands to characterise the marginalised and disruptive other will sound familiar to readers who have engaged with poststructuralist theory in their study of literature and/or theology. There are many affinities between poststructuralism's focus upon the trace of the other in discursive practices and the concerns of religious feminists for the embodied others who are excluded and oppressed within our social order. However, this convergence of interests, and an increasingly similar vocabulary, do not mean that the political objections that have been raised by religious feminists to poststructuralist theory have been overcome. In chapter 4 I consider the reasons why many feminist theologians have displayed a resistance to using poststructuralist theory in their reading of female-authored literary texts. This move necessitates problematising

---

6 The celebrated anthropologist and writer who is widely taken to be the precursor of the current literary awakening among black women in the United States.

such key terms as experience, woman and the body (rendering unstable the foundations of feminist identity politics). More locally, but perhaps equally painfully, it necessitates a questioning of the conventions that govern both *what texts are read* and *the way in which they are read* by religious feminists. We would be required to acknowledge that our own work is disciplined, regulated and constrained and that we are reluctant to be challenged by 'others' that we cannot incorporate or control.

It is at this point that I argue for a greater openness towards the insights of poststructuralist theory in order to create alternative patterns of engagement between women's literature and feminist theology. While the work of male poststructuralist thinkers is becoming an increasingly important resource in contemporary theological thinking (religious feminists have been particularly enthusiastic about the work of Foucault), feminist theologians have been slow to gain a deep appreciation of the religious themes that are so important in the work of women poststructuralist thinkers. This situation is now changing and the use made by Pamela Anderson (1998) and Grace Jantzen (1998) of the work of Irigaray and Kristeva in their attempts to revision the philosophy of religion is an important sign of these changing times.

Feminist religious reading

Having critically surveyed previously unacknowledged constraints under which religious feminists read women's literature, I turn in Part II to exploring how the work of women poststructuralist thinkers and theorists can enrich our reading practices and offer alternative models for an engagement between literature and theology.

Julia Kristeva is best known within the academy for her unorthodox application of Lacanian theory to contemporary culture. She characterises her own work, however, as a quest to discern how the interconnected energies of literature and the sacred represent a vital source of renewal for our deeply ailing political system. Kristeva employs the now familiar device of characterising literature as feminine and placing it in opposition to the excessive authoritarianism of paternal domination. Her work ascribes a greater transformative potential to literature than we have encountered up till now. It thus challenges religious feminists to reassess our utilitarian approaches to literary texts and enquire into whether these might have a more powerful political role when their status as literature is recognised and affirmed.

To assess the significance of Luce Irigaray's work for feminist religious readers requires us to enter into an alternative conceptual space where language is unstable and metaphors perform the work normally ascribed to logical propositions. Irigaray works within the literary/fictional space of the *feminine imaginary*. This is envisaged as a powerful generative resource entirely capable of recreating the world. Irigaray argues that just as the order we inhabit is structured according to a masculine symbolics predicated upon the phallus so it can be remade when the feminine breaks silence and claims its own language, cultural incarnation and divine image. Irigaray does not perform the work of directly associating her vision of female 'becoming divine' with the work of women artists.[7] Thus it is necessary in chapter 6 to make explicit the many implicit connections her project and the concerns of this text. What becomes apparent as I do so is how Irigaray's utopian visions and extreme faith push our understanding of sexual difference in relation to literature and theology beyond the boundaries currently contemplated by religious feminists.

Both Kristeva and Irigaray challenge religious feminists to reassess the political significance of gendered cultural forms and to accord to literature a more powerful feminine voice – which is not only that of everywoman, or those who are marginal to culture, but also an echo of the divine. Helene Cixous develops these themes further, explicitly claiming writing as a 'divine force' but also wrestling with the problem discussed in chapter 1 – namely how to work at writing literature with a full awareness of the challenges human suffering poses for all forms of artistic production. As Maurice Blanchot (1995) frames this question: how do we work at writing 'after the disaster'? It is a particular weakness of feminist theology that it is reluctant to contemplate irredeemable loss and the complicity of the divine in human tragedy. Cixous uses literature to probe these issues and her work is particularly important because she is a celebrated writer herself and a religious reader of other women's texts.

Despite her immense importance as a contemporary feminist visionary, Cixous' work has been neglected by religious feminists and this book offers one of the few close readings of her oeuvre that engages with the political and theological dynamics of her later writings. My hope is not only that her work will be recognised as the creative resource it undoubtedly is but also that feminist theologians will find that the way Cixous brings together literature, theology and politics provides an example of how feminist religious readers can themselves generate exciting, radical and ethically accountable forms of theological thinking.

In chapter 8 the implications of my readings in feminist poststructuralist theory are brought together to form an agenda for future engagements between literature and feminist theology. I do not seek here to set aside the creative inheritance of the past, but to extend the scope of our vision of what literature can contribute to our future work. Suggestions are made in this chapter as to how feminists might begin to read more adventurously. While 'reading in the dark' has its own delights, there is more waiting to be enjoyed when the lights are switched on and this chapter is an invitation to extend the scope of our reading pleasures.

---

7   Indeed she usually adopts the rhetorical position of a generic woman, which relieves her of the responsibility of interacting with other women writers.

Chapter 8 serves as a conclusion in that it completes my intended project in writing this book. However, this work is an invitation to reconsider 'the way we read literature and the literature we read', and in this respect the conclusion should not be seen as an ending but as a point of departure for further explorations. It is for this reason that I allow myself the indulgence of a postscript in which I offer my own feminist religious reading of the work of one of my favourite writers – Elizabeth Smart. Smart is introduced here neither as a heroic feminist author nor as a writer who incarnates a literary style compatible with postmodern sensibilities. Rather I read her work because I love her work. It is my hope that this example will encourage other religious feminists to return to authors they have loved (including male authors) but whose writings may not have seemed immediately relevant to their theological projects. It is my belief that these texts may contain resources vital for the creative development of feminist theology.

PART I

The uses of literature

CHAPTER 1

If literature is a girl

Terms of engagement

Reading in the dark

Why write a book exploring the interface between women's writing and feminist theology? A straightforward answer would be that there is scope to present a more detailed study of interdisciplinary work in this area than has previously been attempted. However, as well as offering a more comprehensive account of existing scholarship than is currently available, I also hope to provoke changes in understanding and practice. I seek to problematise what has been taken for granted and therefore not examined. I hope to challenge religious feminists to reassess the way they read literature and what literature they read. I want the politics of reading to become a matter of concern to the many religious feminists who use literature as a vital resource in their theological work.

With this reconstructive agenda firmly in mind this first chapter will set out to shift the frame in which religious feminists view the relations between literary and theological texts. In the past we have tended unconsciously to assume continuity between feminist theological thinking and women's creative writing. In so doing we have expressed an unexamined assumption that women's writing is distinctive and special, that it 'belongs to us' and that it can be easily seen in isolation from 'male literature'. Perhaps for this reason feminist theologians have not demonstrated a great interest in interdisciplinary debates concerning the proper relations between literature and theology. While male scholars might occupy themselves defining genres and marking disciplinary boundaries we have been quite happy to take down the garden fences and walk on the grass.

Feminist theologians are not alone in their eager appropriation of literary resources. Feminism is a peculiarly literary movement and many of the intellectual and political leaders of the women's struggle have been celebrated writers (e.g. Mary Wollstonecraft, Alexandra Kollontai, Simone de Beauvoir, Virginia Woolf). These women found in literature an accessible space in which it was possible to critique contemporary practice and engage in the imaginative construction of alternative worlds. Works of literature written by women thus form an important resource in *all* fields of feminist scholarship as they represent our most significant textual inheritance. But feminist theologians have another reason to trace their own pre-history back through works of literature. Social and spiritual deviancy are often closely woven together in women's creative writing, which abounds in vivid and unorthodox namings of the divine.

Women's literature has thus been very useful to religious feminists. Our texts are adorned with quotations from favourite authors whose political aspirations and spiritual audacity appear to mirror our own precisely – and yet. Perhaps this easy usefulness masks a difficult problem? Surveying feminist religious scholarship at the end of the 1980s, Carol Christ and Judith Plaskow were moved to declare that Alice Walker's novel *The Color Purple* was the most widely quoted 'theological text' of the day (1989: 5). But what is going on when literature is seen, in Christ and Plaskow's words, as 'theological text'? Does literature then cease to be literature or does theology become a form of creative writing? Do we employ the same sets of reading skills in relation to both categories of discourse? What is the relation between form and content in theological and literary texts? Are questions of political power acknowledged and addressed when texts and traditions are brought into new conjunctions by religious feminists?

These are not issues that have been widely debated and even the raising of such questions might be seen as inimical to the feminist project. Many feminists treasure the dream of a world in which boundaries are transgressed and the traditional disciplinary categories that have regulated knowledge wither away. A creative confusion of literary and theological genres would thus appear something to be welcomed rather than warned against. This is an attractive position that celebrates the fact that it has always been impossible to make a decisive separation between the two worlds. If we rush to celebrate the breaching of traditional boundaries, however, we may fail to address the questions that confront us when we dwell on the borders of these two ancient territories. As a consequence we may not only be accused of critical naivety but we may also miss the opportunity to have our own projects challenged and transformed through a deeper engagement with literary texts *as works of literature*.

So the first move in problematising current assumptions about the use of women's literature in feminist theology is to cut the cords that bind them and make a heuristic distinction between the two fields. This immediately shifts the frame because women's literature then ceases to be the 'pre-text' of feminist theology and reassumes its status as literature. In a situation in which women's creative writing could be conflated with feminist theology its connection to male literature did not need to become the focus of attention. Nor did we need to ask whether feminist theology was repeating, in its own uses of literary texts, gestures established by male theologians in the past. If its literary status is reasserted, then religious feminists can begin to make their own contributions to conversations concerning the proper relations of literature and theology. This is the concern of

11

the rest of this chapter, in which I shall argue that an awareness of sexual politics and our customary 'hermeneutics of suspicion' can generate new insights into some of the disputes that are currently most crucial in theological study. Much is at stake in the apparently simple question, 'What is the relation between literature and theology?': issues that matter to women. Important battles are currently being fought across this terrain, but religious feminists have yet to make their own significant contributions to these debates.

Contesting definitions

To begin to offer a feminist perspective on the interdisciplinary study of literature and theology it is necessary to explore some of the ways in which the relation between the disciplines has been constructed in the past and how these impact upon current scholarship. Immediately questions of definition arise. While a great deal has been written about the relations between literature and theology there remain stubborn difficulties in employing both terms – particularly for women. S.W. Sykes begins his definition of theology with the cautionary proviso that the word 'has had a number of meanings throughout history' (1983: 566). This instability endures and feminist, postcolonialist, queer and liberationist theologians continue actively to dispute and deconstruct the term. Recognition of the significance of human practice for theological reflection has shifted our understanding of theological thinking in recent years. There has also been a growing awareness of the significance of the imagination in the work of the theologian. The fact that narrative, metaphor and allegory are now owned as integral to the discourses of theology has not, however, transformed the dominant consensus that, whatever resources are employed to achieve its ends, theology has a necessary duty to offer coherent, rational, ordered and, by implication, authoritative accounts of faith.

As is immediately apparent, coherence, rationality and authority are not 'buzz words' for feminists. Many women would perceive theology to be a male-centred discourse deeply implicated in sustaining a hierarchical social order. Because of the regulative connotations of the term, and its close ties with Western monotheistic religion (particularly Christianity), many religious feminists would regard 'theology' as simply an inappropriate word to describe their own reflections on the divine. Some would prefer to use the term thealogy to indicate their repudiation of these former traditions and the female-centred nature of their own work.[8]

The ambivalence of the term 'theology' presents a number of specific problems within this text. The varied output of religious feminists, writing out of a number of established religious traditions as well as from the less circumscribed territories of goddess feminism, nature religion and post-Christian feminism, cannot easily be described as theology in the usual sense of the term.

8   This is not to imply that thealogians have abandoned the project of offering coherent and intelligible accounts of their own positions.

The prefixing of 'feminist' to theology does not solve the problem. For some this straightforwardly creates an oxymoron. For others it obscures the diversity within religious feminism. Many Christian, Jewish and post-Christian feminists might be happy to be described as feminist theologians, whereas Buddhist feminists, for example, would have serious problems with the understandings of the divine implicated in this term.

These confessional differences do not mean, however, that there is no recognisable body of scholarship that has been formed out of the work of religious feminists during the past forty years. There is a dialogical relationship between the writings of religious feminists and they contain identifiable political and spiritual convictions that overcome religious divisions. There is no doubt that this body of work constitutes a living tradition, in Alasdair MacIntyre's (1981) understanding of this term as a conversation (or argument) over time. This common ground has meant that it has been perfectly possible to anthologise the writings of women from many faiths in one volume. This practice has continued from the time of Carol Christ's and Judith Plaskow's groundbreaking text *Womanspirit Rising* (1979a [1975]) to the present day. Such works have generically been described as feminist theology, reflecting, no doubt, the hegemonic position of white, Western, Christian women within the academy. How long the expression will continue to have useful currency is in doubt,[9] but there is currently no other commonly recognised term that can be used to describe the collective work of religious feminists. This is one reason why I have continued to refer to the uses of literature within 'feminist theology' while basing my observations on the work of goddess, Jewish, Christian and post-Christian scholars.

While recognising that use of the term 'theology', whether or not the label 'feminist' is attached, creates many difficulties for women, I also believe that there are some advantages in continuing use of this contested term. It signals the conversational relationship of the 'feminist theologian' with the intellectual traditions of the past as well as with the work of male colleagues today. For many religious feminists its continued use marks the fact that we do not repudiate our faith inheritance but cherish the hope that the 'symbols can be turned' to address the needs and concerns of women and more adequately reflect the image of God (see Soskice, 1996). It also indicates that we are eager to contest within the theological arena rather than remove ourselves to another place.

This brief discussion has revealed that the difficulties experienced in employing the term 'theology' are considerable. Those relating to the word 'literature' can, however, appear overwhelming. Terence Wright complains that if 'theology can

---

9 Some feminist theologians believe that the political convictions which have maintained a fragile consensus between religious feminists should now themselves be challenged. They argue that the time has come when women will find new creativity through a return to the doctrines that have shaped their religious traditions. See, for example, essays in Parsons (ed.) *The Blackwell Companion to Feminist Theology* (2002).

only be defined in the most general terms literature seems altogether to defy definition' (1988: 3). It is clearly feasible to construct elaborate sets of related genres in which lyric poetry, gothic novels and tragic drama can be located so that all appear to have their proper place. It is also possible to generate canons of great texts that seem to earn by their merits the title 'literature'. It is much harder to decide what it is about a text that makes it literary. Wright counsels against attempts to hypostasise literature by defining it too closely, believing that the very indiscreteness of the concept is a characteristic feature. However, he follows Auden in the tentative assertion that 'literature "embodies what it indicates" … so that form, content, medium and message, are inseparable' (1988: 6).

This emphasis upon form and the assertion of an intimate relation between what is expressed and the medium of expression is helpful. It points us towards the literary significance of language, of metaphor and genre. It expresses the sense that literature is creative work that continually recreates the world. It identifies something of the particularity, the untranslatable nature, of literature; there is no essence to a work of literature that can be extracted from the medium in which it is incarnated.

Despite the fact that these literary qualities are attractive to many feminists, when we employ the term 'literature' we do so with awareness that this too has not always been a friendly word for women. In previous generations women's significant creative work has not been included within the established literary canons (for a discussion of the dynamics of exclusion see, for example, Spender, 1986). The genres in which many women have chosen to write (e.g. gothic, romance and detective fiction) have always been viewed as of lesser significance – hardly literature at all. When women employ the word 'literature' it carries with it the history of all these exclusions.

The dream of harmony

In a work of this kind it is necessary to spend time exploring and even problematising significant terms. However, it is not necessary to dwell on this for too long. Any reader of the extensive writing on literature and theology will soon become aware that, whatever definitions are being offered, these are of secondary importance to what is implied by the supposed difference between the two categories. There is clearly a relation between actual, what might be termed 'shelvable', texts of literature and theology and what is meant when the words 'theology' or 'literature' are employed in debate. But the words carry with them a wealth of wider associations beyond their library locations and are used heuristically to convey contrasting approaches to issues of fundamental concern. It is vital to grasp that the terms 'literature' and 'theology' are doing a great deal more than identifying particular types of texts or discourses. They have come to signify contrasting ways of apprehending the world and approaching the divine.

Generally speaking the term 'theology' trails in its wake notions of a negotiable and intelligible universe. Because the purposes of God are communicable through revelation, and because human beings are endowed with a rationality that mirrors that of their creator, it is possible to strive towards clarity, universality and reasonable certainty when we give expression to faith. In order to achieve clarity a process of abstraction and a purification of forms is necessary and desirable. While there will always remain a mystery at the heart of things, theology strives towards the light. It seeks to generate the illumination necessary to live by faith in this world.

In contrast 'literature' is employed to evoke what is contrary, particular and resists abstraction or incorporation into systematic thought. In parable, metaphor and allegory it confounds interpretation. Straying from the straight and narrow, literature is profligate in the production of new meanings. Literature overwhelms plain sense with beauty and gives voice to pain that cannot be carried by other forms. It is reckless in its approach to the established conventions of everyday life.

Not only are literature and theology used to signify contrasting world views, as they have done since discussions concerning philosophy and poetry in the work of Plato and Aristotle (see Cupitt, 1991: 40), it also becomes apparent that literature and theology are commonly located on opposite sides of the binary schema through which meaning is generated in Western culture.[10] Theology is placed on the side of spirit, reason, light, truth, order – the masculine virtues. Literature is associated with the body, desire, darkness, mystery – the feminine. Theology is the place where God and 'man' meet. Literature, like Lilith excluded from the garden, endlessly seduces and gives birth. This binary, hierarchical and gendered division has been the unstated supposition behind classical formulations of the relations between the disciplines.

T.S. Eliot is the most widely quoted representative of what might be termed a conservative understanding of the relationship between literature and theology. The subject, of immense personal concern to the poet, was one which he reflected upon in numerous essays and critical articles. Eliot was convinced of the importance of both religion and art to a healthy culture. However, he held that the religious faith of a people sustains and enlivens the whole culture. Without this spiritual base literature itself becomes decadent and unable to make its own particular contribution to the wider nexus. 'As the religious imagination atrophies, the imagination *tout court* disappears also. The arts in their decline pass through the stage of sensationalism and theology and philosophy which cease to be nourished by the imagination descend into verbalism' (Eliot, in Kojecky, 1971: 183).

The harmony which Christians should strive for is to be found in an organic society in which there is a healthily functioning 'social-religious-artistic complex' (Eliot, 1951: 62). However, they should never lose sight of the fact that it is

10 For a fuller discussion of the nature and function of this binary system see Elaine Graham, (1995: 11–16).

theology that should guide literary judgements. It alone can provide the standards and criteria through which all cultural forms are to be judged.

> What I believe to be incumbent on all Christians is the duty of maintaining consciously certain standards and criteria of criticism above those approved by the rest of the world; and that by these criteria and standards everything we read must be tested ... so long as we are conscious of the gulf fixed between ourselves and the greater part of contemporary literature we are more or less protected from it and are in a position to extract what good it has to offer us. (Eliot, 1975: 105)

Literature is thus viewed as having an important role to play but requiring the guiding hand of theology to regulate its energy and potentially harmful influence. Eliot is particularly concerned to warn against the dangers that ensue when literature abandons its appointed place and seeks to usurp the authority of theology. He opposed those 'who would make literature a substitute for a definitive theology or philosophy' and dedicated himself to 'try to keep the old distinction clear' (in Kojecky, 1971: 76). Quoting Jacques Maritain, a thinker he deeply admired, he proclaimed that literature needs theology to save it from itself: 'By showing where moral truth and the genuine supernatural are situated religion saves poetry from the absurdity of believing itself destined to transform ethics and life: saves it from overweening arrogance' (Maritain, in Eliot, 1933: 137).[11]

In Eliot's thought it is clear that theology performs the duties of the good husband and literature represents the wife. If proper relations between the couple are maintained then harmony prevails. Literature in her own sphere is worthy of honour and contributes greatly to a healthy civilisation. Left to herself and unrestrained she has the power to corrupt the common cultural home.[12] While Eliot's work represents perhaps the most clearly articulated understanding of a hierarchy between literature and theology, the idea of a complementary and harmonious relation is one which continues to be widely held.

Terrence Wright is keen to honour both disciplines and his work presents a scholarly and creative exposition of the challenges and insights that literature offers to theology. He writes:

> There will always be a tension between conceptual and creative discourse. Systematic theology will continue the necessary attempt to impose clarity and consistency upon

---

11 Eliot further comments, 'This seems to me to be putting the finger on the great weakness of much poetry and criticism of the nineteenth and twentieth centuries' (Eliot, 1933: 137).

12 T.S. Eliot's views on the proper relations between literature and theology have their counterpart in his views concerning the proper relations between women and men. Commenting upon the Nazi determination to locate the energies of women in the kitchen, childcare and church he argued that this programme should not be abandoned simply because of its fascist origins. 'Might one suggest that the kitchen, children and church could be considered to have a claim upon the attention of married women? Or that no normal married woman would prefer to be a wage earner if she could help it'. (1939: 69–70)

language while literature will no doubt maintain its equally necessary task to complicate and enrich the apparent security of theological concepts. (1988: 13)

Paul Fiddes pictures a similar harmonious division between the literary and theological imaginations. The impulse of theology is to make manifest God's self-disclosure. He quotes Barth to describe a movement in which revelation 'seizes language' in order to move from the mystery of God towards a clarity of communication (Fiddes, 1991: 12). In a contrary manner literature reminds humanity of a reality reason cannot comprehend. Whereas Fiddes endorses the position of Eliot that originality and creativity have no place in doctrine he affirms that in the literary sphere they serve to propel the imagination towards the divine.

Christian theologians, appealing to revelation, and writers employing imagination understanding themselves as working in two rather different directions. The first are following a movement from mystery toward image and story, the second, form image and story *towards* a mystery. (Fiddes, 1991: 27)

In other words, theology seizes language to illuminate and instruct whereas literature leads us back towards the dark and damp, sacred places where words and forms disintegrate.

Although she has largely written on philosophy rather than theology, the work of Martha Nussbaum is important to consider at this point as she presents perhaps the most sustained contemporary reflection on the complementary relations between rational, abstract forms of discourse and creative writing. Her work has been extremely influential in both feminist and theological debate.[13] Nussbaum advocates an opening up of philosophy to receive the insights of literature. Literary texts testify to the mystery and beauty of human life and, what is more, they carry emotion into the world of practical reason. Emotion is another way of knowing the world which has its own genius, and 'narratives contain emotion in their very structure' (1990: 246). Crucial to Nussbaum's advocacy of literature is the acknowledgement that there may be some views of the world, particularly those which emphasise the beauty, mystery, complexity and ambiguity of existence, that cannot be fully and adequately stated in the language of conventional philosophical prose. Style matters, and abstract theoretical forms of discourse are making implicit statements about what is important and what is not.

On an initial reading it might appear that Nussbaum is a defender of the

---

13   To some feminists her use of literature appears to offer the means of transforming intellectual traditions in a manner that would render them more responsive to the material realities of everyday life. Her work is also increasingly significant within the field of theological ethics. Out of her reflections Nussbaum constructs a distinctive Aristotelian discourse on the cultivation of the virtues and the significance of tradition. Nussbaum's work has been widely referenced by theologians. For example, Hauerwas and Jones (1989) include one of her essays in their influential edited collection of work in narrative theology.

genius of literature and adamant in her insistence that 'literature cannot be reduced to philosophical example' (1986: 14). However, a critical consideration of her work reveals that literature is seen as a necessary supplement to philosophy rather than an equal partner.[14] Literature does not change the agenda of philosophy but facilitates a fuller enquiry into the great themes that philosophers have always debated. The emotions that literature supposedly embodies are ones that are harnessed to facilitate more effective intellectual enquiry into these issues. Furthermore, it transpires that literature is not merely a worthy helpmeet for philosophical thinking, she is also good in bed. Novels seduce with 'mysterious and romantic charms', they lure into 'a more shadowy and passionate world'. They require the reader 'to assent, to succumb' (1990: 258). In a devastating critique of Nussbaum's project, Robert Eaglestone concludes that she reinscribes traditional conventions through which the relations between logocentric discourse and literature have always been debated. For Nussbaum, he states, 'Philosophy is rational, abstract, universal, fully present on the page as argument. Literature is emotional, specific, contingent, not present as text, but as "real life" situations' (1997: 57). He concludes that Nussbaum reinstates 'binary oppositions, which can no longer have any value for argument when one side is subsumed in the other' (1997: 58).

What is called woman

I have employed the work of Eliot, Wright, Fiddes and Nussbaum to argue that in discussions of the relationship between literature and the 'logocentric' discourses of theology and philosophy literature is constructed as female; literature is a girl. However, the gendering of literature as female can be understood in a variety of ways. For Eliot it implies that theology has a magisterial role and literature can best serve her purposes through submission to a higher authority. Wright, Fiddes and Nussbaum are concerned to portray a relationship in which the differences between literature and theology/philosophy are mutually enriching. Both partners benefit from recognition of their complementarity. However, it remains difficult for these scholars to escape the power connotations of the binary scheme that structures their work. This accords primacy always to one term for, as Derrida argues, in Western thinking 'we do not have a peaceful co-existence of facing terms but a violent hierarchy. One dominates the other' (in Roemer 1995: 196). Feminists negotiating these discussions may find themselves irritated by the heterosexual matrix in which the whole debate is framed and unwilling to enter a discussion predicated on these terms. However, once an awareness of the

---

14 She is selective in the forms of literature she employs and has demonstrated a preference for texts portraying what philosophy has traditionally identified as the great dilemmas of the human condition. She shows less interest in innovatory use of literary form or poetic language – both of which have been significant for women writers as they have sought to reconstruct the symbolic order.

gendered significance accorded to the terms 'theology' and 'literature' has been achieved it does have some critical potential. We can use this understanding to look with fresh eyes at the current theological landscape. Applying the insights of deconstruction we will identify the ways in which the binary schema through which meaning is generated can disclose how power functions within theological thinking. We will note how logocentric discourse subordinates those terms that challenge its singular authority. However, we will also note how dependent this discourse is upon the elements which it excludes or denies. Furthermore, we will celebrate the fact that the construction of literature as feminine can no longer signify, as it did for Eliot, a complementary and subservient role.

In her groundbreaking and celebrated work, *Gynesis: Configurations of Women and Modernity* (1985), Alice Jardine analyses how, in the cultural exhaustion surrounding the collapse of modernist aspirations, postmodernist scholars sought out a 'place' which had been obscured and silenced in enlightenment discourse as the only point from which it is now possible to speak a new world. The place of the body, desire, of things beyond language has been ciphered 'woman'.

'Woman' as a new rhetorical space is inseparable from the most radical moments of most contemporary disciplines. To limit ourselves to the general set of writers in focus here, 'she' may be found in Lacan's pronouncements on desire; Derrida's internal explorations of writing; Deleuze's work on becoming woman; Jean Francois Lyotard's calls for a feminine analytic relation; Jean Baudrillard's work on seduction; Foucault's on madness; Goux's on the new femininity; Barthe's in general. (1985: 38)

Jardine, alongside Braidotti (1991: 10), has been concerned to show how the feminisation of theory cannot be understood without a corresponding analysis of the often unacknowledged influence of feminist writers from de Beauvoir to the present day. Feminist poststructuralist writers are working to make manifest the relation between 'woman' as a trope or rhetorical device and the creative struggles of women to refigure social and symbolic systems. These issues are explored further in chapter 3. What it is significant to emphasise at this point is that the gendering of literature as female now implies something more than once it did. It has become associated with the assault that poststructuralist theory is making upon the symbolic conventions that are complicit in sustaining our current social relations. In the following pages I shall demonstrate how, if we turn our gaze to places where literature and theology are placed in conjunction in contemporary theological thinking, we can see quite clearly the ways in which theologians are turning to the feminised resources of literature to sustain a masculine symbolic system in deep crisis.

In the remaining pages of this chapter I explore three contrasting approaches to the use of literature in contemporary theology. First I examine canonical narrative theology; a movement that places theology in opposition to contemporary culture. I then explore constructive narrative theology, which emphasises the importance of literary creativity but uses literature as a means of securing theological discourse. Finally I turn to the work of scholars, influenced by post-structuralist theory, who are seeking to respond to the political failures of theological endeavour. These 'religious readers' seek, through literature, to voice a protest against the exclusion of the suffering flesh from the grammar of theology.

The use of literature in canonical narrative theology

Behind the Bible

I begin my discussion of canonical narrative theology with Hans Frei's important book, *The Decline of Biblical Narrative*. Published in 1974, this work was to be of great significance in restoring an authority to theology which had been severely challenged during the previous tumultuous decade. It was Frei's main argument that, owing to the rise of historical criticism in the eighteenth century, the Western churches had lost their sense of the trustworthy and 'realistic' nature of biblical narratives. Before this faith was shattered, Frei argued, it was widely assumed that the Bible was interpreted by believers as being based upon real events which happened in temporal sequence and had a coherent plot; diverse biblical stories contributed to a 'common narrative referring to a single history and its patterns of meaning' (1974: 2).

In articulating this perspective and pleading for a 'return' to biblical narratives Frei draws upon the work of the theologian Karl Barth. Frei's reading of Barth centres upon the notion of God's unique self-revelation in the *story* of Jesus. This story becomes the norm for interpreting scripture; the parts can be combined into a single narratable whole and the story of Jesus functions as the lens through which all else is viewed.[15] This same story is the basis of all doctrinal thinking and consequently discloses the reality of human history and personal identity. Barth argues that in this story we discover our own true story. 'His history as such is our history. It is our own true history (incomparably more direct and intimate than anything we know as our history)' (Barth, in Ford, 1981: 165). It is Barth's conviction that we can be gripped by the power of this narrative that leads David Kelsey to conclude that Barth reads the Bible as if it were a 'vast, loosely scripted, non-fictional novel' (in Lindbeck 1984: 121).

As well as Barth, Frei drew upon a classic text of literary theory to construct his understanding of biblical narrative. Erich Auerbach's *Mimesis: The Representation of Reality in Western Literature* (1953) portrays the Bible as a distinctive text in the ancient world. It creates its own universe of meaning which those who encounter it are compelled to enter.

The Bible's claim to truth is not only far more urgent than Homer's it is tyrannical – it excludes all other claims. The world of the scripture stories is not satisfied with claiming to be a historically true reality – it claims that it is the only real world. (1953: 14–15)

15   See Ford (1981) for a fuller discussion of Barth's narrative theology.

And, significantly, Auerbach suggests that the gospel narratives share an extraordinary affinity with the realistic novels of the nineteenth century which sets them apart from other ancient texts (see Loughlin, 1996: 75).

By integrating the work of Barth and Auerbach, Frei constructed an alternative to the modern trajectory in biblical studies. He refused the critical impulse continually to dissect and analyse the disparate traditions within the text as well as the liberal option, to view the scriptures as a source of timeless spiritual truths. Clearly a return to historical literalism was not a credible scholarly option but, he believed, a reawakened sense of the Bible as coherent, 'realistic' narrative might restore its use to the churches and generate new grounds for authority in theological thinking. Frei demonstrated a particular devotion to the passion narratives and the plain sense of these, he believed, provided the criteria against which all theological claims could be tested and authenticated.

The project Frei initiated stands in contrast to the attempts of liberal and liberation theologians to discover, through conversation with secular culture, an appropriate register in which to reiterate Christian convictions. Rather than finding a voice which resonates with common concerns, Christians are to speak in a language that is distinctly their own and distinguishes them from others.[16] With a rediscovered sense of the significance of their own narrative traditions, Christians need no longer justify their own beliefs on the basis of what is acceptable to the culture in which they are located. Too much energy, Frei believed, has been wasted upon the attempts to sustain the illusion that there is a compatibility between the Christian faith and the intellectual traditions of the Western world. What is now required is an intercommunal or 'intratextual'[17] effort to generate identity out of the resources of the foundational narratives,

The most fateful issue for Christian self-description is that of regaining its autonomous vocation as a religion after its defeat in its secondary vocation of providing ideological coherence, foundation and stability to Western culture ... one never knows what this community might then contribute once again to that culture or its residues including its political life, its quest for justice and freedom and even its literature. (1993: 149)

There are many problems with Frei's project,[18] but it is the relation between theology and literature that is of specific concern here. Frei's small aside, 'and even its literature', is of immense significance. What is being implied is that

16 In his later writing Frei draws increasingly upon the work of Lindbeck, who likens religious traditions to languages with their own distinctive idioms, symbols and grammatical procedures. It is Lindbeck's conviction that in a situation of 'dechristianization' Christians will be compelled to cultivate their own discursive resources, their 'native tongue', rather than seeking common mediums of cultural exchange (Lindbeck, 1984: 33–34).

17 A significant term which is used by Frei and his supporters to signify that the Christian narrative contains all that is necessary for the self-definition of the Christian community.

18 Most criticisms focus around either the cultural specificity of the reading practice Frei advocates or the problems of engaging in the public sphere on the basis of a self-authenticating narrative.

biblical narratives generate out of themselves the resources required for authentic Christian theology and practice, and that a return to this authentic theology and practice might consequently have the power to regenerate the creative imagination. However, a feminist hermeneutics of suspicion will quickly identify that Frei's position is dependent upon literary rather than biblical foundations.

As a passionate reader, Frei has been instructed through his study of the great nineteenth century novels to approach the text with attention to plot, character, event and action. His Jesus is an agent in a 'narratable plot' (1993). 'The form of the gospel is so novel-like' that Jesus must be understood in the same way as we would understand a character in a realist novel (1993: 46). Frei has learnt to surrender himself to the panoramic view of the world presented in the novelistic text and to trust that its 'realism' guarantees the authenticity of all that is there encountered. On all these matters he is quite candid.

In trying to work out the hermeneutical principles of this program of interpretation, I found that a certain kind of understanding is involved which is perhaps best exemplified by what goes on in the 19th century realistic novel and the attempts to understand it (George Eliot's Adam Bede and Middlemarch come to mind). (1993: 32)

What enables him to rehearse this position so innocently is the presumption, based on his reading of Auerbach, that it is the Bible which has generated, or pre-empted this particular literary genre (1993: 46). Indeed, viewed in this light, the nineteenth-century novel is not really literature at all. It somehow borrows its 'realism' from the Bible. Frei's critics have poured scorn on the notion that Christians throughout the centuries have employed the conventions appropriate to realistic fiction in their readings of the Bible. Is it not much more likely that Frei, as a child of a culture which has embraced empiricism and equated realism with true knowledge, is bringing these post-enlightenment, Anglo-Saxon sensibilities to his readings both of nineteenth-century literature and the Bible? What is interesting for the purposes of this text is that a project which is pursued in order to rescue theology from its cultural dependence requires the (invisible) support of literature to sustain it. The concept of biblical narrative employed by Frei is constructed out of the very resources it is employed to critique. It is here that a feminist hermeneutics of suspicion enables us to discern how theology is sustained through its illicit alliance with literature. The masculine discourse requires the feminised genius of literature in order to overcome its current impotence.[19] Frei, however, is not alone in proclaiming the absolute authority of Christian discourse over cultural constructions while at the same time turning to literature as his helpmeet in overcoming the world.

---

19 I am informed by a colleague that for a period Frei had a notice proclaiming he 'would rather be reading Jane Austen' displayed on his office door.

Before virtue

The work of Frei, particularly as it has been further developed through the encounter with the post-liberal theology of George Lindbeck (1984), has been significant to a number of scholars who, from radical or conservative positions, are currently seeking to re-form theology after its long captivity in secular cultural forms. A parallel path has been taken in Christian ethics by Stanley Hauerwas. In his work we will also observe peculiar dependencies upon literature which curiously destabilise his thinking from within.

Hauerwas was an attentive reader of Frei's work – although the debt he owes to this scholarship is rather understated in his texts. In his early works Hauerwas employs Frei's readings of the work of Barth and Auerbach to construct a model of the Christian community as the location in which the 'story of Jesus' is embodied and continually retold (1981: 55). In later works he is increasingly influenced by his friend and colleague Alasdair MacIntyre. In *After Virtue* (1981) MacIntyre discusses the relation of ethics to communal narrative traditions and the impossibility of cultivating ethical character outside such traditions. Following this trajectory Hauerwas begins to describe the church as a story-formed community which cultivates moral predispositions in its members as part of their conformity/submission to the stories they hear, tell and embody. It is through being a community of character in concordance with these stories that the church challenges the social order. Not by political action, or by espousing progressive causes, or by campaigning on specific issues. Instead Christians who are in faithful conformity with their narrative are advised to engage in works of personal care and to 'take time to enjoy a walk with a friend, to read all of Trollope's novels, to maintain universities, to have and care for children and, most importantly, to worship God' (Hauerwas, in Albrecht, 1995: 117).

Take time to read all of Trollope's novels: once again a small aside, but of great signifi-cance. It is a striking feature of Hauerwas's reflections on the specificity of the Christian tradition and the distinctiveness of the Christian community that he draws so heavily upon literary texts. In fact his early manifesto, *A Community of Character* (1981), is not fabricated around the stories of Jesus at all but around Richard Adams's novel *Watership Down* (1974).[20] In his later work it is the novels of Trollope which provide the supplementary material to display the formation of the Christian virtues. The following quotations are illustrative:

I use Trollope because I love to read Trollope. Yet Trollope also helps me display Christian convictions at work ... Trollope-like novels are my best allies and resource for the display of the kind of redescriptions required to live as a Christian, particularly in a liberal society. (1995: 8)

Thus the very reading of the novel is moral training. (1995: 55)

20 A novel about a group of rabbits (bucks) seeking to establish a new warren and attract breeding does. I find this choice of text pleasantly ironic.

Trollope would never assume that our task is to reject convention but rather the task is to live out the substance of our conventions. (1995: 57)

Apart from raising intriguing questions about what exactly a 'Trollope-like' novel might be, the extracts above prompt questions about the relation between 'narrative' and 'literature'. 'Narrative' is a term that holds no threats for Hauerwas. It can be confidently employed.[21] Christians can be certain that they inhabit a 'true narrative' (1981: 149) whose revelatory and ethical status is clear. Such assumptions raise many problems for feminists for, as Gloria Albrecht observes:

Hauerwas does not need to acknowledge the difference in the proverbs, prophecies, legends, laws and traditions that fathers pass on to their sons and that mothers whisper to their daughters. Hauerwas seems not to recognise the reality of relationships of domination within the Christian narrative and its tradition, nor the multiplicity of voices, nor the silencing throughout history of many Christian's stories. (Albrecht 1995: 100–101)

However, it is not the inherently fragmented, unstable and politically contested nature of narrative that is most problematic. It is the assumption Hauerwas shares with Frei that 'narrative' is a fully baptised term inherently compatible with the exclusivity of the Christian community. Narrative lives happily with doctrine, theology and magisterial authority. Indeed this authority becomes increasingly attractive to Hauerwas in his later writings as he increasingly stresses the importance of Christians' submitting themselves to the authority of those who decide how their story should be told. And yet, as his own work demonstrates, the discreteness of the Christian narrative is illusory.

It is not the intention of this work to deny that narrative plays a significant role in contemporary theology, but rather to enquire what household gods are hidden under narrative's skirts. Although narrative might be conceptually distinguished from literature, in reality, once narrative is employed as a significant category of analysis it is literary terms and forms that must be used to explicate its function. The use of a story about rabbits in Hauerwas's seminal work is not merely illustrative. He cannot embody his convictions concerning the significance of narrative without the use of such literary texts. In this sense he is quite right, 'novels are my best allies and resource'. However, once literature is employed we are no longer inhabiting a world of true stories, we are living in the realms of fiction. As Paul Ricoeur points out, literature may proclaim its faithfulness to reality but this fragile realism is continually undermined by the nature of literary construction.[22]

If indeed resemblance is only a semblance of truth, what then is fiction under the rule of this semblance but the ability to create the belief that this artifice *stands* for genuine

---

21   In the recently published *Hauerwas Reader* (2001) the index contains long lists of references to narrative and story. There are only three references to literature in the index to this weighty text.

22   This process is, in fact, particularly evident in the great realistic novels of the nineteenth century so favoured by Nussbaum, MacIntyre, Frei and Hauerwas.

testimony about reality and life? The art of fiction then turns out to be the art of illusion. From here on awareness of the artifice involved undermines from within the realist motivation finally turning against it and destroying it. (1985: 158)

Once again a feminist hermeneutics of suspicion will allow us to discern in Hauerwas's literary dependence the deconstructive feminine function which undermines the precarious power of the master narrative.

Constructive narrative theology

The primal home
In the canonical narrative theologies of Frei and Hauerwas a distinction is being implicitly drawn between the realistic narrative[23] (which is presumed to be inherently compatible with Christian theology because of its self-evident authenticity or truth) and the values of contemporary culture which are illusory, seductive, immoral and dangerous. Through making this distinction literature becomes available as a resource that can be used to construct a theological position which then erases its vital contribution. Theology is still assumed to be generative and literature supportive or illustrative. Although it is impossible to make claims concerning the realism and authenticity of the Christian narrative without drawing upon literary conventions, nevertheless, literature remains the wife of a self-made man. As Ricoeur has argued, however, realistic narrative cannot be disassociated from the literary tradition out of which it developed. Milan Kundera goes further and argues that the very style of novelistic realism undermines its own claims to intelligibility and authority. He writes, 'The novel is, by definition, the ironic art: its 'truth' is concealed, undeclared, undeclarable ... It denies our certainties by unmasking the world as an ambiguity' (in Roemer, 1995: 145). I shall now explore some very different understandings of the importance of narrative within theology, which continue to rely upon similarly gendered conventions but employ these in a markedly dissimilar way. The question I shall be asking here is whether, despite the apparent differences between 'orthodox' and 'liberal' approaches to theology, an analysis of the way that literature is used in both reveals a similar tendency to establish the authority of theological discourse in a cultural context suspicious of its claims by incorporating literature into the foundations of the temple.

In 'The Narrative Quality of Experience' (1989 [1971]), an evocative essay which was to inspire an entirely different trajectory in narrative theology from those described above, Stephen Crites refuses to disengage narrative from its literary associations and affirms that 'art is involved in all storytelling. It no longer appears natural and innocent in our eyes' (1989: 69). His paper was concerned

23 Established as a genre by the rise of the novel in the modern era and not, I believe, to be transported backwards into the texts of ancient cultures.

to establish the culturally generated nature of human identity – 'The way people speak, dance, build, dream, embellish is to be sure always culturally particular: it bears the imprint of a time and a place' (1989: 65) – and to argue that this identity is formed through narrative trajectories which structure the very nature of experience. We apprehend the world in narrative form.[24]

Crites' understanding of the role of narrative in structuring human experience led him to the conclusion that the form of narrative is 'primitive' (1989: 82). Our narrative propensity enables consciousness to form identity both in the sense of personal history and of communal belonging.

> It is not as though a man [sic] begins as a purely individual consciousness ... and then casts about for a satisfying tale to lend it some higher significance. People awaken to consciousness in a society, with the inner story of experience and its enveloping musicality already infused with cultural forms (1989: 80).

As well as forming cultural identity, narrative sustains, nourishes and protects it. Narrative, as a means of structuring experience, preserves us from both immediacy and abstraction – present in our times in the political threat of totalitarianism (in either fascistic or global-capitalist forms). In times of danger or rapid cultural change, the permeability of narrative forms enables people to perceive new configurations of their experience and the sacred stories of their culture. These together may generate new symbols, 'causing a burst of light like a comet entering our atmosphere' (1989: 81), which enable human beings to reorientate their cultural identity to meet the challenge of new times. Literature, as the most significant representative of narrativity, has a crucial role to play in this process of spiritual and social renewal.

The power of Crites's essay lies in the link he proposes between personal biography, sacred traditions and contemporary literary forms. All of these mediate in distinct but not separate ways the sense of personal and corporate identity, and provide the resources necessary to negotiate social and political change. His work has been hugely influential in the development of biographical theology and other forms of narrative theology which emphasise the importance of the cultural construction of identity. As literature is read as a privileged mirror of identity his work paved the way for feminist and black theologians to use literary texts as a theological resource giving voice to those whose reflections on the

---

24 In making this argument Crites distinguishes three forms of narrative. First there are sacred stories which lie 'deep in the consciousness of a people' (1989: 69), forming a mythopoetic inheritance which is anonymous and communal. These stories are 'not like monuments ... but like dwelling places. People live in them' (1989: 69) and they orientate the life of a people through time. Secondly, there are mundane stories which consist both of the literary resources of culture and the everyday narrative communications that facilitate daily living. 'Here we find stories composed as works of art as well as the much more modest narrative communications that pass between people' (1989: 71). Between sacred and mundane stories there is distinction without separation, and mediating between these narrative forms is a third type – that of experience as consciously grasped always in narrative form.

divine had not been represented in traditional theological discourse (see Goldberg, 1991: 12–16).

Previous discussions, however, have been based upon a hermeneutics of suspicion regarding the gendered nature of the discourse concerning literature and theology. With this critical awareness we can perceive in the work of Crites that what he terms 'narrative' (a territory largely occupied by literature)[25] functions as primary matter, primitive form, maternal home, nurturer and protector – in other words as a *good mother*. Clearly this is, in some ways, a more attractive role than subjected wife; however, there are also many problems inherent in this positioning. Literature might easily become associated with a kind of primal goodness that stands in timeless opposition to historical, intellectual and political movements. In an age in which nostalgia for the natural is a symptom of distrust in human potential it is tempting to reinstate the traditional binary distinctions between literature and logocentric discourse in reverse order. We need narrative to rescue us from a culture that has lost its roots in traditional wisdom and to return us to our true selves.

Having pointed out that this danger arises from the way Crites accords a primal role to narrative it is only fair to concede that this is a pitfall that he attempts to avoid. Perhaps because narrative is so closely associated with the artifices of literature in his thinking it is never straightforward, transparent or unambiguously benign; 'narrative form is by no means innocent' (1989: 82).[26] Some of those who have followed in the trajectory of Crites, however, have been less careful to avoid the implications that narrative radiates a primal goodness.

In *What Is a Story?* Don Cupitt follows Crites in arguing that it is through stories that 'our social selves, which are our real selves' (1991: ix) are produced. In contrast, philosophy offers the alienation of 'non narrative reason' and theology, which could have chosen the narrative path, has 'fallen' with philosophy through rejecting its own origins in story and drama (1991: x). In Cupitt's opinion the current parlous state of philosophy and theology reflects the consequences of a deep antipathy towards the creative and imaginative arts. Cupitt recognises, and makes plain, that this is a symptom of hostility towards all that has been gendered feminine within culture. He also argues that the maintenance of this gynophobia is profoundly dangerous in the current context. If we are to survive at all human beings must embrace a feminisation of knowledge. Narrative, as feminine art, structures experience in such a way that it enables us to inhabit it safely. Just as children draw a house in the style of a human face 'with a central doorway representing the mouth … a little above it windows representing the eyes, and the roof – especially when it is thatched – is like a head of hair' (1991: 58), so narrative makes inhabitable a formless and potentially unfriendly world,

25 He writes 'narrative is artifice … there have been many forms of narrative epic, drama, history, the novel and so on' (1989: 69).
26 Thus Crites avoids some of the problems identified in the work of Frei and Hauerwas.

and keeps darkness and death at bay — at least for a while. We are listening to Scheherazade again. Putting off death by telling tales through the night. Narrative, only narrative conquers darkness and the void. (1991: 80)

Cupitt's work abounds in celebratory feminine imagery extolling the virtues of narrative. In contrast, philosophy and theology are imaged as impotent, inadequate and male:

Hulme remained an unmarried male contemplative like virtually every other philosopher from Plato to Kant. He still felt the need to look for philosophical happiness in the same direction as all his predecessors had done, namely towards a timeless and universal, objective order of Reason. This order of Reason had always been a kind of exalted and spiritualised and generalised masculinity, phallogocentrism. (1991: 58)

We can discern here a developing symbolic system in which narrative and literature — with the sheltering and nurturing functions which Cupitt ascribes to them — function as the last guarantors of identity and coherence in a world where the pillars of other temples have been torn down. This is a most attractive notion for Christian theologians who have been challenged to relinquish former forms of 'foundational thinking' rooted in revelation or the rational capacities of the human subject, and who are searching for an alternative basis for theological thinking (see, for example, Peter Hodgson's recent work on George Eliot, 2001). Narrative can be employed to construct coherence in a world of chaotic circumstances and, through the same process, to generate self-identity. Such ideas have been particularly powerfully articulated in the work of Paul Ricoeur.

Narrative and the making of the world

Ricoeur's early writings were constructed in conversational relation to those of Crites (1991: 141)[27] and, like Crites, he is concerned with both the cultural and theological import of storytelling, particularly through the literary tradition. Ricoeur presents a process of plot creation as the manner in which human beings 'provide "shape" to what remains chaotic obscure and mute' (1991: 115). The operation of plotting synthesises the heterogeneous elements of existence and 'Narration organises them into an intelligible whole' (1991: 426). This narrative propensity is the basis of our subjectivity, as human beings seek to impose the same form of coherence upon the discordances of personal existence. Entangled in stories from birth we learn to become 'the narrator of our own story without completely becoming the author of our life' (1991: 437). Subjectivity is not pre-existent but is rather the achievement of narrative identity.

The *subject* is never given at the beginning ... a *self* is born, taught by the cultural symbols, first among which are the stories received in the literary tradition. These stories give unity — not unity of substance but narrative wholeness. (1991: 445)

---

27 Although there are significant differences between the two thinkers, particularly regarding the relation between narratives and symbols in cultural production.

Whereas the canonical narrative theology of Frei and Hauerwas has not proved to be a theological position attractive to women[28] – it is definitely a 'boy thing'- constructive forms of narrative theology have been welcomed by many religious feminists. It is part of the folk wisdom of feminism that women have always been suspicious of abstract thinking. Adriana Cavarero's comment that the 'the discourse of the universal … is always a matter for men only' (2000: 53) reflects this popular understanding. Eschewing the flight into abstraction, women are pictured as surviving extreme hardships through their storytelling activities:

Cornered in weaving rooms, like Penelope, they have, since ancient times woven plots with the thread of storytelling … Whether ancient or modern, their art aspires to a wise repudiation of the abstract universal and follows an everyday practice where the tale is existence, relation and attention. (Cavarero, 2000: 53)

In this frame storytelling is a heroic activity through which women have repaired the broken threads of circumstances and created meaningful self-definitions despite their exclusion from patriarchal systems of knowledge and belief.[29] The influential feminist theologian Rebecca Chopp understands 'narrativity' as the primary means through which women 'are composing their lives' (1995: 43) in relation to the divine.[30] As such it is a vital theological activity which now deserves a space in the academy as well as around the kitchen table. Chopp's work is a celebration of what can be achieved when theology is remade as women begin to tell their stories. In the United States the image of the 'crazy quilt' (crafted from worn and irregular scraps of old clothing) is frequently used to describe the process through which women create form and beauty from obscure and care-worn lives.

Such images have a powerful appeal, but feminists must always be aware that the reclamation of domestic images may prove domesticating. Once again I should emphasise that it is no sense the intention of this text to deny the significant role that narrative plays in all areas of contemporary theology. My intention is rather to problematise this in two ways. First, I intend to make visible the ties that bind narrative to literature. Just as in Derrida's argument, speech and writing can never be disassociated, so narrative cannot be separated from the literary constructions of culture. Narrative cannot be positioned as primal, natural and authentic while literature is presented as artificial and deceptive. My second intention is to question the political significance of engaging the feminised

---

28 Carol Christ writes that women 'find that self-identification with the sons and other male images and symbols in the language of the Bible and tradition requires us to reject our particular identities as women – the very identities that we are engaged in recovering and affirming in all the other important areas of our lives … the exclusion of our experience from the funding of sacred stories may point to a basic defect in the perception of ultimate power and reality provided by the traditional stories' (1979a: 230).

29 Women's literature is taken as the culmination of this tradition, bringing women's experience out of the private sphere and manifesting it for public attention.

30 Chopp is particularly indebted to Crites in this understanding (Chopp, 1995: 33).

resources of narrative/literature to sustain theological thinking. The supposedly natural and primal force of storytelling may be pictured as restoring to women what men have always had: a sense of the power of their own agency, the coherence of the social world, the stability of their own identity and an identification with the divine. These functions are important for women, and for other non-dominant groups who are struggling to achieve a position from which it is possible to enter into a political dialogue with others. However, it is important to be aware that women's stories, when used in this way, are only another form of the constructed foundationalism discussed previously. Narrative constructionists like Ricoeur and Crites have been criticised for replacing the stable identity located in Cartesian rationality with a 'narratable self' which functions in a similar way to shore up personal identity and make sense of history (see Cavarero, 2000: 40). What if, however, identity is radically plural and fragmented? What if the events of our times are out of joint and cannot be incorporated into a narratable plot? What if God assumes the form of absolute alterity? And what if literature, far from restoring coherence, lends its energies to the unweaving of the world? What form should theology take in these circumstances? And, if these conditions apply, religious feminists might be better engaged in using literature to pull the tapestry to pieces than in forever weaving together the threads. Penelope, I believe, performed both roles.

Religious reading

Reading the Disaster
Walter Benjamin writes:

Less and less frequently do we encounter people with the ability to tell a tale properly ... It as if something that seemed inalienable to us, the securest among our possessions, were taken from us: the ability to exchange experiences. (Benjamin, 1973 [1940]: 83)

In the previous section I explored the ways in which narrative is currently being used to restore coherence, identity and hope among those who have lost faith in traditional forms of foundationalism. I have argued with Crites that 'narrative form is by no means innocent' (1989: 82) but that its ambivalence is overlooked by theologians from conservative and radical traditions, who have found a turn to narrative immensely useful as it has enabled them to continue their work as if little had changed as a result of the century of holocausts that preceded our own. This 'narrative turn' is not limited or confined to theological circles. Wherever foundational truths are challenged in social or personal life, 'narrative' is prescribed as a means to restore coherence to existence. Such faith has been placed in narrative's power to remake the world that the term 'redemptive' is frequently used to describe its healing power. However, the assumption that the re-establishment of order is to be understood in this quasi-religious sense has not gone unchallenged.

In *Telling Stories: Postmodernism and the Invalidation of Traditional Narrative* (1995), Michael Roemer mounts a sustained critique of this position. Roemer maintains that after the twentieth century's genocides 'we no longer believe in character' (1995: 16) and the plot of history has become unintelligible. This being the case, contemporary attempts to establish that story creates order out of chaos are not only misguided but immoral. However, for Roemer this does not imply that storytelling should cease. It is rather that the power of storytelling should be reassessed in a quite contrary form.

Roemer argues that an examination of traditional folk narratives reveals that they do not function to make the world a safe home but rather to allow humanity to encounter what is strange, unmanageable and *sacred*. In his opinion, stories do not in fact order existence. 'The plot of a traditional story is not really "intelligible". In human terms it often makes no sense whatsoever' (1995: 44). Plot-making does not signify a fragile mastery of circumstances but enables the often tragic encounter with the 'other'. This other 'is necessity, the sacred, fate, nature, process, time, the past, the generic, and the unconscious – all those things from outside that govern our lives' (1995: 56). In reversing the assumption that narrative brings order to human affairs Roemer is offering his own version of the distinction between literature and theology/philosophy – a distinction that he believes is necessary if we are to avoid the dangers of totalising systems that seek to establish an illusory wholeness.[31] Fiction may become strangely redemptive precisely because it resists the reconciliation of differences within the subject, in social affairs or between humanity and the sacred.

> Unlike theology it does not comfort us with the presence of an all-knowing, all-powerful deity – who very likely is fashioned from our own needs and who, in turn, often serves for a model of domination and control. Story insists on the utter alterity of the 'other'. (1995: 151)

Trauma and testimony

Roemer is offering a vision of literature as no longer incarcerated within the walls of the theological palace but able to make an assault against the forces of domination and control in the name of what theology resists: the utter alterity of the other. His passionate and eclectic text protests against attempts to establish narrative coherence in a wide variety of cultural arenas. Recently, however, very significant criticisms of narrative as redemptive practice have begun to emerge from among the writings of those who are specifically concerned with studying the effects of trauma. In the introduction to their edited collection *Tense*

---

31 He writes, 'Heidegger's conflation of poetry and philosophy and his implied rejection of self-division as an inescapable element in the human condition surely make him susceptible to fascism, which too, claimed a single realm and an actualised wholeness ... not only must we pay a steep price for our "wholeness"; but so must all those whose "otherness" sustains it. For there is no *Volk*, no *Reich*, and very likely no *Führer* without the Jew or his equivalent' (1995: 237).

Past: Cultural Essays in Trauma and Memory (1996b) Paul Antze and Michael Lambek argue that there is nothing redemptive about subsuming the chaotic symbolic/embodied symptoms of trauma into a coherent narrative script. Such scripts are often generated in conventional forms by medical/psychological or social authorities who are not only seeking to heal but also to control those who have experienced trauma.[32] In the same text Laurence Kirmayer speaks of trauma memories in holocaust survivors and those who have experienced childhood sexual abuse (these two instances of trauma are often taken as paradigmatic). He argues that these are located on the edges of consciousness 'to be worked around or told in fragments ... *There is no narrative of trauma*' (1996: 175, my emphasis). What are circulated as trauma narratives are often attempts by those who have not been subject to such overwhelming circumstances to repair the social fabric by restoring comprehensibility and communication.[33]

Scholars who focus upon the experience of trauma often use the term 'testimony' rather than 'narrative' to describe the discourse of trauma survivors themselves.[34] Shoshona Felman writes,

As a relation to events, testimony seems to be composed of bits and pieces of a memory that has been overwhelmed by occurrences that have not settled into understanding or remembrance, acts that cannot be constructed as knowledge nor assimilated into full cognition, events in excess of our frames of reference. (1992a: 5)

By making this distinction, Felman is attempting to mark a separation between experiences that can be 'told' and those which are incommunicable in realistic terms—the experience exceeds the frame – but which nevertheless may be given voice through other means. This 'giving of voice' Felman describes as poesis, a translation of experience into strange forms so that inexpressible suffering is 'not given a voice that redeems it from muteness and says it properly but the power to address us in its very silence' (1992b: 163).

In addressing the question 'how can suffering speak?' and suggesting that this may happen through a process of poesis in which metaphor mediates what can never be fully present as coherent narrative, Felman stands in a tradition that has

---

32 They defy the dominant understanding that to speak one's symptoms is to achieve a release from their disturbing power; 'there is nothing liberating in narrative per se ... merely to transfer the story from embodied symptoms to words is not necessarily to exercise it. Development may be foreclosed when a particular version is given complete authority' (Antze and Lambek,1996: xix).

33 Quoting Greenspan he argues that such trauma narratives are attempts to make sense of what 'for the survivors live on as the negation of comprehensible and communicable form. Set against those memories all such accounts are attempts to "make a story" out of what is "not a story"' (Greenspan, in Kirmayer,1996: 185).

34 This was the term used by Elie Weisel to describe his hugely influential autobiographical novel *Night* (1960 [1958]). Weisel has continued to refer to his work as testimony (see Cargas, 1976) and there is no doubt that his preference for this term has been significant in subsequent scholarly use of the word to refer to the narratives of trauma survivors.

engaged with this problem over the past half century. The scandal of representing unbearable experience was articulated most powerfully in Theodor Adorno's reflections upon the Holocaust. His initial judgement was that writing lyrical verses (or indeed engaging in any form of writing) had become impossible after Auschwitz because the world had ceased to be representable in coherent form. He later concluded that the imperative to let suffering speak could only be fulfilled by the metamorphosis of reality which takes place through art and literature.[35]

Adorno's reassessment reflects the artistic achievements of the post-war years and the literature of testimony which emerged out of the horrors of the Second World War. Paul Celan is a representative figure for those writers who strove to make a mediation of suffering through poetry.[36] Reflecting on this process in a public address given in 1960 he stated,

But I think – and this thought will scarcely come as a surprise to you – I think it has always belonged to the expectations of the poem to speak in the cause of the strange – no I can no longer use this word – in precisely this manner to speak in the cause of an other – who knows perhaps in the cause of a wholly other. (1978: 35)

Maurice Blanchot's famous fragmented text, The Writing of the Disaster, articulates similar themes. The disaster is so huge that it is 'the limit of writing' (1995: 7) and de-scribes the world. After such a horror what is it to work at writing?

To write is to renounce being in command of oneself or having any proper name and at the same time it is not to renounce but to announce, welcoming without recognition the absent. Or is it to be in relation through words in their absence with what one cannot remember – a witness to the unencountered, answerable not only for the void in the subject, but for the subject as a void, its disappearance in the imminence of death ... To keep still preserving silence: that is what, all unknowing we all want to do, writing. (1995: 121–122)

What both Celan and Blanchot are reaching towards is an understanding of literature as testimony to what is lost, silent or strange – the other who, for Celan, might indeed be 'wholly other'. This, I would argue, is the last way in which we can see the gendering of literature as female in contemporary debate. As Elaine Marks has observed, 'women have always been on the side that has been repressed. Women are the absent, the unacknowledged, the different and the dead' (in Yorke, 1991: 113). But to think alterity only in these terms would

35 He wrote, 'I have no wish to soften the saying that to write lyric poetry after Auschwitz is barbaric ... But Enzenberger's retort also remains true, that literature must resist the verdict ... It is now virtually in art alone that suffering can still find its own voice, consolation, without immediately being betrayed by it' (Adorno, in Felman, 1992a: 34).
36 The mediation of suffering through literature is a costly process as is evident in the fact that many of the creators of testimony literature eventually find that the struggle to express horror through poesis overwhelms them. What is being described here is not a reconciliation of suffering but rather its brief epiphany.

be to circumscribe literature as the voice of the powerless female victim, always lamenting on the margins and without the power to effect any form of challenge to logocentric power.

By contrast Celan evokes a more active power in poesis, that which makes possible 'the mystery of an encounter' (1978: 37) with the other who confronts and addresses us. Carl Raschke (1988) has termed this sense of being addressed by the other the 'epiphany of darkness'. He argues that it is this strange epiphany which is the ethical concern of poststructuralist theory. The concern with 'the other' has dominated contemporary theoretical debate. According to Raschke, in the work of Jacques Derrida and others we are not catching the faint echoes of a voice from the margins but confronting a cataclysm of syntax which signals the overwhelming of logocentric power by those forces it has long excluded (1988: 110). Raschke is fascinated by the fact that Derrida has hypostasised the deconstructive processes at work in contemporary theory in female form, indeed as a female divine (1992: 95). This, however, has been a controversial move in the eyes of many feminists who are suspicious of claims by male theorists to identify the 'feminine' with what is unrepresentable and appears in their work, as far from benign.

Poetry and obligation

Raschke is one of a number of theologians working on the frontiers of literature, theology and critical theory who are signalling the emergence of a new under-standing of the relations between the disciplines which is very different from those which have dominated discussions in the past. Poststructuralist theory, as the pre-eminent discourse of alterity in our times, has provided a conceptual vocabulary in which literature is seen as an embodiment in textuality of the 'other' who disrupts the order of the Word. Mark Ledbetter writes that literature has the ability 'to violate the reader and writer of texts ... imposing on us a story unfamiliarly shocking enough that we cannot live our lives outside the victim's untold story' (1997: 123). Ledbetter here uses the word 'violation' to describe the experience of a shocking encounter with alterity. David Pacini expresses the same sense of a traumatic bonding in his reflections upon the nature of Christian doctrine in the light of the death of his baby son:[37]

I am connected to a silence, an ellipsis ... Hence I am bound by an obligation of transfer-ence, mobilised by the energies of the silenced to become a debtor to the foreign place that static tradition refuses to claim. I am called to the interminable political labour of speaking in the name of the site of the excluded. (1994: 148)

---

37 Pacini's reflections are prompted by the death of his infant son and the effect it has had upon his own understanding of faith. The symbolics of poststructuralism give him a voice to express protest, grief and commitment in a radically different form from that of orthodox credal formulas.

In Pacini's understanding, 'being bound by an obligation' is political witness, and this theme is further developed by John Caputo in *Against Ethics* (1993). This text develops the notion of obligation as being laid hold of, seized or claimed by the other. The other is encountered in the midst of a disaster. Caputo refuses the singularity of the word 'disaster' in Blanchot's writing – for him 'life is a disaster' (1993: 8) and 'Disasters are places where *poems* cluster like leaves rapped in the fissures of windswept walls' (1993: 181, my emphasis). Caputo's reflections are framed in terms of a poetics of obligation. This is a poesis which might be regarded as the embodiment of obligation. 'It is a matter of writing other histories, telling other stories, of worrying over other oblivions, of answering other calls' (1993: 166). It involves siding with 'disastrous, disfigured, ill-formed, ill-fated, star-crossed, damaged bodies – with everything that the discourses call flesh' (1993: 194).

Everything that the discourses call flesh. That which is bodily, fragile, fertile, desiring, disruptive – female. That which now seizes hold of us and obliges us to respond to its claims. Literature is here imaged as confronting theology with the challenge of those things which David Jasper has argued, are 'too often excluded by its systematic claims – laughter, expenditure, meaninglessness, loss … the scandal and the stumbling block must be reintroduced to overturn the rhetorical machinery of religious power' (Jasper, 1993c: 9).

Jasper believes that instead of settling back into the conservative traditions through which an understanding of the relations between literature and theology has been constructed in the past (1992: 2), it is now necessary to recognise that literature might offer theology its best, perhaps only chance, to cease from the futile theodical exercises through which it has sought to extricate itself from the guilt of genocide. Theology must open itself up to the challenge to embrace that which it continually flees. This would be both an end and a beginning.

But that means bearing to think the unthinkable: embodying in textuality the unbearable so that embodiment and incarnation endures and embraces its own fragmentation and dismemberment (1993: 161)

The book and the body

Although we must never lose sight of the fact that the gendered terms 'literature' and 'theology' are used heuristically (a book is not a body; a book is not a girl – really) it is apparent that in each of the three theological projects I have explored very significant issues are being negotiated under the cover of what might be dismissed as a marginal academic concern: 'How do we study literature and theology today?' It will also be evident that I am deeply dissatisfied with attempts to use literature to restore theology's failing powers. My own sympathies lie with the third approach in which literature is imaged as laying hold of theology and confronting it with the claims of the feminised other. These claims are practical and political but they also lead beyond themselves towards what is

35

variously described as the silenced, the absent and the unbearable. In this frame the trajectory that is followed is through politics towards a mystery. The journey begins at the point of pain where we are challenged to ask how we may write the divine after the disaster.

In aligning myself with this approach to literature I am espousing a perspective that has been powerfully championed by male scholars but has not yet featured significantly in the work of religious feminists. Furthermore, whereas male colleagues have drawn upon the work of male poststructuralist writers in their reflections upon literature, religious feminists have largely ignored the important work of women poststructuralist theorists on the significance of literature as a feminine sphere. This body of work has much to contribute to the development of our own thinking and in the second part of this text I hope to demonstrate how our reading practices might be enriched through engaging with this important resource. Before doing so I turn, in the next two chapters, to interrogating the two approaches to the use of literature in feminist theology that have predominated up till now. Both of these are dependent upon characterising literature as a feminine voice disputing logocentric authority. However, the manner in which literature is constructed as feminine, while drawing upon the conventions described in this chapter, takes a rather different form in feminist theology than elsewhere in theological discourse. Both approaches to literature have influenced the development of feminist theology in significant ways – although I shall argue that, unless subjected to critical scrutiny, they also have the potential to limit and circumscribe the role that literature is assigned within feminist religious thinking in the future.

CHAPTER 2

Visions and revisions

Carol Christ and women on the spiritual quest

Losing innocence

In the previous chapter I set out to occupy a different vantage point from which to view the relation between literature and theology from those that have been favoured by feminist theologians in the past. In so doing it was my intention to locate an examination of the use of women's writing in feminist theology in a much wider frame than usual. When surveying the various approaches to literature within the work of religious feminists it soon becomes apparent that debates concerning appropriate relations between literature and theology are not a primary concern. There are many reasons why this is so. Chief among these is the fact that literature written by women is so rich in its references to the divine.

Early works of feminist criticism celebrated the discovery of this remarkable spiritual legacy and demonstrated how the spiritual radicalism of women's creative writing posed a direct challenge to the conventions of domestic piety usually deemed appropriate to women. For this reason women authors often found it necessary to dissemble and communicate their audacious visions in the language of the family hearth and schoolroom (see, for example, Gilbert and Gubar, 1979).

In the twentieth century women authors became more audacious in their spiritual experimentation. This new confidence was fuelled by burgeoning research on female deities in antiquity, a growing awareness of Eastern religions in which the sacred feminine continued to be venerated and anthropological studies which revealed the spiritual traditions of women in many cultures. Virginia Woolf was an eager reader of such literature and her representation of dazzling but ambivalent women characters, such as Mrs Ramsey and Mrs Dalloway, are experiments in the representation of female sacred power (see Carpentier, 1998). P.L. Travers drew upon her extensive readings of Hindu traditions to create the playful but dangerous maternal surrogate, Mary Poppins. The poet H.D. was particularly bold in her scholarly reappropriation of ancient religious symbols. She combined these alien forms with the folk beliefs of her Mennonite forebears and conceived an idiosyncratic theosophical awareness of the female divine. This 'lady' had been known in many forms throughout history. H.D. held that she could be discovered anew amid the crises and disasters of modern times. She is not 'imprisoned in leaden bars in a coloured window/ She is Psyche, the butterfly/ Out of the cocoon' (1983 [1946]: 571).

It is clearly evident why religious feminists have turned to writers such as these in order to demonstrate how women outside the theological guild were actively engaged in confronting male-centred spiritual traditions before the emergence of feminist theological scholarship. However, the work of contemporary women writers, in continuity with this heterodox tradition, is also seen as a parallel discourse that can be easily merged with our own and incorporated into our own work. This appropriation seems all the more natural because we appear to speak the same language.

Feminist critics have demonstrated how the employment of a 'female sublime' had become an established convention in women's writing by the latter part of the twentieth century.[38] This female sublime appropriates the tremendous power of religious symbolism but articulates it in a distinctively feminine voice and with emancipatory intent. Its use is widespread. Novelists such as Michelle Roberts and Sarah Maitland creatively revision the Christian heritage. Toni Morrison, Amy Tan and Isabel Allende are among the best-selling authors who employ female religious traditions marginalised by the dominant culture. Jeanette Winterson and Elizabeth Smart construct a sacred discourse elaborated around female sexuality. A woman-centred ecological spirituality animates much of the poetry and prose of Margaret Atwood.

All these uses of 'sublime' discourse are literary devices that may be employed as a means of articulating insights that are inexpressible in the common currency of everyday language. It is because religious symbolism remains so highly charged and is familiar-while-becoming-strange that it has the power to carry what other words cannot. Its employment within literature is thus not necessarily confessional, and it would be inappropriate to claim that every woman who employs the female sublime is a 'religious' writer. Nevertheless, women's writing, with its abundant spiritual images, functions as a rich and accessible resource for religious feminists who have found that Western theological and ethical traditions do not furnish them with the necessary resources to address the divine in ways that express their specificity, or their passion for justice. What appears to be missing from the common store of the faithful can apparently be readily supplied from an alternative source.

Women's literature has served religious feminists so well that it has not been judged necessary to engage in the kind of interdisciplinary explorations

---

38 For a discussion of the 'female sublime' in women's writing see Patricia Yaeger's classic text *Honey-Mad Women: Emancipatory Strategies in Women's Writing* (1988).

outlined at the beginning of chapter 1. It must also be admitted that there are some disadvantages in re-marking traditional disciplinary borders when we have become accustomed to enjoying the privileges of unrestricted access. We lose an innocence, a sense that we inherit an open garden in which we can freely eat of all the fruits. And there is a further loss of innocence involved in focusing upon the processes that result in the gendering of cultural forms. We risk the fall into theory. The concerns of feminist theologians in the Anglo-American context have always displayed the pragmatism of the domestic cultural and political traditions in which their work developed. Thus we have been much less inclined to ask 'what is a text?' than 'how can I use this book?' The political agenda which has inspired much religious feminism has seemed to confirm the legitimacy of this pragmatic approach to knowledge (see, for example, Curti, 1998 and Rowley and Grosz, 1990). There has been a suspicion that the liberating ideals of feminism might be compromised by too deep an entanglement in theoretical debate. The language of literary theory can seem particularly abstruse and there has been a suspicion that this is a male discourse that threatens to subvert the energies of women.[39]

Neither has it proved necessary to resort to theoretical arguments in order to claim that women's writing represents a female counterpart to the 'male' texts of theology and philosophy. No doubt cultural assumptions concerning the feminised status of fiction have been operative within feminist theology as elsewhere. However, it is the traditions of liberal humanism that have shaped the approach of religious feminists to literature written by women. Deep within the unspoken conventions of this 'common sense' tradition is the assumption that texts somehow participate in the identity of their authors.[40] Women's literature is seen as uniquely illuminating for women readers because it speaks with the voice of one woman talking to another. More than this, books written by women have also come to be regarded as 'female' texts. Within this frame it is *authorship*, rather than the classification of a text as literature or theology, that assigns a work its gender. The slippage between author, text and reader that is integral to this way of thinking has resulted in a conceptual elision. From the assertion of a common female identity between author, reader and text is generated a further claim that women's writing has a natural and legitimate authority. It can claim to testify to the realities of women's experience and thus speak with the voice of everywoman.

In this chapter I shall demonstrate, through a critical reading of the work of Carol Christ and Alicia Ostriker, how this 'common sense' approach has shaped the

39 Feminist theologians have retained a deep commitment to the democratisation of knowledge and cherish a certain pride in the 'kitchen table' production of theology. There has been a concern not to separate the language of theology from the ordinary speech of women or to allow our agendas to be set by concerns that appear remote from the issues of those who suffer poverty, oppression or violence.

40 See pp. 88–90

development of feminist theological thinking. I shall make plain how important it has been, and how far it has taken us, in shaping our critique of male-centred theological traditions. However, I shall also question whether the apparent transparency of this approach has prevented religious feminists from perceiving how the conventions structuring relations between literature and theology, which were discussed in chapter 1, continue to impact upon our own work in ways that may be unhelpful, restricting and potentially harmful to our project.

Searching for maps

It is appropriate that this interrogation of the use of literature within feminist theology begins by considering the pioneering work of Carol Christ since her work has so decisively influenced the approach of religious feminists to women's writing. Christ began her work in the early days of feminist scholarship, and works that explore the relation between women's writing and theology still continue to engage her thinking.

In the late 1960s and early 1970s, women academics, particularly those engaged in theological research, experienced many problems in articulating concerns specific to women. They were also frequently isolated and marginalised within their faculties. In their joint preface to *Womanspirit Rising* (1979b), Christ and her friend Judith Plaskow reminisce about their time at Yale:[41]

> We remember the day we proposed to a professor that we might take one of our comprehensives on the history of Christian attitudes towards women. Although we were armed with seven or eight pages of sources on the subject we had no sooner mentioned the topic than he slammed his fist down on the table and shouted 'not for me, you're not!' We also remember Carol's turning in a seminar paper on Barth's view of women to a professor who glanced at the title and remarked that he had never considered that a very important topic. He then went on to discuss the papers presented by the males in the class. (1979b: ix)

Not only were women lacking mentors and colleagues, feminists had yet to hollow out their own discursive space in which to test and debate new ideas. There was no easily accessible body of feminist writing. A tiny number of scholars, notable among them Simone de Beauvoir (1972 [1949]) and Margaret Mead (1977 [1949]), exercised an extraordinary influence. This was not only because of their appeal to enquiring women in search of intellectual maps but also because their thinking had achieved acknowledgement and some degree of acceptance both within and beyond the academy. However, feminist scholarship needed to move beyond an extended commentary upon the work of those very few women whose critique of gendered culture was judged worthy of serious attention. A younger generation of scholars sought to establish the legitimacy of

41 The place where the canonical narrative theology practised by Frei and others first began to exert its powerful influence upon contemporary theology.

their own critical perspectives. One of the ways in which they did so was by the gradual staking out of a new autonomous space – 'women's experience'.[42]

Literature and women's experience

The claim to this independent territory was crucial in the development of women's theological critique. Valerie Saiving's article, 'The Human Situation: A Feminine View' (1979 [1960]) is taken by Christ and Plaskow to signal the birth of feminist theology (1979c: 19–24), and is an exemplary prototype of later critical incursions. Saiving is careful to ground her arguments in the anthropological writings of acknowledged women scholars and makes particular reference to Margaret Mead. However, she does so with the intention of legitimising her appeal to 'women's experience' as a valid hermeneutical key. 'I propose to criticise, from the viewpoint of feminine experience, the estimate of the human situation made by certain contemporary theologians' (1979: 25).

While conciliatory and cautious in tone, Saiving's essay represents a radical challenge to established theological method:

It is my contention that there are significant differences between masculine and feminine experience and that feminine experience reveals in more emphatic fashion certain aspects of the human situation which are present but less obvious in the experience of men. Contemporary theological doctrines of love have, I believe, been constructed primarily upon the basis of masculine experience and thus view the human condition from a male standpoint. Consequently these doctrines do not provide an adequate interpretation of the situation of women. (1979: 27)

Saiving's contention is that theology is mutilated by its failure to consider the insights of women. Only through their incorporation might it cease to be a dangerous and damaging force and have a future in a world in which 'a theology based solely upon masculine experience may well be irrelevant' (1979: 41).

The work of Saiving was influential in shaping the later writing of Christ and Plaskow. However, the two women introduced a new dimension to the debate

---

42 As well as being a useful theoretical strategy the appeal to experience also carried particularly powerful associations for feminists. The 'consciousness raising group', in which women friends shared their personal histories and forged them into shared political analysis, generated much of the early energy of the movement. Christ testifies to the power identified with this activity: 'In consciousness raising groups ... women are engaged in the extremely important and exciting task of recovering and discovering the shapes and contours of our own experience. We tell each other stories which have never been told before, stories utterly unlike the stories we have all learned from the culture ... we have gained the power to create new being' (1979a: 229). The writers whose work had proved inspirational in the early development of the women's liberation movement came to be recast less as individual visionaries and more as participants in the shared task of articulating a new consciousness. Christ describes de Beauvoir as a 'theorist of women's experience', and in so doing she both incorporates her inheritance into the new feminist movement and democratises the project. What is being described is no longer the contribution of a few women 'good enough' to enter the male world of reasonable debate but an entirely different location from which to speak.

by using *women's literature as a privileged medium of access to women's experience.*[43] It is read as communicating with directness and authenticity the truth as women see it. This understanding of women's writing was born from an unprecedented encounter with Doris Lessing's five novel series *Children of Violence* (1990a-e) and their central character, Martha Quest. Christ and Plaskow spent many hours reading and discussing these texts. Christ writes 'When I first read *The Four Gated City* I dreamed about it for weeks' (1979: 231). More soberly, Plaskow writes that Martha embodied their critical insights enabling them to give form and 'content to the idea of women's experience' (1980: 49). It is interesting to note that beyond theological circles Lessing's writing was exerting an extraordinary influence among women readers at this time (see Greene, 1991: 106). The writer responsible for the first tampon in English literature offered models of creative and intelligent women struggling with the realities of everyday life in a society deeply hostile to their personal and political aspirations. Her work was massively important to women coming to feminist awareness.

Both Plaskow and Christ produced important books from their shared reflections, first upon Lessing and then upon other women writers. Plaskow chose to follow the agenda set by Saiving, and in *Sex, Sin and Grace: Women's Experience and the Theology of Reinhold Niebuhr and Paul Tillich* (1980) she sets out to employ women's experience to challenge the fundamental assumptions of these male theologians concerning human nature. Like Saiving she sought to establish her credentials by appealing to the authority of Mead and de Beauvoir. However, these theorists are now seen as offering a limited perspective. Their accounts of womanhood must be confirmed and deepened 'by recent literature by and about women ... it is only through literature that the dynamic of *women's experience can begin to emerge in all its complexity*' (1980: 34, my emphasis).

Although they remained friends and colleagues, Christ's encounter with women's writing provided her with the energy to undertake a voyage of greater distance than Plaskow's. For Plaskow in *Sex, Sin and Grace*, literature was the powerful means to 'add a final layer to our vision of women's experience' (1980: 38) which could then take its place alongside the experience of men as a valid resource in theological thinking. For Christ, women's writing provided the evidence for an altogether different spiritual awareness among women that could not be contained within the boundaries of theology at all.

Christ's short essay 'Spiritual Quest and Women's Experience' (1979a [1975]) is an attempt to formulate a response to Lessing's impact upon her. She begins negatively by describing her alienation from male religious narratives. Women's experience 'has not funded the sacred stories of biblical tradition ... We will no longer be content to read ourselves sideways into stories in which the daughters

---

43 The concept of 'women's experience' quickly became one of the most contentious issues in feminist theology. For a fuller discussion of this subject see chapter 4, pp. 79–83.

do not exist' (1979a: 230). Women need what men have always had access to: a treasury containing powerful myths which can be used to mirror and interpret their lives. To satisfy this hunger they 'must devour literature which reflects our experience' (1979a: 231). In Lessing's writing can be discerned 'a structure of a quest myth from the perspective of women's experience which strikes a chord with many women' (1979a: 238). This quest, Christ suggests, has a number of stages which are repeated in the everyday lives of women everywhere and attested to in the fiction of women writers. Having 'discovered' the parameters of a quest which she believed to be common, or even archetypal, in women's experience, Christ set out to test this hypothesis by 'comparing Martha's quest to the quests of other women, both in literature and in life' (1979a: 238). This is the project of Christ's most famous work, *Diving Deep and Surfacing: Women Writers on the Spiritual Quest* (1980).

From nothingness to new naming

Christ's book contains an expanded exploration of the four significant moments in the spiritual quest which are now termed *nothingness*,[44] *awakening, insight* and *new naming*.

In describing *nothingness* Christ uses the language and concepts of her time to explore women's feelings of cultural invisibility and lack of self worth. She comments upon their confinement to the domestic sphere where their creative energies are dissipated in trivial and repetitive tasks. She notes their educational and occupational disadvantages as well as the unease women feel about their bodies. Christ contends that women suffer greatly because of the restrictions placed upon them but that their travails are deemed petty, boring and self-induced – not to be compared to the weighty, existential dilemmas of significant males which are well documented in spiritual writings.

Women need a literature that names their pain and allows them to use the emptiness of their lives as an occasion for insight rather than as one more indication of their worthlessness. (1979a: 17)

The spiritual strength that can be gained through confronting nothingness Christ terms *awakening*.[45] This is a word she regards as more appropriate than *conversion* to describe the experience of women who are beginning to sense another dimension impressing upon their mundane reality. A man achieving spiritual awareness is commonly portrayed as turning from one source of authority to another, renouncing an overdeveloped sense of pride in self and involvement in the material order in submission to a higher power. Like Saiving (1979) and

44 This is an ambivalent concept referring both to the current emptiness of women's lives and the possibility of entering uncharted space to create new forms. The word is borrowed from the work of Mary Daly, who employs it in *Beyond God the Father* (1986 [1973]). Daly in turn has adapted the thinking of Michael Novak in *The Experience of Nothingness* (1970).
45 This term refers back to Kate Chopin's novel *The Awakening* (1972 [1899]).

Plaskow (1980), Christ asserts that women have a need to achieve, rather than relinquish, identity and power. They will do so through becoming awake to the 'powers of being' in themselves, in other women and in the material forces of the natural world.[46]

It is their *insight* into ultimate connectedness, 'union or integration with powers' (1979a: 19), which Christ sees as the particular hallmark of women's spiritual quest. They are likely to discern this connection in particular circumstances. Of prime importance to those deprived of an image in culture are perceptions of transcendence in nature. 'Women's experiences in nature are extremely significant because they can occur in solitude when a woman feels isolated from other people and has nowhere to turn' (1980: 23). Spiritual awareness can also be the result of a woman sensing the power of being in her own body as she unites with other creative forces to produce life. However, Christ does not totally locate the sources of spiritual power in the realms of nature. Women simply enjoying each other's company, or involved in political movements, may sense that 'the quest for truth or justice or being which they embody are rooted in the powers of being' (1980: 23). The sources of power identified here reflect Christ's deepening devotion to the goddess.

The final stage in women's spiritual quest is *new naming*. This entails resisting what Mary Daly has termed 'false naming' – the description of the world from a male perspective. Women are called upon to employ their insights to shape the world anew. In particular women are called to resist dualism through a re-evaluation of the negative poles of the Western binary system. However, Christ has no wish to abolish difference through enforcing 'a new monism' (1980: 129) but rather to end the definition of existence in hierarchical or oppositional categories.

The quest in women's literature

Having outlined the features of women's distinctive spiritual quest Christ goes on to describe the evidence she has found to support her description of this common journey in women's literature. She begins with Kate Chopin's novel *The Awakening* (1972 [1899]), one of the most significant rediscoveries of the feminist movement.[47] In it the passive heroine, Edna, awakens to her own power through immersion in nature – she learns to swim. Edna begins to seek sexual freedom and rebels against her social confinement in domesticity and motherhood. However, although she can achieve a certain degree of autonomy, the social forces ranged against her prove too strong to conquer. Rather than conform to them she swims out to sea from the same beach where she awoke to the potential of freedom. Christ sees Chopin's work as confirming her description of women's spiritual quest but criticises the author for failing to unite spiritual and

46 For a more recent discussion of this issue see Coakley (1996).

47 It received much critical abuse on first publication but has now become a feminist classic.

social liberation. 'Edna's suicide is a spiritual triumph but a social defeat' (1980: 39). She states that today's feminist readers require that authors,

write stories in which the spiritual and social quest can be combined in the life of a re-alistic woman. And also one task facing readers is not to be fully satisfied with women's literature until it does so. (Christ, 1980: 40)

In her analysis of Margaret Atwood's *Surfacing* (1985), Christ discerns a similarly valiant but flawed attempt to describe women's quest. The sufferings of the unnamed protagonist after a traumatic abortion are linked to the laying waste of the generative powers of the Canadian wilderness. The hero regains her power when she dives into the deep lake and reclaims her link to the chain of being by conceiving a child. The protagonist recognises her body as both *revelation* and *incarnation* of the great powers of life and death (1980: 47). Although Atwood succeeds in allowing her heroine to overcome the alienation that has separated her from her roots, she does so in a stereotypical manner through becoming a mother. Christ argues the question of the impetus towards social change is unresolved.

Although it was Lessing who initially inspired Christ to consider literature as revelatory in *Diving Deep and Surfacing*, she is not uncritical of her mentor. Lessing is still to be admired for the concreteness of her writing and for rooting Martha's quest in the violence of a generation travelling between the holocaust and environmental catastrophe – but Christ is less convinced that Lessing offers a way forward into the future. Martha begins her awakening in mire and motherhood, 'she and her friend, both pregnant, take off their clothes and luxuriate in the rich red mud created by a summer rainstorm' (Christ, 1980: 57). However, it is through learning the desperate patience of the insane that she becomes able to decipher the inchoate sounds of the future. It is Martha's psychic discernment of the voices of the future that Christ finds most problematic. On first reading it seemed to Christ that this interpretative ability offered real hope for a mystical mediation of political disaster. Upon reflection though, Christ is disappointed with Martha's eventual occupation in rearing 'new children' who have evolved powers that appear to promise that humanity may survive the coming disaster. Christ writes, 'I find more to hope for in the new naming that emerges from the sisterhood of women than in Lessing's vision of the miraculous new children' (1980: 73).

The poetry of Adrienne Rich presents a different agenda for Christ from that raised by the previously mentioned writers. There can be no doubt of Rich's feminist credentials. What is less evident is that her writing can be seen as spiritual. Christ asserts that, particularly in *The Dream of a Common Language* (1978a), Rich has moved beyond describing the violence and disintegration (nothingness) of patriarchy towards a new focus upon women's beauty and strength. This lesbian vision is a *new naming* because woman-love had formerly been excluded from representation. Christ focuses upon Rich's declaration: 'There are words I cannot choose again: *humanism, androgyny*' (in Christ, 1980: 84). This is an option for difference which Christ herself affirms as pointing towards the transformation of culture.

Christ's study of her final author, Ntozake Shange, is the section which is most criticised today (see, for example Thistlethwaite, 1989: 6). Shange's choreopoem, *for colored girls who have considered suicide/ when the rainbow is enuf* (1986) is straightforwardly appropriated as the cultural property of all women 'who feel they have actually lived through the stories they have heard' (Christ, 1980: 97). The work is interpreted as triumphant confirmation of a successful spiritual journey from nothingness to new naming. Shange's statement out of adversity 'i found god in myself/ and I loved her', is universalised to read 'in this case women' (Christ, 1980: 116) rather than remaining a message to the 'colored girls' whom Shange explicitly addresses.

The limits of experience

At the climax of her work the archetype that Christ has laboriously constructed displays its most evident weakness. Her critics have argued that the distillation of 'women's experience' into the form of an archetypal quest has served to obscure the social, economic and ethnic differences between women.

Annalies van Heijst (1995) elaborates this accusation, not only in relation to Shange but also through a detailed analysis of Christ's reading of Atwood's *Surfacing*. In her novel Atwood makes reference to the exploitative use the United States has made of the Canadian wilderness. Christ makes light of this important theme, preferring instead to emphasise gender differences that unite women in a common relationship to men and to the environment. Atwood felt compelled to respond to the interpretation Christ (and Plaskow) place upon her work. Van Heijst writes:

In Atwood's 'A Reply', a commentary of only a page and a half, she says that she finds the discussion of both women highly interesting. She adds two notes. The first is that a novel is not a statement of ideas. The second is that the theologians Christ and Plaskow have viewed the central metaphor of the novel, the opposition between technology and nature, as an analogy for the relationships between the sexes. Canadian critics, Atwood (herself a Canadian) remarks neatly, knew they should read this metaphor as a reference to the relation between exploitative America and Canada. (1995: 258)

In the light of her analysis, van Heijst asserts that Christ's commitment to visionary feminist interpretations leads her to distort the testimony of those who do not share her assumptions/experience. She conceals her own rigid framework by a critique of orthodox Christianity but allows no similar testing of the violence of her own method. Van Heijst discerns in Christ's work the operation of a new feminist orthodoxy which is similar in its repressive tendencies to the order it seeks to abolish:

The urge to ascribe feminist meanings can lead to new repressions, i.e. repressions of other kind of differences. Such interpretations are inclined towards moralism: simple prescriptions of good and evil. (1995: 267)

Furthermore, Christ is accused of not modifying her perspective in the light of criticism.

Critiques of how Christ uses women's experience such as those rehearsed above are compelling. While retaining a deep commitment to their heuristic method, however, Christ and Plaskow have made clear (for example, in their 'Introduction' to *Weaving theVisions: New Patterns in Feminist Spirituality*, 1989) the grave weaknesses they see in their early work:

In *Womanspirit Rising* ... [we] often wrote of women's experience in universalising terms. Ten years later we recognise that 'women's experience' too often means 'white middle class women's experience' in just the same way that 'human' too often means male ... To continue using the concept of women's experience under these circumstance obligates us to uncover and describe the diversity it encompasses. The notion of women's experience must be taken as an invitation to explore particularity rather than homogenise significant differences. (Christ and Plaskow, 1989: 3)

Whether it is possible to claim the authority of women's experience while avoiding its universalising claims is debatable. Feminists are still struggling with this difficult problem (see chapter 4). However, recognition of this dilemma should not obscure the crucial role played by Christ in establishing the importance of gender difference as a valid critical perspective in theological thinking. Where there is no place to stand it is a political imperative to create new ground. Christ's use of women's literature to confirm the authority of 'women's experience' enabled a decisive leap forward to take place in feminist scholarship. In struggling to understand what defines scholarship as 'feminist writing' Elizabeth Grosz has written, 'It must help, in whatever way, to facilitate the production of new and perhaps unknown, unthought discursive spaces ... that contest the limits and constraints currently at work in the regulation of textual production and reception' (1995: 23). Christ's use of literature to embody 'women's experience' has certainly achieved this and I concur with the judgement of Kathleen Sands that this was crucial in 'suspending androcentric assumptions about generic humanity and inclusive truth in order to clear a space in which women's questions could be asked' (1994: 135). Seen in this light, Christ's failure to perceive the implicit racism in her use of experience places her alongside, rather than apart from, other white women scholars then and now. As Sands states, it reflects the sad imprint of 'a long moment through which we have yet to finish passing' (1994: 124).

We cannot thus be dismissive of the hugely significant contribution Christ made to the early development of feminist theology through her insistence upon the authority of experience. However, we will have many questions concerning the use of women's literature to serve her strategic purposes and the precedent that this has set for other religious feminists. The appeal to experience fails to note the strangeness of literary discourse. Christ fails to recognise that 'realism' is a literary device and believes she can transparently appropriate literary texts for her own political/spiritual ends. As van Heijst argues,

Christ reads literary texts ... as testimonies to experience and as statements. She erases both the fictional as well as the literary character of the text: life and literature overflow into each other ... The difference between persons and characters fades. Literature appears to be a realistic reflection of experiences: the notion that literature is a constructed representation appears to be absent. (1995: 261)

Van Heijst sees Christ's commitment to feminist identity politics based upon 'women's experience' and her realistic readings of literary texts as inextricably intertwined and contributing together to an oppressive naivety in feminist theological readings. She accuses her not only of obscuring women's social differences, but also of developing a tradition of highly restrictive reading practices and of generating a realist canon of literature deemed appropriate for theological reflection. Ironically, this has resulted in a situation in which theology, albeit feminist theology, is once again placed in a position of dominance over literature, 'the literary text is an aid for another better theology. In that sense Christ is a more faithful follower of the theological tradition of reading than she herself acknowledges' (1995: 266). Perhaps the legacy of Christ's time at Yale is more important than has been recognised. It is certainly the case that Christ repeats the gesture used by Frei, Hauerwas and other canonical narrative theologians when she insists that narrative realism as a genre can operate as an intermediary between literary and theological discourse.

These accusations are serious. It is certainly the case that feminist theologians following Christ have not tended to inquire into the legitimacy of their fictional readings on any other basis than whether the 'women's experience' they incarnate can be viewed as authentic. However, Christ's pioneering work in raising fundamental challenges to androcentric traditions through her readings of women's literature cannot be dismissed. Her major contribution has been to encourage religious feminists to view works of literature written by women as strong texts capable of challenging male-centred theological discourse.

By refusing to assimilate women's stories to the doctrines of men she has established women's literature as a theological source that while still largely ignored by androcentric religious studies has become vital to most religious feminists. (Sands,1994: 124)

Alicia Ostriker and the love relations of literature and theology

Coils of the serpent
I turn now turn to examine the work of Alicia Ostriker, whose approach to literature I have paired with Christ's since both women are united in their characterisation of women's literature as representing distinctively female experiences

and apprehensions of the divine. Both Christ and Ostriker rhetorically employ women's literature as the 'voice of woman'[48] and contrast it with the male tones of established religious traditions. For Christ this contrast implies contradiction. Contemporary women's writing heralds the coming into being of an alternative spiritual consciousness among women. This is the direct consequence of the feminist awakening that has generated insight and new naming. Women are now able to 'tell each other stories *which have never been told before*' (Christ, 1979a: 229, my emphasis) and women's writing is to be trusted because it stands somehow apart from the works of men.

In contrast Ostriker believes there is the possibility of a complementary relationship between male and female wisdom. Instead of seeking to establish women's literature as a separate source of spiritual authority she seeks to engage with male-centred theological traditions – to shift, subvert and seduce dominant forms rather than supplant them. She argues that women do not need to turn their backs upon the past because within tradition can be found the evidence that women have always been active in cultural production. There has never been a time when they have not sought to modify and subvert dominant understandings. Our cultural inheritance is thus not monological but contains the submerged evidence of women's traditions upon which today's feminists can continue to build. Contemporary women's literature finds its place within an ancient chain of creative interventions. The serpent has always coiled itself around the rod and its spiral forms are engraved upon the cross. There has always been a conversational relationship between male and female traditions which has frequently been acrimonious but has the potential to generate political and cultural renewal.

Reading our own writing

Ostriker has only recently been acknowledged as an important theological thinker, and the reputation she enjoys in feminist circles is largely founded upon her work in literary criticism and as an award-winning poet. Her early work is the product of her fascination with William Blake and in particular his prophetic writings. These stimulated Ostriker as much because of their rare and complex verse form as their subversive and esoteric content. Significantly, even in her earliest published writing (for example, *Vision and Verse in William Blake*, 1965), she interprets the conjunction of constraint and anarchy as an implicit acknowledgement of the need to pay deep homage to custom and order when attempting radical and disruptive reinterpretations of tradition. Ostriker shifted her attention to the work of women poets as a growing interest in feminism alerted her to the misogyny of Blake's romanticism and excited her with examples of women poets wrestling with traditional forms and symbols in the attempt to create a new imaginary order.

48 Although in her later work Ostriker increasingly uses the particularity of her Jewish identity as a creative resource and speaks quite specifically as a Jewish feminist.

Ostriker acknowledges a continuing debt to the critics who prompted this change of direction in her thinking and particularly to those who stimulated her efforts to discover the contours of an emerging tradition in American women's poetry. It is worth mentioning three contributions in particular because of their impact upon her work. The first comes from Elaine Showalter and especially her pioneering work of gynocriticism,[49] *A Literature of their Own: From Charlotte Bronte to Doris Lessing* (1977). Showalter took as the motif for her work John Stuart Mill's assertion that if women had lived in a country of their own they would have created a literature of their own. Like many male scholars, then and now, Mill regarded the work of women writers as imitative and dependent upon the work of men. In contrast Showalter argued that women writers have created a tradition in which 'female culture is a center … Beyond fantasy, beyond androgyny, beyond assimilation' (1977: 319). Showalter cites many examples of female authors saw it as their duty to end the silence of literature on subjects of importance to women; and demonstrates how they were encouraged to do so by a perceptive female readership. This process has resulted in the development of a shared literary culture among women which has become progressively more confident of its 'Feminine, Feminist and Female' voice (1997: 13).

A second major influence upon Ostriker's developing thinking was Sandra Gilbert's and Susan Gubar's *The Madwoman in the Attic: The Woman Writer and the Nineteenth Century Literary Imagination* (1979). Whereas Showalter draws upon sociological and anthropological thinking to analyse a literary tradition born from women's marginality in culture, Gilbert and Gubar employ a psychoanalytic paradigm in this monumental work. Their thinking owes much to the work of Harold Bloom (1973), who offered a disturbing picture of the forces driving male artistic production. These he pictured as being generated out of a desperate and lonely struggle to assert individual creativity in relation to powerful father figures and all-pervasive inherited tradition.[50]

In contrast to their male counterparts, Gilbert and Gubar argue, women writers have found themselves deprived of role models validating their audacious claims to authorship. They have possessed no publicly acknowledged matrilineal descent in which to locate their own creative work. Gilbert and Gubar argue that without

---

49 Gynocriticism is a term that was employed by feminist critics in the 1970s and 1980s to signal their concern to explore women's experience, culture and literary traditions in their critical work.

50 Gilbert and Gubar write: 'Applying Freudian structures to literary genealogies, Bloom has postulated that the dynamics of literary history arise from the artist's 'anxiety of influence', his fear that he is not his own creator and that the works of his predecessors, existing before and beyond him, assume essential priority over his own writings. In fact, as we pointed out in our discussion of the metaphor of literary paternity, Bloom's paradigm of the sequential historical relationship between literary artists is the relationship of father and son, specifically that relationship as it was defined by Freud. Thus Bloom explains that a 'strong poet' must engage in heroic warfare with his precursor', for, involved as he is in a literary Oedipal struggle, a man can only become a poet by somehow invalidating his poetic father' (1979: 46–47).

such a genealogy women struggle less with the anxiety to assert their own originality and more with an intense psychic alienation, an 'anxiety of authorship'
which comes from their sense of usurping a forbidden role. In order to write at
all women have participated in a sustained undermining of the received tradition
which has denied women place. The woman writer must 'overtly or covertly free
herself from the despair she inhaled from some "Wrinkled Maker" and she can
only do this by revising the Maker's texts' (1979: 76). A feature which marks
women's creative work distinct from men's is the willingness women display to
acknowledge, rather than repudiate, the weighty impact of the past upon them
and the debt they owe to their female predecessors. Other women writers are the
proof that revolt is possible. Gilbert and Gubar do not see isolation and individu-
ality as the proofs of creativity. They quote Anaïs Nin:

This 'I am God', which makes creation an act of solitude and pride, this image of God
alone making sky, earth, sea, it is this image which has confused women. (in Gilbert and
Gubar, 1979: 3)

Ostriker uses the work of Gilbert and Gubar to construct an image of women
authors emerging from their intense isolation and beginning to co-create a
literary movement which positively values mutuality and co-operative effort.

The poetry and essays of Adrienne Rich are a third significant source used by
Ostriker to construct her own literary vision. Rich has moved through a number
of stages in her writing life and in the work most admired by Christ (see p.
45) she assumes a lesbian voice and seeks to create a new language between
women from what has not yet been spoken – from the 'whiteness of the wall' (in
Christ, 1980: 85). However, in the early 1970s (the period of her work which
is most important for Ostriker) she was exploring the potential of the concept
of androgyny. This was envisioned as a quest to create cultural forms which
reflected the image of both sexes and allowed individuals to become reconciled
to the lost twins of divided gender. The creation of this new culture entails a
painful rereading of the past in which women begin to decipher the symbols
previously interpreted only by men. In *Diving into the Wreck* she writes

> I came to explore the wreck
> The words are purposes
> The words are maps
> I came to see the damage that was done
> and the treasures that prevail
> I stroke the beam of my lamp
> slowly along the flank
> of something more permanent
> than fish or weed. (1973: 23)

The same message is to be found in her famous essay 'When We Dead Awaken:
Writing as Re-Vision' (1978b), in which she states that the work of locating and
identifying the legacy of the past is crucial when seeking to build a new future.

Re-vision – the act of looking back, of seeing with fresh eyes, of entering an old text from a new critical direction – is for women more than a chapter in cultural history: it is an act of survival … We need to know the writing of the past and know it differently than we have ever known it; not to pass on a tradition but to break its hold over us. (1978b: 35)

Re-vision is an act of concentrated reading that cannot afford to omit from its scrutiny any of the signs women need to interpret in their serious and pains-taking effort to weave again the fabric of culture. Although its political and theoretical groundings are very different, the reading process described by Rich resonates with the accounts of reading that have become familiar since the impact of deconstruction upon critical theory.

To question everything. To remember what it has been forbidden even to mention. To come together telling our stories, to look afresh at, and then to describe for ourselves, the frescoes of the Ice Age, the nudes of 'high art', the Minoan seals and figurines, the moon landscape embossed with the booted print of a male foot, the microscopic virus, the scarred and tortured body of the planet Earth. To do this kind of work takes a capacity for constant active presence, a naturalist's attention to minute phenomena, for reading between the lines, watching closely for symbolic arrangements, decoding difficult and complex messages left for us by women of the past. (1978b: 13)

Stealing the language

The related concerns of Showalter, Gilbert and Gubar and Rich are creatively combined and then developed further in Ostriker's most famous work to date: *Stealing the Language: The Emergence of Women's Poetry in America* (1987). Ostriker presents her work as a critical experiment to test her thesis that a distinct literary culture exists among women. Whereas this was formerly a hidden tradition, women have now achieved the confidence actively to engage in the forensic examination of the male tradition and the reformulation of the male cultural canon. If this understanding is correct it should be possible to discern the impact of this development through a panoramic reading of the work of contemporary women poets. Ostriker describes her method as 'radically inductive'. She studies approximately 300 volumes of poetry written in the post-1960s period and argues that these do in fact display the features of a shared tradition among women writers engaged in radical revisionary work.

The new assertive trend that Ostriker claims to have discerned in modern women's poetry has a number of defining characteristics. It celebrates a specific female identity which becomes the basis for a distinctive style of writing, 'women poets begin to draw maps of the female body, the female passions, the female mind and spirit, demystifying these mysteries' (1987: 90). It employs a symbolism drawn from women's bodies to represent an embodied subjectivity that bleeds, suckles, shares in the cycles of nature – and grows old. It presents women as confident in their erotic power and uses a different love-language to describe a sexuality that is otherwise than penetrative and erect. Lovers have 'permeable membranes' and 'The motion of love is down, not up: down toward the earth and water, down into the flesh, easily' (1987: 176).[51]

The way in which a poetry that expresses the particularity of women's embodied identity relates to the traditionally segregated sphere of 'the sacred' is the theme that Ostriker tackles in the final chapter of her work, entitled 'Women Poets and Revisionist Mythology'. Ostriker argues that those very experiences which were often seen as inimical to spiritual understanding are now used in women's writing to point to new ways of understanding the divine. Furthermore, when such experiences are given figurative expression through the introduction of transgressive metaphors into authoritative stories the effect is to promote change. Myths are particularly significant sites of cultural struggle: [52]

Whenever a poet employs a figure or story previously accepted and defined by a culture, the poet is using myth, and the potential is always present that the use will be revisionist: that is, the figure or tale will be appropriated for altered ends, the old vessel filled with new wine, initially satisfying the thirst of the individual poet but ultimately making change possible ... Myth belongs to 'high' culture and is handed 'down' through the ages by religious, literary and educational authority. At the same time, myth is quintessentially intimate material, the stuff of dream life, forbidden desire, inexplicable motivation – everything in the psyche that to rational consciousness is unreal, crazed, or abominable. (1987: 212–213)

From suspicion to desire

The ways in which women are engaging with myth as a means of promoting social and spiritual change are more fully explored in Ostriker's later text *Feminist Revision and the Bible* (1993). In this she argues that creative women are engaged in an 'erotic' relation with the dominant culture. This perspective requires a,

less monolithic view of the dominant culture, one which would take into account its fragmentary nature ... I can no longer assume that women are entrapped in an oppressor's language without loopholes. I argue that the woman writer can write from a stance of pleasure, and can intervene in the creation of culture ... We assume that the language, the culture, one's own experience are always already so capacious as to make room for female pleasure and female reality. (1993: 116)

An illustration of the processes Ostriker sees at work in feminist revisionist myth making is best found in her assessment of H.D., a poet who most satisfactorily represents for her the approach she advocates and whose work she cites as exemplary both in *Stealing the Language* and *Feminist Revision and the Bible*. H.D. is contrasted with Ezra Pound,[53] whose approach to the mythology is to cram his poems with

51 The influence of Blake is evident in Ostriker's discussion of the political impact of such loving 'as gratified desire emerges from beings who are equivalent rather than polarised' (1987: 176).
52 For a more recent discussion of this subject and its significance for feminist politics see Pamela Sue Anderson (1998: 127–164).
53 The two poets collaborated intimately in their early work and were for a time engaged to be married.

'chunks of authorized, authoritative history'. For H.D. the tradition is always powerful but 'never authoritative ... always to be deciphered, tangential' (1987: 228). Likewise she is distinguished from Eliot, whose *Four Quartets* offers a basis for spiritual renewal after the Second World War in an indestructible heritage transcribed in the eternal. H.D.'s equivalent work, *Trilogy* (1983 [1944–1946]), places the hope for renewal in what that heritage has marginalised, what has been 'overwritten' but nevertheless continues to imprint upon the future.

For H.D., the work of the poet is akin to that of the diviner who assembles signs from the past to interpret the future. She uses the image of the *palimpsest*, scarred with the traces of what has already been written and yet also the surface upon which the future will be inscribed. She has a mystical vision of the larger space below the surface of the text and refuses the dissociation of past and future in describing a new *and* ancient wisdom. In her poetic manifesto 'Notes on Thought and Vision' (1988), written out of the trauma of the First World War and her own near death in pregnancy, H.D. celebrates a syncretising spirituality which promises personal and social regeneration. Christianity is not rejected but reconceived.

Christ and his father, or as the Eleusinian mystic would have said, his mother, were one. Christ was the grapes that hung against the sunlit walls of that mountain garden, Nazareth. He was the white hyacinth of Sparta and the narcissus of the islands. He was the conch shell and the purple fish left by the lake tides. He was the body of nature, the vine, the Dionysus, as he was the soul of nature.

He was the gulls screaming at low tide and tearing the small crabs from among the knotted weeds. (1988: 52)

In her later work Christ often appears, but rarely alone. He is accompanied by the Lady. She is a composite of Madonna and Magdalene. She is mother and daughter and bride and has been known in many forms before. Ostriker delights in the way H.D. invites her readers to interrogate the visions she shares in *Trilogy* rather than proclaim them authoritative.

Her Christ will cease to represent 'pain-worship and death-symbol' and be recovered as resurrected avatar of Osiris, her Virgin is one with Aphrodite and Isis ... her Magdalen will be a figure for the poet herself, 'unseemly', 'an unbalanced, neurotic woman' ... Dialogic not only with past texts but with a despairing self, with twentieth-century materialism and death-worship, with father-figures who alternatively support and condescend, the poem from its outset is dialogic as well with the reader. We are directly addressed, made intimate with the poet's struggles, invited to share her visions, as she reopens the closed Book, reconceives a story we thought was finished. (1993: 72)

H.D.'s poems, like her loves, are addressed with reverence and desire to the divine in male and female form. H.D.'s most enduring relations were with women but, as her intercourse with male lovers and mentors like Pound, Lawrence and Freud shows, she was willing to enter fully into dialogue with the body-texts of men. Ostriker finds this comprehensive bisexuality attractive. Like Rich's early pursuit of androgyny, this bisexuality stands as a figure for the pleasure Ostriker finds in texts. It is a borderline position between male and female traditions and it desires both.[54]

The erotic imagery that Ostriker uses to refer to the relationship between writers and texts in her more recent work (1993, 1997) reflects her deepening fascination with the inherited tradition. Our sacred stories are too precious, too desirable, to be discarded. The female revisionist is both seduced by them and seduces them. Ostriker uses the image of interpenetration to describe a moment of vulnerability and intimacy. 'To love is to enter and be entered, both at once … to penetrate the other and be penetrated by the other' (1993: 118–119).

I cease to posit a simple polarity or adversarial relationship between male text and female re/writers. Instead, I want to take up that thread of my argument which claims that what may seem outrageous, blasphemous and irreligious about woman's re-imaginings of the Bible is both forbidden and invited by the very text and tradition she is challenging. (1993: 56–57)

In claiming that the text invites reimagining rather than submission, Ostriker locates her work in the Jewish Midrashic tradition – women poets become Midrashists offering their own commentary on a tradition which they can claim as their inheritance. Although feminist theology has necessarily engaged in the hermeneutics of suspicion in order to highlight the misogyny of the inherited narratives it should now be recognised that, in women's revisionist/Midrashic literature, we can identify a 'hermeneutics of desire' through which women have borne numerous illegitimate offspring to the ur-texts of patriarchy. What Ostriker now sees as the next significant step forward is a 'hermeneutics of indeterminacy' which takes seriously the rabbinic saying 'There is always another interpretation'. Such an approach proliferates innumerable rereadings and revisions of texts, without seeking to replace one with another.

Human civilisation has a stake in plural readings … Most people haven't caught on though. Most people need 'right' answers just as they need 'superior' races … At this particular moment it happens to be feminists and other socially marginal types who are battling for cultural pluralism. Still, this is an activity which we're undertaking on behalf of humanity, all of whom would be the happier, I believe, were they to throw away their addiction to final solutions. (1993: 123)

Queer loves

The work of Ostriker represents an approach to the narrative traditions of faith that is appealing to those women who wish to challenge their inheritance without separating themselves from it. The use of Midrash and the concept of a 'hermeneutics of indeterminacy' represents an acknowledgement of difference

---

54   It is a position Liz Yorke describes as 'contrary' rather than 'oppositional'. It allows space to reinstate the concept of difference 'as multiplicity, ambiguity and heterogeneity' (1991: 12) rather than as 'the other of the same'.

that is dialogical rather than oppositional. The fact that Ostriker locates her own work as a critic and theologian within a company of feminist scholars and her work as a poet within an emerging female tradition gives her entire work a conversational tone. This dialogical model also emerges as paradigmatic for her understanding of the relationship between literature and theology which is represented by many erotic metaphors of communication. The complex relation between women and men is a figure for the uneasy relation of the woman poet to the dominant tradition. The woman writer penetrates and is penetrated by the theological forms of her culture. Ideally she is bisexual/androgynous, located in a borderland and enjoying her 'two loves separate'. She is able to couple fruitfully with male lovers as sister and bride yet also invokes, by her sacred devotion, the repressed female divine 'shimmering and struggling at the liminal threshold of consciousness' (1993: 50).

While appreciating the many pleasures Ostriker offers her readers we must question, however, her optimism concerning the potential of revisionist writers to affect a fundamental shift in the way predominantly misogynist theological traditions construct women within culture. As Mieke Bal argues, while interpretations of tradition abound there nevertheless abides within the Western tradition a continuing adherence to the dominant reading. This results in an apparent pluralism while, nevertheless, preserving as central a 'monolithically misogynist' perspective (1987: 2). The dominant reading may be strengthened rather than overturned by the plurality of interpretative strategies which surround it and which it can easily accommodate (in the same way as the Western economic and political system is upheld by the pluralism of postmodern culture). Those of us who have placed faith in the creative power of women to reimagine tradition in ways that are less destructive for us must reflect upon the challenge that these revisionist processes might sustain rather than overthrow the 'dominant regime'.

Perhaps Ostriker's faith can be justified, however, on the basis of her appreciation of the desperate struggle in which her favourite women poets are engaged to birth the new out of the inheritance of the past. This is no sweet nativity. Matthew Arnold, writing on 'Dover Beach' (1974 [1853]), is famously sorrowful about his inability to figure a creative relation between the religious past and the literary configurations which promise, but seemingly cannot deliver, a new foundation for human living (Jasper, 1996: 14). He stands alone contemplating what has died and what is powerless to be born. In a re-visioning of this image, Adrienne Rich places the work of creating new form in the hands of a woman poet who unites past present and future – who is mother, child and midwife:

> your mother dead and you unborn
> your two hands grasping your head
> drawing it down against the blade of life
> your nerves the nerves of a midwife learning her trade. (1973: 16)

Such a painful birthing process is always accomplished at great cost. The work of creating a living word out of intercourse with the traditions of the past is not to be compared to the work of some Egyptologist poring in academic concentration over ancient hieroglyphics. H.D.'s palimpsests are etched and overetched with violent efforts to obscure and rewrite tradition. In 'The Walls Do Not Fall' (1973) the palimpsest is imaged as the walls of a bombed-out home where the fragments of past life can be read in rainsoaked tatters. Pursuing the materiality of this metaphor further, Adrienne Rich pictures the face of a child who has somehow escaped attempted infanticide and grown up in the dangerous protection of the wilderness. The marks of the first violence are overscored with other scars which have been received as a consequence of inhabiting a place beyond the boundaries. On being brought back into human culture, speech is impossible, but the face is writing:

> A cave of scars!
> ancient, archaic wallpaper
> built up, layer on layer
> from the earliest, dream-white
> to yesterdays, a red black scrawl
> a red mouth slowly closing ...
>
> these scars bear witness
> but whether to repair
> or to destruction
> I no longer know. (1973: 57–58)

It is the painful seriousness of deciphering the cave of scars and its political intent that brings the work of re-vision described and practised by Ostriker very close to the obligation, rehearsed by Caputo, to write other histories, to tell other stories, to worry about what might be lost to oblivion and respond to unheard calls.[55] Her practice has the potential to decentre authority, declaring that there is no truth or 'at least not a single one ... where truth is absent women can creep in and write themselves back into history' (Bal, 1987: 132). It also has the potential to deregulate theology and disauthorize the work of doing theology. In 'Everywoman Her Own Theology', Ostriker describes her own version of the poet's labour. Her palimpsest is the family bulletin board on which is pinned her own version of Luther's theses. These are not displayed to challenge a faithless people but to entice an elusive divinity:

> This piece of paper is going to be
> Spattered with wine one night at a party
> And covered with newer pieces of paper
> That is how it goes with bulletin boards
> Nevertheless it will be there ...
> My paper will tell this being where to find me. (1990b: 83)

55 See p. 35.

What women and men have written

This chapter has explored the ways in which Carol Christ and Alicia Ostriker have presented women's literature as the voice of woman. I have shown how this rhetorical strategy is predicated upon assumptions concerning the relations between female author, female reader and female text. In requiring that (women's) literature contest with (male) theology Christ generated a dynamic impetus which simultaneously fuelled the development of feminist theology and dangerously circumscribed the reading practices of religious feminists.

In the work of Alicia Ostriker the terms 'literature' and 'theology' lose much of their currency and are supplanted by references to male and female traditions. It is 'men's writing' which has authored the dominant religious and cultural narratives and 'women's writing' which opposes and engages with the dominant regime. Ostriker's work, which I very much admire, represents an excellent example of how a hermeneutical strategy primarily based upon the differences between male and female experience subverts traditional disciplinarity. A rejection of disciplinary authority has many advantages. It is clear that theology, whatever its systematic pretensions, has always incorporated myth, metaphor and poetry. It is equally clear that women's writing does contain explicit theological and philosophical statements and has often performed precisely the revisioning role that Ostriker identifies.

And yet when gender supplants genre we may begin to lose a sense of the real and significant affinities between literary and theological texts created by women and men. In relation to literature, without a sense of women's writing 'as literature' we read without an awareness of the significance of literary traditions and devices *for women authors*, causing us to expect a transparent clarity on the surface of their texts. I am particularly concerned that when women's literature is called upon to represent women's experience, to be authentic and truthful, it may also begin to stand for us as a substitute for the logocentric disciplines of sure knowledge – and only certain kinds of women's writing may be judged appropriate for this task. Difficult literature, avant-garde literature, literature in which content collapses into form, not to mention romantic or gothic literature, may not appear as good spokeswomen for the feminist cause. However, it may be precisely these unsuitable sources which offer feminist theology its most challenging partners, provoking new developments in our thinking and continually resisting the closure of our own forms of orthodoxy.

In relation to theology, if we cease to inquire into the connections between women's theological work and the tradition we may fail to perceive the ways in which feminist theology all too easily settles back into established patterns of male stream thinking establishing its own canons and conventions. We may also fail to discern the way in which women repeat the gestures of male theologians in using (women's) literary texts for (feminist) theological ends.

These questions remain as I turn to examine a second approach to women's writing which has been influential in the development of feminist theology. The work of Katie Cannon and Kathleen Sands is taken as representative of an alternative trajectory in feminist theology. Here particularity and identity are emphasised rather than the commonality of women's experience. In this context women's literature is called upon to fulfil a rather different role. Rather than as the emerging voice of culture's female other, women's literature is portrayed as opening the reader to a world of difference that has been systematically eradicated from the theological tradition.

CHAPTER 3

Beyond the one and the other

Katie Cannon and black womanist ethics

Every-other-woman

In the work of Christ and Ostriker the female voice, speaking through literature, testifies to an alternative spiritual wisdom based upon women's experience. In the works of other religious feminists, however, women's literature is prized because of the diversity of understandings it contains and the many tongues with which it speaks. Literature is contrasted with theology not because the one is female writing and the other male writing, but rather because theology is a totalising system whereas literature is always particular, differentiated and located.

This is another way of characterising the fluid (albeit permanently gendered) relationship between literature and theology. It deploys the familiar associations of theology with order and restraint and of literature with rebellion which we have already encountered. However, these are given a new slant. Theology here represents the abstract and universal. Women's literature opposes this regime with the claims of the material and the embodied. What is particularly interesting in this development is that feminist theology is itself critiqued for acquiring male theologies, totalising tendencies. Furthermore, in the move away from Christ's 'in this case women' towards a feminist politics based upon difference, new questions concerning the legitimate uses of literary texts are raised. Do works of literature belong particularly to certain groups, who are best able to understand and interpret their meanings? Alternatively, can they be valued as precious media of communication, disclosing particularity in a political situation in which it is necessary to come to a better understanding of the multiple, overlapping communities within our plural culture? This chapter will consider different perspectives on this issue as they are expressed in the work of Katie Cannon and Kathleen Sands.

A black woman's tradition

Katie Cannon's famous work *Black Womanist Ethics* (1988) begins with arguments aimed at establishing the existence of a 'Black woman's literary tradition' and the cultural specificity of black women's writing. Works written by black women are identified as emerging from a context that is understood by black women readers and thus able to communicate especially with them in a way that is simply inaccessible to white feminists. Cannon sees this as a necessary first step because in the early days of feminist theological scholarship white theorists paid little attention to the differing social locations of black and white women. Black women's literature was both extensively quoted (when helpful) and strategically ignored (when challenging). The issues raised by this appropriation were not considered until black women protested against this treatment (see, for example, Lorde, 1984: and hooks, 1991). Unfortunately, a new acknowledgement of racism frequently resulted in an equally dangerous counter-tendency. In their analyses of black literature, white women have often fallen into the trap of regarding black life as entirely predicated upon the sad need to respond to the violent agenda of white oppressors.

In contrast to this position, Cannon asserts, black women authors have demonstrated that their concerns are *primarily* intracommunal. Writers like Zora Neale Hurston, Alice Walker, Audre Lorde and Toni Morrison have sought to transcribe the internal dynamics of black social life. Love and conflict *between* black characters are the immediate concern of their protagonists. They portray the ambivalence experienced in forming relationships of intensity within a community that is both deeply wounded and dynamically regenerative. Within such a context white oppression simply does not have the power to rob them of a perpetually returning past. As Sherley Williams has argued, when black women writers explore their heritage it is not merely to demonstrate how their mothers suffered but to discover how they survived and re-membered their people.[56]

When we go in search of our mother's gardens, it's not really to learn who trampled on them or how or even why – we usually know that already. Rather it's to learn what our mothers planted there, what they thought as they sowed, and how they survived the blighting of so many fruits. (Williams, in Cannon 1988: 9)

Once black women's writing is located within the distinctive agenda of the black community and understood as part of the political work of creating an oppositional stance in relation to white society, it becomes quite clear how

---

56 To insist that black women's writing gives primary attention to the particularity of black life does not mean, however, that intercommunal concerns are absent from their work. Relations of friendship and antagonism are explored between black and white characters (e.g. Walker, 1976: 181) and efforts are made to show white people struggling with their own social constraint in a binary culture sustained by racism (e.g. Morrison, 1987: 8–9). Yet it is not primarily in order to explore personal relationships or psychological struggle that white culture is invoked. It is rather to position black culture as oppositional to white hegemony.

inappropriate it is to read such writing as expressing truths universal to women's experience. Similarly, Cannon implies, black women's writing should not be brought into immediate comparison with a white, male-centred theological tradition while ignoring the fact that its primary referent is the spiritual dynamic of African Americans.

Reference points

Having argued that black women's writing should be viewed principally as an intracommunal discourse, Cannon's second concern is to display that the literary tradition she has identified is a faithful witness to the deepest concerns of the black community and speaks of its material and spiritual struggles for identity:

> The Black woman's literary tradition documents the 'living space' carved out of the intricate web of racism, sexism and poverty. The literary tradition parallels Black history. It conveys the assumed values in the Black oral tradition … It cryptically records the specificity of the Afro-American life. (1988: 7)

Controversially, she insists that there is a difference to be discerned between the writing of black women and men – and that women's writing is more 'authentic' than that of male authors. Black male writers 'tend to focus their literary energies upon the confrontation between the white and Black worlds' (1988: 89) and the most significant action in their work often takes place once the characters have 'moved away from their natal roots' (1988: 88). Many black male writers have set their fiction in the cityscapes of Northern states and have been keen to engage in intertextual dialogue with white fiction. In contrast, black women have paid more attention to the rural culture and traditions of the South. They have been more willing to use the language, idioms and folklore of 'the cultural tradition transmitted by the oral mode from one generation to the next' (1988: 84). And they have re-membered in powerful new forms the ancestral traditions of African religion. For these reasons their literature 'can be trusted as seriously mirroring Black reality' (Canon, 1989: 291).

Whether the 'reality' of black life has been more accurately reflected in the work of one sex than another must surely be open to question. That being said, Cannon does not stand alone among black womanist critics in the claims she makes concerning the ancestral voice in black women's fiction. This writing has been regarded as a privileged medium of self-definition for black women, uniting them to their past and offering resources to sustain them in the present. Literature has been the primary form of written expression used by black women and is understood not only as literature but also as integrally intertextual and inter-generic. The black women's literary tradition is looked to for historical, anthropological, philosophical and theological resources that can aid black women in establishing an identity which is self-affirming and socially liberating (see, for example, Caroline Boyce Davies' critical text *Black Women, Writing and Identity*, 1994). However, Cannon makes a bold and original move in representing the black women's literary tradition through a particular woman. Cannon embodies black women's writing through the ancestral figure of Zorah Neale Hurston (1891–1960).

Searching for truth

Hurston's enormous influence upon contemporary black women's fiction is widely documented (see, for example, Walker, 1984: 83–116 and hooks, 1991: 135–144). In Black Womanist Ethics she comes rhetorically to incarnate the literary tradition she has decisively influenced. Her life and literature, her *person*, become illustrative of Cannon's convictions concerning the specificity, veracity and particularity of the black women's literary tradition and are presented as exemplary of the dynamics of black culture as articulated through a woman's writing. This is a vivid and exciting textual device. Women's writing is not patterned according to an archetypal female form, it is given a specific identity, body and voice. To establish this trope Cannon devotes a major section of her text to constructing a biographical picture of Hurston. Helpfully, her life history contains the elements necessary to sustain Cannon's argument.

After struggling to have her academic gifts recognised, Hurston worked with the most famous of all American anthropologists, Franz Boas, in the late 1920s. Early in her career she strove to record the folk tales and songs of the black rural South. This anthropological work overlapped with a period of artistic involvement with the 'Harlem renaissance' during which Hurston's creative powers, and the personal tensions they engendered, became evident. She eventually located herself within a black Southern community that turned upon its own axis – having only marginal contact with the white society existing beyond its borders. Hurston published numerous articles, wrote plays, stories and three novels. Two of the novels are devoted almost entirely to the specific dynamics of black life, and use the language of Southern black society as well as the vehicles of expression created by this community. The sermon recorded in Jonah's Gourd Vine (1971 [1934]) was such a powerful example of the genius of this oral tradition that critics of the time refused to believe that it could have been uttered from the mouth of an unlettered black preacher.

Despite her many talents, Hurston lived a life that was riven by personal and political conflicts. She experienced periods of social humiliation and grinding poverty which her scholarly and literary reputation could not remedy. And yet, Cannon claims, she continued to display personal integrity and conviction despite these hardships, displaying a resilience which makes her life and literature 'paradigmatic of Black culture and Black women's lives' (1988: 8).

Cannon's account of Hurston's life is crafted to present Hurston as progenitor of a particular literary tradition which in turn offers 'the sharpest available view of the Black community's soul' (1989: 291). Through her ancestral form the community becomes newly visible to itself and able to articulate its concerns. In her writing is to be discerned the implicit ethics that transforms mere survival into creative living:

> I have found that this literary tradition is the nexus between the real lived texture of black life and the oral-aural cultural values implicitly passed on and received from one generation to the next. The ethical character of Black folk culture is strongly and unmistakably present in Zora Neale Hurston's life and literature. (1988: 5)

It is in her description of the 'ethical' impact of Hurston's writing that Cannon's work is most persuasive.

She argues that dominant ethical systems presuppose a degree of freedom and a wide range of choices that prove null and void in situations of oppression. Lacking the self-directing agency assumed of the moral subject, black women display instead what Cannon, following Mary Burgher (1979), describes as quiet grace. Such grace is the quality which enables existence to continue to be meaningful in situations of moral ambiguity and constraint. Having no means to avoid moral compromise and frequently unable to meet obligations towards loved ones, black women find ways to compensate: to mend and restore relationships. Dignity and self-worth are not given but precariously achieved, and the testimony to black women's 'unshouted courage' is the survival of their people.

> Black women writers authenticate in an economy of expressions how Black people creatively strain against the external limits of their lives, how they affirm their humanity by inverting assumptions, and how they balance the continual struggles and interplay of paradoxes. Blacks win by losing, retain their blessings by giving them away. (1988: 174)

What is particularly significant for Cannon is the way in which Hurston has portrayed 'quiet grace' at work: the 'basic assumption of all her work is that quiet grace is manifested in the search for truth' (1988: 127). This search involves confronting the myths, stereotypes and prejudices that define black life from outside but *also* sustaining personal integrity despite lacking the autonomy to act according to one's own best desires. Life must be made the best of. Janie, the hero of *Their Eyes Were Watching God* (Hurston, 1978 [1939]) declares, 'If you kin see de light at daybreak, you don't ker if you die at dust. Its so many people never seen de light at all' (1978: 236).

The ethical insights generated by Cannon from her readings of Hurston are powerfully articulated. However, when Cannon moves from the ethical to the theological arena many tensions begin to emerge within her argument. There are points where she appears to suggest that African American theology should be fundamentally shaped by black women's writing because it functions as a mirror of the black community's soul. This is a radical gesture, but at other points she suggests that it is not black women's literature itself which is important but rather the fact that it is shaped by an energy that is also active in the work of the male theologians she most admires. Howard Thurman and Martin Luther King Junior are described as drawing from the same source as Hurston, that is, from contact with the 'The Negro farthest down' (1988: 9). Cannon believes that this common energy comes directly from the culture and experience of the black poor.

Utilising a similar slippage between categories, Cannon sometimes argues that Hurston's literature is implicitly theological because:

Implicit, not yet explicit, in Hurston's literary vision (i.e. her love of black life, her sense of the value of community, her search for truth, etc.) is the theological vision: human beings are united in a bond of divine love which enables them to live justly; and the overarching mandate calls for all people to live co-operatively in an inclusive human community. (1988: 174)

At other times Cannon laments that Hurston did not herself have access to the 'balm of the Black religious heritage' (1988: 160) to sustain her in periods of personal difficulty. If she had been able to supplement her insights into the ethical character of black communal life with the 'resources available in the theological vision' (1988: 160) then her gift to future generations would have been somehow more complete. As it is, contemporary black women must struggle to make real what Hurston never saw.

What Hurston was denied, Black women of today must have. Black women intellectuals must transform the tradition so as to enable Black women, who celebrate Black life, to make a reaffirmation of their spiritual roots. (1988: 174)

Writing real theology
Cannon seems unable to resolve the tension between responding to black women's writing as 'theopoesis', a literary embodiment of the divine, and arguing that these texts must be distilled or dissected to reveal the historical facts and the socio-political values they carry (1988: 174). These facts and insights are then to be incorporated into the development of a distinctive black theological tradition which rises above its own roots in folklore, myth and the everyday passions of black women's lives. This dilemma is probably the result of Cannon's own divided loyalties. She has become convinced that Hurston has bequeathed an inheritance which enables contemporary black women authors to explore their spiritual roots in audacious narratives and metaphors.[57] It is difficult, however, to see how this growing company of iconoclastic women who are the feisty inheritors of Hurston's mantle can be easily subsumed within the black Christian tradition to which Cannon gives allegiance.[58] She poses the question,

are the fundamental dispositions that Black women possess as they transcend their oppression and transform their lives part of the faith tradition which the Black Church confesses and teaches? (1988: 9)

57 The collection of autobiographical testimonies from black women writers edited by Barbara Christian (1985) contains many examples of black women self-identifying with this legacy.
58 This dilemma recalls for me the unsatisfactory adaptations made in the screen version of Alice Walker's *The Color Purple* (1983). In the film, Shug's audacious body-theology is downplayed and her energy is brought into reconciliation with the black church.

But this cannot be adequately answered within the limits of her text.

To argue that there are unresolved tensions within Cannon's work, however, is not to deny the significance of her writing. The ideas she articulates have been widely debated. Her move to celebrate the specificity of black women's writing has been of great significance within womanist theology, and white feminist theologians have also responded to her critiques of their appropriation of black women's literature by examining their own reading practices. An example of this reflexive trend within white women's theology is found in Susan Thistlethwaite's important book, *Sex, Race and God* (1989). Thistlethwaite edited the series in which *Black Womanist Ethics* appeared and responded to its challenges shortly afterwards with her own attempt to articulate what black women's writing might mean for white feminists once they have ceased to read themselves into the lives of black women and learned to see themselves always as outsiders and often as oppressors.

Race and God

Thistlethwaite begins her work by echoing Cannon's argument that 'the writing of black women functions as an articulation of not only black women's experience but of their theological, political, sociological and anthropological viewpoints as well' (1989: 4). She also acknowledges the cultural specificity of black literature and that, when using it as a theological resource, she must be aware of the political minefield she is crossing. Thistlethwaite then goes on to identify ways in which white feminists' emphases upon commonality between women are challenged by novels like Morrison's *The Bluest Eye* (1970) and Walker's *Meridian* (1976). She argues that a growing awareness of a violent disharmony between women raises new theological questions for white religious feminists. In its diverse forms, white feminist theology has too easily assumed common ground with creation-centred process theology emphasising connectedness, fruitfulness and cosmic unity. Thistlethwaite's reading of black women's passionate but painful relation to nature, their bodies and their children, compels her to recognise the cultural specificity of these theological presuppositions. She makes an important discovery from her encounter. 'I as a white feminist must stop trying to belong to nature and its harmonies and begin to see myself as an other in order to transform society' (1989: 67).

Such a social transformation can no longer be based upon an assumption of female innocence. Compelled to recognise the legacy of racism within themselves, white women must now look with new eyes upon the deep ambiguities inherent within human living and reflected throughout the created order:

Evil and good, destruction and creation are more intertwined than I as a white feminist theologian have so far allowed ... I now know that I need to spend more time coming to terms with the profound ambiguity of evil and to imbue my embrace of nature with a consciousness of its cultural interpretations. (1989: 74)

An encounter with black women's writing has provoked Thistlethwaite to critique white feminist theology, but she remains unwilling to concede that radical difference might be the basis of a new ethics – a complete reversal of norms in theology and practice. Sensing the links between her struggle against the violence of universalism and similar poststructuralist critiques of totalising systems, Thistlethwaite nevertheless feels compelled to distance herself from contemporary critical theory. She believes that it is necessary to appeal to self-evident truths when fighting oppression:

What concerns me is that as I employ poststructuralism to loosen the absolutist hold on 'women's experience' ... I may be opening the door to a denial of the truths of my experience in the movement to end violence against women ... I find that postcritical theory does not always allow me to declare that violence against women is wrong in all circumstances. (1989: 15)

Thistlethwaite is voicing a concern which is shared by many feminists and has been the subject of intense theoretical debate. The unease she registers remains a common response of feminist theologians to poststructuralism. Thistlethwaite has acknowledged the challenge of difference but despite this retains a commitment to the logocentric authority of her own prophetic voice. It is a painful dilemma.

Despite its creative challenge, similar problems haunt Black Womanist Ethics. In Cannon's text, Hurston embodies the power of black women writers who are now speaking with their own distinctive voice. Less helpfully Hurston is used to eliminate the space between fiction and reality, imagination and history. The specific truth Hurston embodies may not be assimilated but neither can it be critically challenged. The book and the body are firmly wedded in hypostatic union. Both Cannon's writing and Thistlethwaite's response represent a growing awareness of the need to bring to theology and ethics an encounter with difference, and readings of black women's literature have been of great significance in this development. However, both theologians seek to limit and contain the encounter – fearful of the massive challenge disturbingly implicit in their own arguments.

Kathleen Sands: literature and tragedy

Theology in the post-age

In this chapter so far we have traced a trajectory away from representing women's literature as 'everywoman' in cultural form towards a recognition that literature may embody rather the specific, the located and the particular. To discern a trajectory is not the same as assuming a progressive development in which primitive understandings are displaced by more sophisticated later developments; former positions are modified in the light of criticism. I have stressed that more recent work continues in dialogue with earlier texts. Through an attention to gender difference rather than critical theory we can see feminist and womanist religious

67

thinkers begin to articulate similar objections to theology as those articulated by the male theologians influenced by poststructuralism which were discussed at the close of the last chapter.

It is clear that both Cannon and Thistlethwaite are aware that the articulation of difference through the reading of black women's literature has the potential to generate a more radical critique of the theological traditions within which they work than they themselves are willing to accommodate. This fact has resulted in deep fissures in Cannon's text. Thistlethwaite articulates her dilemmas more openly. At the end of the 1980s poststructuralism was for her a step too far. It might offer attractive critical resources but the feminist theologian working out of the justice-seeking traditions of liberal humanism has far too much to lose to be seduced by its fascinating obscurity. In the best traditions of emancipatory theology, she is far more interested in pragmatic responses that challenge the everyday violence women suffer than in a theoretical critique of cultural forms. The work of Kathleen Sands (1994), however, carries the engagement of feminist theology with women's writing into a new epoch in which a cautious engagement with critical theory is brought into dialogue with the liberative traditions of religious feminism.

Sands's intention in approaching women's literature is to illuminate her thesis that theology has established its power through a denial of the realities of human suffering and the theodical questions such suffering raises. For her the circumstances of the current 'post-age'[59] mean that the theological edifice can no longer avoid a confrontation with that which it has repressed. It stands like some fantastic winter palace about to be overwhelmed by a deluge which its own rapacious vandalism and colossal bulwarks have contributed to creating. Flooded with elements it was meant to exclude, theology too is 'catching its death'. In post-time, there will be no clean or peaceful resurrection.

What survives will be as disruptive as the beggars at the wedding banquet, as disturbing as the footprints of the past in this morning's snow, as magical as the mermaid in the ship's cabin, drowned but still alive. In the shrinking light, the ultimate defeat of evil, irrationality, and death shows itself to have been a bad dream. Immersed in negativity, we may awaken to a better one. (1994: 1–2)

Knowledge of evil

Sands outlines how Christian theology has sought to protect itself from knowledge of evil using two main strategies. She terms these the 'rationalist' and 'dualist' responses. The rationalist maintains faith in the supreme power and goodness of the creator and dismisses the havoc caused by evil as a necessary and ultimately beneficial consequence of creative activity 'never beyond comprehension or

---

59 An evocative term which Sands uses in preference to terms such as 'postmodernism' which are deeply embedded in cultural analyses that take little cognisance of the historical agency of non-dominant groups.

rehabilitation' (1994: 3). In contrast dualist explanations see reality as a battle-field between good and evil. Evil cannot be accommodated or brought within the light of the family hearth. It must be resisted until it is overcome either by revolution, apocalypse or gnosis. Sands maintains that although these responses appear to be contradictory they are in fact twins born of the same parent. 'Under pressure rationalism splits into dualism; at ease dualism softens into rationalism. Always one pattern shadows the other' (1994: 4). Their progenitor is a benefi-cent and ultimately triumphant divine power.

In a kaleidoscopic examination of the theodical enterprise from Augustine through Kant to Barth, Tillich and the theologians of liberation, Sands shows the rationalist and dualist defences at work as twin pillars guarding the entrance to the dwelling place of the divine: 'these twin passions guard the gates of the Christian paradise against the incursion of the tragic' (1994: 3). She then goes on to argue that feminist theology has relied upon the support of these same two explanatory systems in its own attempts to describe and explain the sufferings of women.

Sands illustrates this thesis with reference to the alternative trajectories of Ruether and Christ (chosen as foremost representatives of Christian and goddess-centred feminist religious thinking). Ruether wrestles to make evil both intel-ligible and redeemable in a hermeneutical framework suspended between what 'is' and what 'ought to be'. Her faith is both rational and eschatological; rooted in the highest traditions of a transcendent theism it also legitimates women in a quest for social justice and the vanquishing of darkness.

Christ's theology also contains both totalising and dualistic elements. Patriar-chal attempts to create a division between soul and body, spiritual and natural, are critiqued. However, a corresponding tendency to elevate the despised female partner in the binary pairings of culture represents a reinscription of dualism's divisive power – albeit within a new aesthetic and spiritual milieu. What disturbs Sands about both women's work is that they are creating new paths for religious feminists to repeat male theologians' flight away from the all-pervasive experi-ence of evil. They are both seeking a 'higher ground' from which to observe the desperate struggles of human existence. It is this search for a 'higher place' which is the common impulse of all metaphysics and which Sands seeks to challenge through a confrontation with the tragic.

As a theological heuristic, the tragic highlights elemental conflicts as questionworthy, holding open the telling wounds of absurdity and fault rather than closing them with preemptive appeals to faith. (1994: 11)

Sands' understanding of the tragic contains a rich complex of associated themes which it is important to explore before proceeding further.

Thinking through the tragic

First, tragedy is a way 'of telling stories that highlights elemental conflicts of truths which I also call conflicts of powers' (1994: 10). Tragedy presents to view the inescapable suffering that characterises human life. 'Tragic speech is about irrecoverable loss and irresolvable contradiction' (1994: 2). From the mouth of such a wound issues the indictment of the deities.

The language of tragedy dispossesses us of the logos of Theo, insofar as that logos has served to fix meaning on an Absolute referent and cover up the absence that is tragedy. (1994: 2)

The challenge of tragedy is not merely that the fullness of human experience has not been acknowledged by theology. There is also a fundamental link between repressing certain knowledges and the process of political domination by particular groups over others, 'the rationale for suppressing resistance is still the assumption that fundamental contradictions or conflicting orders do not really exist' (1994: 3).

Significantly, it is when religious feminists have based their writing upon attentive listening to the abused and dispossessed that they have come closest to articulating a tragic narrative. Sands finds the work of Sharon Welch particularly helpful as it enables her to bring together her tragic and postmodern concerns. Welch is commended because of her attempts (1985, 1990) to construct models of 'resisting knowledges which do not fund their power through a bank of transcendent truth' (Sands, 1994: 63). Sands approves her adoption of a Foucauldian analysis which rejects alien moral absolutes and which locates knowledge and power in the discursive activities of dominating or subjugated groups.[60]

Sands, following Welch, envisages women and other marginalised groups drawing power from their local knowledge: the shared narratives of remembrance, mourning, rage, resistance and jouissance which challenge the established cultural order. Appealing to Foucault's vision of a potential insurrection of subjugated knowledge, Sands envisages feminist theologians discovering a means of escape from the compulsion to retranscribe the old rationalisations of the evil they encounter. Women must, rather, find a way of immersing themselves in the flow of life that is powerful and celebratory. According to Sands, Welch has pointed towards the way in which this might be achieved:

Lacking absolute grounding of any kind, Welch's theology can neither avoid the risk of nihilism nor withdraw into the 'cultured despair of the middle class'. In the face of tragedy and loss, especially the loss of innocence about the moral powers of humanity, she risks commitment to the possible good … Welch recognises that in the postmodern era truth is breaking loose from goodness and instead becoming attached to the fractured, multiple

---

60 Foucault writes: 'We should admit rather that power produces knowledge … that power and knowledge directly imply one another; that there is no power relation without the correlative constitution of a field of knowledge, nor any knowledge that does not at the same time presuppose and constitute power relations' (1991: 27).

discourses of power. Choosing a side, she identifies the divine with goodness as a moral quality, not with ontic structures or processes. The goodness for which she stands possesses its own kind of power, but that power is only one among many, just as the good of a particular community of accountability remains one of a plurality of goods. (1994: 63)

The use of the phrase 'plurality of goods' is of great significance here. It is an expression characteristic of Sands. Good and evil are no longer to be thought of as unitary oppositional forces but multiform and adaptable configurations of meaning and experience. Tragedy confronts both the single voice of the divine logos and the binary opposition of dualism. 'No better than the One can the Two name the existential manyness of which tragedy speaks so eloquently' (1994: 5). Postmodernism bears testimony to 'the radical plurality of goods and powers that has become the truth at the end of modernity' (1994: 38).

Joining the chorus

In the face of this profligate plurality new beginnings are possible for theology. Sands begins to redraw her theological map by refusing old reference points and polar forces. She begins by affirming that God is dead. 'He' is so long dead that even the space of an absence has closed for her. In the present post-time she believes we recognise our deities as household familiars – the creation of our own hands (1994: 14). Unusually, even among those who share this perspective, there is no hint of nostalgia in this bereavement. For Sands it has straightfor-wardly liberating potential. Women theologians may now enter more deeply into the power that can be discovered in the 'meaning making activity of a historical community' (1994: 138). They will do so in companionship with others who have also been made to bear the stamp and wear the form of evil. They will show that what 'has been called evil can indeed think … has voices, desires and intel-ligibilities of its own' (1994: 136).

There is, for Sands, nothing to be gained by raising old ghosts or hoisting the empty sheets of transcendence. The tragic stage is now flooded with actors. The chorus has drowned out with its cacophonous cries the hero's soliloquy; his solitary wrestle with Olympian decrees. It is through joining this chorus that the theologian is able to assume her mediating and divining function.

Immersed in a living community and participating critically in its vital functions, a theology sensitive to the tragic might begin to speak in ways that cross more worlds … Entering those worlds, searching for what is absent, we may discern the sites where a healing disturbance gathers to reemerge. (1994: 16)

It is from this perspective that Sands approaches literature as a 'theological source to which a tragic heuristic might be applied' (1994: 138, my emphasis). As with the other religious feminists whose work we have explored previously, no boundary is made between works of literature and other feminist texts. She reflects upon women's writing because she believes it offers insights into how women with diverse backgrounds and experience attempt to knot together circumstances into provisional knowledge. It reveals how they can generate their own identity and pursue political ends through this process. In this respect her concerns are similar to those of the constructive theologians, discussed in chapter 1, who are concerned with the achievement of a narrative nature for identity after the collapse of foundational epistemologies.[61]

The texts she studies are sites where meaning is negotiated and invented. The theological dynamic consists in placing these stories next to her own and reflecting upon the familiarity and strangeness this intertextuality reveals:

> In that spirit I turn to literature by women though without presupposing that other women's stories are in fact my stories. My model, rather, is one of dialogue with these novels, putting my story next to theirs … For in fact the stories of women have been woven next to each other, and it is a task of religious feminists to inquire what this has meant and might be made to mean. (1994: 138)

The four novels that Sands chooses to use are tragic and non-hegemonic. They contain the subjugated knowledge of marginalised people in which Sands seeks to identify some hope for the future.

Between the story and the subject

In Toni Morrison's Beloved (1987) she finds the deepest possible acknowledgement of humanity's lost innocence. White readers are made to view their own guilt without cure as though from a distance; the view is of a terrible and unchangeable tableau. The black characters they are observing cannot redeem by their suffering what white civilisation has brought to pass. White readers must acknowledge that they cannot seek salvation here. (Sands, 1994: 140)

Black readers are also compelled to look upon a petrifying image, to gaze upon a mother who takes murderous responsibility for her child: 'she cannot mistake passivity for innocence. The mother who gave life must therefore choose how it will end' (1994: 142). Through choosing to kill her child rather than return her to slavery Sethe's remaining days are soaked in red, the colour of a love which is too thick, which leaves an irradicable stain both upon her and those who witness or recount the act.

What Sands learns from placing this story beside her own is that 'inescapable guilt can be a source of moral information' (1994: 145). The code of this text differs for the oppressed and the oppressor but is there to be read clearly by both.

> For all of us goodness is a fragile and costly thing to be fostered in our own communities not imported from above or imputed from beyond … in the thickness of uneasy love, it returns us as well to our own communities where the scars of racism must be faced. (1994: 145)

61 See pp. 28–30.

Bastard Out of Carolina (1992) by Dorothy Allison is autobiographical fiction by a lesbian writer from a poor, white Southern background. The hero, Bone, who is illegitimate, 'white-trash' and a victim of childhood sexual abuse, must struggle to create her own identity by acknowledging the violence of her own desires. She forms her self-image through the refracted reflection of herself in the lives of other characters: 'niggers', abusers, failing mothers, friends and lovers, people whose struggles are similar to but different from her own.

Good and bad, female and male, dark and light – Bone tries to sort them out but in the end finds strength in the mixture. Feeling the resonance between the words 'nigger' and 'trash' she finds that black is not pure 'other' but is like her with her black hair and her anger. (1994: 150)

As a lesbian, Bone's sexuality is also not simply a given. It is woven from what she encounters to hand. Sands places Bone's story next to her own and ponders upon the similarities. She reflects upon her own lesbian identity and finds it not to be a simple or defined sexual category. She has been formed by the influence of others. In particular, Sands concedes that she was shaped by the scarred and swollen hands of a mother who 'did not mean to raise a lesbian but she did' (1994: 150). Those hands were not soothing and gentle. They were ugly hands which were never young. However, Sands now recognises that she has inherited both the shape of the fingers and their anarchic creative potential to form beyond what is desired or intended. Bone is the child of an order descended into a chaos of creative fragments, and Sands portrays herself in the same way.

I look down at my keyboard now and I see those hands, my mother's hands, saying things that she would never say. It is evidence to me that creativity gets out of our hands, that desire, uncountenanced and unforeseen, may speak new stories. (1994: 152)

The third work Sands examines is *Love Medicine* (1993) by Louise Erdrich. This is a series of connected stories exploring the relationship of descendants of the Chippewa people to their religious and cultural inheritance, to dominant American culture – and to each other. In a situation in which ethnic identity is fractured, resemblances, character, 'gifts' continue to be handed down from generation to generation. Similarly the same pains, dilemmas and passions return to be confronted. Some characters will succumb to the pressures that overwhelm them but always 'these human disasters leave behind someone who might do more than endure or repeat' (1994: 159). Sands draws from these examples renewed faith in the importance of people and events that appear to slip between the words of recorded history. What future exists for the Chippewa is uncertain but as long as the past continues to imprint upon the present there is a possibility of taking responsibility for the active remembering that creates form out of the tornado of experience.

Sands' last choice of literary text is *Housekeeping* (1991 [1980]) by Marilynne Robinson. This is the story of a community living on the water's edge. It is a loving lament for those who drown – and a celebration of those who make the grey darkness their own element.

Ruthie's family has a particular association with water, since her grandfather, Edmund Foster, lodges in the deepest part of the lake ... Helen, mother of Ruthie and Lucille, elopes with a Reginald Stone and, after he leaves or is left by her, sinks like a stone into water. In a suicide shocking for its nonchalance, she snacks on wild strawberries then drives her borrowed car into the lake where her father reposes. (1994: 161)

After their mother's death Ruthie and Lucille are cared for by her sister Sylvie. She is a 'transient'; a human creature adapted to living in elemental chaos. The home she makes for the girls is flooded with those things houses are meant to exclude: rubbish, cobwebs, wild things, cold, darkness and sorrow. The other women of the community see Sylvie's domain turning from a house to a floating vessel 'overrun by the elements and undocked from its neighbours' (1994: 164). Growing up in this place prepares Ruthie herself for a transient life in which she becomes lost to the conventions of the community and views its life as though through a series of images reflected upon the surface of deep waters.

Housekeeping is a richly symbolic work and provides Sands with many fruitful images to place alongside her own narrative. She ponders upon the character of Sylvie and the simultaneous challenge and threat she represents. Although she was initially fearful of the Sylvies she has known:

As the years go by, I too am relieved by my eccentricities and breaches of femininity, and I grow less embarrassed to be seen with tilted head, listening for the whisper of perished things. (1994: 162)

Of particular poignancy for Sands is the way the novel portrays Ruthie's choice to embrace a life in shadows as an extended form of mourning for her mother. Sands lost a brother in tragic circumstances and initially felt separated from him by her own fear of death. However, one night in a dream she experienced this barrier flooding over. She embraced her mortality and loss and met her brother. 'He and I were fish gliding along the ocean floor ... I felt my lungs breathe water, but there was no struggle in my drowning' (1994: 163–164). She goes on to say, in a passage reminiscent of Pacini's lament for his lost child (see chapter 1), that this experience transformed her own garden of remembrance. She became both the gardener and the gravedigger. Attentive to the regeneration and the decay that surround her:

I had thought that in the vacuum of my loss every little pleasure and beauty would disintegrate, but against that open horizon they grew sharp and piercing instead. I was not prepared for the shock of joy in the spring when my eyes reopened on the world which suddenly seemed like a vast and beautiful graveyard, where even every fallen bird is still beneath our feet. (1994: 164)

What Sands achieves in her readings of these four novels is a dialogue between their concerns and the plot of her own life. She is empowered by their specific accounts of survival in the face of tragedy. They enable her both to face the personal tragedies she has experienced and to support the political struggles of suffering communities whose texts have touched her deeply. This personal encounter points towards her vision of the emerging new theology she believes religious feminists should cherish. This is a fully dialogical theology, immersed in and emerging from living communities. A theology that will 'cross more worlds ... searching for what is absent' (1994: 1).

Beggars at the banquet

Escape from Paradise is an eloquent appeal to other religious feminists to climb over the wall and enter the real world. Sands' tragic heuristic highlights 'some of the colours that flood theology after the death of the one and the Other' (1994: 167). She has forged a powerful link between 'post-age' thinking and the tragic in order to challenge a theological discourse which turns its face away from evil. Her work is poignantly resonant with some of the most difficult dilemmas that religious feminists face today. Sands' approach to literature draws close, indeed, to what I am reaching towards in this work. There are two particular points of resemblance. She uses poststructuralist theory as a discourse of difference to identify the regulatory powers of theology and she makes human pain the impetus for developing a reading practice which begins in politics but reaches beyond the political to another horizon, crossing worlds in the search for what is absent. Yet despite the considerable similarities between us, there are important differences in both our use of poststructuralist theory and our understandings of where our political readings might lead us.

Sands chooses to employ the work of Michel Foucault alone from the assorted band of contemporary continental theorists as her guide and mentor in the construction of post-age theological thinking. This may be (I think it is) because Foucault appears to be the most assimilable of all the poststructuralist thinkers. His work is clearly applicable to concrete social problems. His writing contains the most recognisable ethical landmarks in its concern for those marginalised by dominant discourses. His vocabulary of power and subjugation is reassuringly familiar for those raised in the humanist/Marxist tradition which values freedom, equality and self-expression. It is a most valuable stepping stone for those moving from an understanding of domination and resistance which emphasises the visible machinery of political power to one which also attends to the significance of microcultural processes.

To identify the familiarity (comfort) that is to be found in some aspects of Foucault's thinking is not to deny his massive importance or the major impact he has had upon contemporary thinking. Works like *Madness and Civilisation* (1965) and *Discipline and Punish* (1991) present the strange world of the silenced to view, making it impossible to view 'normal life' without seeking to understand the exclusions upon which health, sanity and order are based. It is easy to understand why Sands welcomes Foucault's 'ship of fools' to harbour with its skeleton crew of the mad, the sick, the deviant and the dead. These are for her the 'Others', beyond the 'one' and the 'Other', whose plural presence provokes her reflection upon difference. She dines 'on board' at the beggars' feast.

And yet. Although it takes courage to sit and eat with such an assorted company there is no sense of the haunting of the banquet. There is no uneasy presentiment of a *danger* beyond the repressive social forces or the chaotic power of the natural world with which to reckon. True, these are terrifying in themselves, and Sands has ably shown how theology has sought to banish both human difference and elemental chaos from its Eucharists. She also acknowledges that these forces can only be embraced by a theological thinking that has stretched to its limits to embrace mystical and aesthetic images of difference (1994: 163). But there is nothing in Sands' writing to indicate a concern for something that can never be spoken. There appears to be nothing to fear or desire which is ultimately unknowable, inexpressibly other.

This may be regarded as a strength. Some would argue that the mystery of evil is best approached through the laboriously constructed human edifices which are its theological monuments and that we should look no further. However, it is also possible that Sands' thinking here may represent a containment or naturalising of evil which too easily recalls the resolution of suffering within the dominant theodical concord. Once radical alterity is relinquished it becomes easier to accommodate evil into the historical/natural cycle of events. Something is lost in this process. Is 'what is very sad' or 'desperately unfortunate' really tragic? Or is it the case that there is no appreciation of tragedy which is not also a dark epiphany? David Jasper writes 'Over the tragic vision broods in one way or another … the grim presence of God' (1993b: 146).

At the banquet that literature sets before us perhaps a strange hand writes unintelligible words high on the wall and the company falls silent not knowing who wrote or how to read.[62] To be a guest at this meal might require a more radical reappraisal of our approach to women's literature than has yet been attempted – including the possibility that literature might mediate for us an unknown and uncanny power. In the chapters that follow I shall argue that there are resources in the work of women poststructuralist theorists that enable religious feminists to stand in awe before literary texts. I shall set out the configurations of the literary and the sacred that are presented in the work of Kristeva, Irigaray and Cixous which I consider offer ways of reading which both reinscribe the 'femininity' of literary texts and leave us open to the mystery they carry. However, before attempting this task I take a step back and enquire as to why religious feminists have been so cautious about using poststructuralist theory in their literary readings thus far. What is it about poststructuralist theory that is problematic for us?

62 Daniel, chapter 5

CHAPTER 4

The problems with poststructuralism

Real politics

Feminism in the wilderness

Poststructuralist theory is the pre-eminent discourse of alterity in our time. It offers a language through which to explore the mechanisms which silence and violate the 'others' of dominant regimes. It has unmasked a benign-seeming liberal humanism in order to critique the totalising grip of the capitalist world-system for which it provides ideological support. Poststructuralism is held by many to be a means through which the sacred is reinhabiting the cultural order. And yet many feminists, in particular many religious feminists, have responded with caution and distaste to this critical movement, believing that it threatens those things they cherish and hold most dear. As literature occupies a very special place in feminist theological thinking we should not be surprised to discover that there has been a particular resistance to bringing poststructuralist insights to the reading of women's texts (see, for example, Ostriker, 1993: 115). This chapter examines how the threat of poststructuralism has been constructed in feminist thinking and what is at stake in exploring another way of reading texts.

The encounter of feminists within the Anglo/American tradition with post-structuralist theory is marked by a series of important publications which introduced the work of so-called 'French feminists'[63] to an audience unfamiliar with the theoretical debates taking place in France (Marks and de Courtivron, 1980; Moi, 1985; Jardine, 1985). These had a profound impact. Women conscious of belonging to a vibrant and successful movement recoiled in shock at writing which appeared to undermine both their interpretative categories and eman-cipatory objectives. Jardine describes the challenge thus:

Feminism, as a concept, as inherited from the humanist and rationalist eighteenth century, is traditionally about a group of human beings in history whose identity is defined by that history's representation of sexual decidability. And every term of that definition has been put into question by contemporary French thought. (1985: 20)

---

63 For a discussion of how Kristeva, Irigaray and Cixous came to be nominated as the representa-tives of 'French feminism' by those outside France see Martin (2000: 11–18).

After the shock of first encounter many influential feminists responded by actively opposing perspectives which, to their frustration, appeared both too complex and too naive, too abstract and too close to the body, too tied to 'male' theory and too fixated upon the feminine. Hazel Rowley and Elizabeth Grosz (1990: 198–200) offer a fascinating account of how leading American feminists wrestled with unfamiliar concepts and attempted to demonstrate their inadequacy, revealing both an embarrassing lack of comprehension and the real intellectual concern that a major threat had emerged to the feminist movement.

In the turmoil some optimistic attempts were made to annex the new thinking to the existing body of feminist scholarship. It was assigned the ambiguous place of a 'cultural unconscious' – important in its own way but of less significance than interventions in the political and social realm. Elaine Showalter's important essay 'Feminist Criticism in the Wilderness'[64] (1986: 243–270) is a good example of this strategy and represents a serious attempt to unify a feminist movement facing the challenges of competing epistemologies. The effort is undermined by a misunderstanding of the nature of the challenge represented by 'French feminism' and a barely disguised irritation with this troublesome movement which had emerged 'after our revolution' (1986: 255).

The strategy of cautious incorporation illustrated above by Showalter was an attractive option to many religious feminists seeking to preserve the gains of the past but excited by the exotic creativity of the new French thought. To this day Rebecca Chopp's text, *The Power to Speak: Feminism, Language and God* (1989), remains one of the most important engagements between feminist theology and poststructuralism. As a popular, and highly respected, feminist scholar Chopp's cautious endorsement of the new theories, as an echo of the marginalised voices within culture and a challenge to resymbolise dominant traditions of faith, was timely and influential. However, Chopp's optimistic work does not admit the violence of the poststructuralist challenge. In this work she appears confident that the logos can be reconfigured as the perfectly open sign and a radical reformation of Christianity can be achieved without the necessity of bloodshed (1989: 125). At this stage Chopp was repeating Showalter's synthesising attempt to incorporate poststructuralism into an existing framework established within a humanist political tradition.[65] She, too, employed the wilderness metaphor to express the hope that, through a process of exploring unfamiliar territory, feminism will emerge strengthened and renewed: 'in the wandering and movement of a sojourn in the wilderness feminism can discover and create new ways of dwelling' (1989: 128).

While the mediating strategies illustrated above enabled the work of the 'French

---

64 Showalter borrows the wilderness metaphor from Geoffrey Hartman's *Criticism in the Wilderness: The Study of Literature Today* (1980).

65 Chopp's later work shows a more critical approach to her inheritance as her engagement with poststructuralist theory has deepened.

feminists' to be debated within a certain context without women running the risk of appearing to betray their feminist principles, they could not long prevent fissures deepening between feminist scholars. As understanding of the key terms of the debate deepened it became increasingly apparent that the new theoretical approach could not be successfully grafted onto feminist thinking rooted in the enlightenment project. Yet it continued to exercise a powerful fascination. Many feminists began the long discipline of 'learning a new language' in an attempt to respond to challenges recognised to be very significant indeed.

The innocence of experience and the seduction of theory

As we have seen, the early encounters between English-speaking feminists and poststructuralism were marred by misunderstandings which needed to be rectified before a genuine dialogue could take place. One of the chief barriers to overcome was the 'theoretical' nature of the discourse employed by the French thinkers. Of course it could be reasonably asserted that all ways of producing knowledge are theoretical in that all rely upon a system of shared assumptions in order to be intelligible. However, the 'common sense' empiricism of English-speaking political discourse disguises, for those who use it, the 'theoretical' consensus upon which it is based (see Eagleton, 1996: 190).

And this form of political rhetoric was the mother tongue of the pioneering feminist thinkers of the 1970s and 1980s. It was taken for granted that their knowledge of the world arose directly from women's experience without the necessity of any mediating devices. Anxious to maintain the accessibility of their analyses to all women they were suspicious of any moves away from straightforward plain speaking. Theory was associated with a disembodied rationalism that was damaging and disempowering for women. Linda Curti argues that the 'denunciation of the male character of theory – from psychoanalysis to structuralism – reflected the need for differentiation in the first phase of the movement'. Within what she describes as 'a general hostility to theory' poststructuralism was particularly suspect because of its apparent undue 'stress on language and its neglect of the social' (1998: 13).

We have already noted some of the problems inherent in the attempt to claim the authority of women's experience. The universalist/essentialist presuppositions that legitimised the early claims of feminists to speak on behalf of all women were quickly challenged and refined. An acknowledgement of difference led women to become much more circumspect in their claims to experiential knowledge. Repeated attempts to differentiate particular boundaries of identity/experience, however, could not entirely restore the stability of women's experience as a foundation for feminist politics. Towards the end of the 1980s Denise Riley observed, 'the move to replace the tacit universal with the qualified "some women's experience" is both necessary yet in the end inadequate. Below the newly pluralized surfaces the old problems still linger' (1988: 99).

79

There is now a general acknowledgement that 'women's experience' is a contested term. Today's generation of feminist scholars continue to search for ways of thinking that acknowledge difference but do not treat as theoretically suspect what emerges as significant from women's lives (see, for example, Jantzen, 1998: 100–127). It is no easier to resolve the tensions between theory and experience now than it was in the past but it is now widely recognised that experience is not 'innocent' and that theory can be of positive political use to women. While the debates in wider feminist circles have thus become more nuanced, within the discourse of religious feminism a strong romantic attachment to the term 'experience' remains. Its powerful appeal is probably due to the crucial role it played in the development of feminist theology.[66] In the early work of Saiving, Christ and Plaskow it functions as the fulcrum that can be used to shift the world out of its traditional orbit and into a new trajectory. By the time Rosemary Ruether published the first systematic attempt to define the new territory of feminist theology in *Sexism and God Talk* (1983) it had become the source and norm for feminist theological thinking (1983: 12). This privileged status has been continually reaffirmed by women theologians. Pamela Young, for example, argues that 'if women's experience is not taken seriously; theology is incredible' (1990: 114).

In an article highly critical of feminist theological thinking Linda Woodhead notes that, given the importance of women's experience for the whole feminist theological enterprise, it is 'remarkable how little space is given by feminist theology to its defence and exploration' (1997: 197). Woodhead maintains that women's identity is neither simple, universal, transparent nor easily accounted for (1997: 199), and thus claims to speak from experience are frequently hopelessly naive. However, this critique fails to take into account the significant attempts made by some religious feminists in recent years to reform the concept by admitting its provisionality and stressing the dialogical nature of the knowledge experience generates (e.g. Graham, 1996: 159). It seems likely that religious feminists will continue to defend the use of experience while increasingly joining with other women in attempts to figure its authority in new ways.[67] However, while the generalisability and authenticity of women's experience continues to be the subject of intense debate among us, we have been less quick to respond to another, perhaps more serious, challenge that poststructuralism raises to our confident use of this key term.

When experience is unaccountable

A common assumption in feminist theological writing is that those aspects of women's experience that have been silenced in the past have transforming

---

66 See p. 47.
67 For an excellent contemporary discussion of the claims of women's experience in feminist politics see Ramazanoglu and Holland (2000).

potential when given public voice. It is also believed that those who have suffered violence and oppression can be empowered through the voicing of their experience (see, for example, Riet Bons-Storm, 1996). Poststructuralism questions this assumption by amplifying the problems of speaking from experience in a context in which consciousness has been seared and scarred through trauma.[68] This trauma, whether expressed as primal (as in the work of Lacan and Kristeva) or explicitly related to the events of the past century (in Lyotard and Levinas), confounds attempts to unite knowledge with experience in an organic whole. In this frame, experience is recast as that which contests with language, frustrating the reconciliation of events into narrative unity. It is in this aporetic space that poststructuralism emerges as a poesis of trauma. But, as Alice Jardine has argued, the liberal humanist politics of English-speaking feminism proved strongly resistant to disruption by the 'crisis-in-narrative' (Jardine, 1985: 146) poststructuralism represents.

In French thought over the past 30 years the question of exactly how 'experience', 'know-ledge', and 'truth' are so out of kilter for modernists has not been set aside as it has tended to be in Anglo American theory. (1985: 146)

The focus of feminist theology remains 'hearing into speech' and great emphasis is placed on the healing and redemptive power of women's narrative work. Post-structuralism introduces ambivalence into this process by maintaining a distinction between what has been silenced and what is 'unspeakable'. To make this distinction, theoretical concepts and language are employed which are necessarily strange and challenging. But esoteric terms and unfamiliar concepts are not used merely in order to confuse the uninitiated and introduce hierarchies of understanding. Rather it is the very unfamiliarity of the words and concepts employed which serves a violent assault upon taken-for-granted forgetful existence.[69] As Gerald Graff has argued 'Theory ... is what erupts when what was once silently agreed to in a community becomes disputed forcing its members to formulate and defend assumptions that they did not even have to be aware of' (1992: 11–31).

I have referred to poststructuralism as a poesis of trauma, making a connection

68 Walter Lowe is among the theologians influenced by poststructuralism who has begun to address this problem. He writes: 'For experience to emerge as experience there is required a kind of psychic space. In this century of total war that space has collapsed ... In contemporary appeals to experience one senses a note of urgency, even desperation which reflects the inherent bind. Experience has become overwhelming: therefore we seek the sign of grace. But because experience has become so overwhelming, the very possibility of confirming experience, the psychic space in which it might take place can no longer be assumed. That is the testimony of the walking wounded from Verdun to Vietnam. What is at stake is not this or that experience but the possibility of experience itself' (1993: 1).
69 Lyotard articulates the need for 'writing that does not forget there is the forgotten; which instead of saving the memory; tries to preserve the remainder, the unforgettable forgotten' (in King, 2000: 24).

between this body of theory and the literature of testimony which emerged from the same epistemological context.[70] In common with poetic writing, much use is made of neologisms, tropes, hyperbole and richly metaphoric language in order to communicate a challenge to the conventional realism of the humanist tradition. Rosi Braidotti argues that poststructuralist theory has strategically adopted these literary forms because poetry was discovered to be an effective instrument of liberation by those who wished to represent the world in new ways (1994: 36).

Women poststructuralist writers struggling to find means to express ideas which are contrary to the deep values undergirding Western culture have been particularly bold in breaking the conventions of traditional academic discourse (again, see Braidotti 1991: 165). Ironically, it is partly because their work has blurred the distinctions between theory (assumed to be empirically grounded) and fiction (assumed to be imaginative construction) that they were initially greeted with such misunderstanding by English-speaking feminists. For example, Hélène Cixous' rhetorical calls for women to write their bodies (1975a) were read quite literally as a call for women to abandon the picket line or political meeting for the creative writing class. They were thus easily dismissed as a diversionary option for middle-class women who had only a dilettante commitment to the women's movement.

It is an ironic fact that it is partly the literary nature of poststructuralism that has prevented religious feminists from employing it in their readings of women's writing. As Alice Jardine has argued, the denaturalising strategies of poststructuralist thinkers render alien what is taken to be most familiar:

> The clearest way, perhaps, to contain in one word the gesture they have performed on the texts and contexts of humanist ideology is to focus on the word *denaturalization*. They have denaturalized a world whose anthro-pology and anthro-centrism no longer make sense. It is a strange new world they have invented, a world that is *unheimlich*. And such strangeness has necessitated speaking and writing in new and strange ways, (1985: 24)

This process of denaturalisation runs contrary to the impulses of religious feminists who have most frequently sought in women's writing the naturalisation of their own social aspirations. Alienated from male-centred religious traditions, we have sought to fashion women's literature into a home in which we might feel secure. The last thing that is desired is dislocation to a strange territory, without secure shelter and with insecure boundaries. However, it was not only a

---

70 It is becoming increasingly difficult to define who are poststructuralist thinkers; the list seems to be growing all the time. However, this connection is particularly evident in the work of two of the women poststructuralist writers whose work is discussed in this book. Hélène Cixous has made a particular study of the work of Paul Celan and frequently uses the war time journals of Ettie Hillesum as a source of inspiration. Julia Kristeva reflects upon the personal and social trauma of living in an epoch of unprecedented violence. She writes 'the second world war brutalised consciousness in an outbreak of death and madness' (1989: 222).

desire for security that prevented us from wandering in the wild woods. It was also the conviction that there are important practical tasks to hand and that post-structuralism represents a potential diversion from political responsibility.

Women and the political real

In 1993 Judith Butler drew attention to an increasingly common refrain in feminist circles:

One hears warnings like the following: If everything is discourse, what happens to the body? If everything is a text, what about violence and bodily injury? Does anything matter in or for poststructuralism? (Butler, 1993: 28)

Her remarks highlighted the dilemma of those feminists who were becoming increasingly convinced by poststructuralist analyses that linked enlightenment thinking with totalising political systems (see for example, Braidotti, 1991: 53 and van Heijst 1995: 281) but who felt that poststructuralism deprived them of a usable basis for political action. Their difficulty was that forms of thinking which problematised the suppression of difference simultaneously appeared to disenfranchise those who would challenge logocentric authority. Poststructuralism deprives women of a politics built upon a sure foundation (such as reason, justice or truth). It also appears to undermine the political agency of women by contesting their common identity. This dilemma, Lidia Curti asserts, has led to a nostalgic 'preoccupation with the abandonment of the real, particularly the political real' and has presented women with what can appear to be irreconcilable choices, 'exclusion versus commitment, the images of women versus real women, the renewal of languages as opposed to changes in the condition of women' (1998: 1).

With a strong tradition of political activism, religious feminists have been particularly uncomfortable about anything that appears to threaten commitment to the political real. If there is a dominant rhetorical gesture in feminist religious scholarship it is one of obligation to this sacred place. The political real is made manifest for us in the figure of a flesh and blood woman, pictured in living relationships with others and in suffering material oppression. This rhetorical figure remains central and it is assumed that this 'woman's' interests are what generate our political agenda and provide the criteria upon which all our actions are judged. It is thus particularly unsettling to read poststructuralist writing in which the term 'woman' does not appear to refer to this heroic and abused historical subject at all (see Hogan, 1995: 60). In the work of poststructuralist thinkers 'woman' is frequently used as a trope, a literary device to signify that which is repressed or absent from representation. In the cultural trauma from which poststructuralism emerges, the absence of 'woman' from the symbolic order becomes the source of a creative possibility that the signifying system might be challenged and subverted by what currently lies beyond its claim. Woman's difference is seen as 'the only solution to the problem of how to rethink the unrepresentable' (Jardine, 1985: 144).

The feminine has assumed this figurative role through the historical construction of Western philosophical discourse within which woman has functioned as the powerful negative pole of culture propelling all away from herself. Derrida writes:

There is no such thing as the essence of woman because woman averts, she is averted of herself. Out of the depths, endless and unfathomable, she engulfs and distorts all vestige of essentiality, of identity, of property. And the philosophical discourse, blinded, flounders on these shoals and is hurled down these depthless depths to its ruin. (in Braidotti, 1991: 102)

As well as possessing the blinding power to petrify the symbolic order, this Medusa's absence from representation means that her potential is held in reserve. She is the last virgin territory; a dark continent ready for discursive colonisation. Braidotti pictures 'man' in his historical exhaustion at the end of the modern age turning to 'woman' as his last remaining hope, 'will this new woman be man's future?' (1991: 10). But if male theorists are able to employ the signifier 'woman' as what Jardine terms a *gynema*, a writing effect, does this mean the claims of women to this identity are invalid? Teresa de Lauretis protests the irony of woman being turned out of her last cultural home, the female body, in order to valorise the space of her absence; if Derrida can 'occupy and speak from the position of woman, it is because that position is vacant and, what is more, cannot be claimed by women' (de Lauretis, 1987: 33). Furthermore, although the cipher 'woman' is not to be equated with 'women', as feminists may have naively supposed, does not a valorisation of alterity deflect attention away from the material injustices experienced by living women? 'What is repressed is not otherness but specific, historically constructed agents' argues Toril Moi (1990: 373). There is a real danger that, through the rhetorical enchantment of poststructuralism, women might find themselves removed from the site of social struggle and transported to some timeless desert: 'we must be careful that, like Helen, we are not left in Egypt with only an image of ourselves transported to Troy as an excuse for war' (Jardine, 1985: 40).

The problems inherent in the poststructuralist exploitation of woman as a negative symbol, a cultural black hole, can seem overwhelming. They raise serious questions about any possible feminist use of such thinking. However, those women theorists who have been most articulate in warning of the dangers of conceptualising woman as space, limit or excess are also those who recognise the political potential for women to engage in new explorations of this disputed territory. Indeed the whole controversy concerning the place of the feminine in culture has opened up a new conceptual space between 'women' and 'woman' which it is in the interests of feminists to make plain. De Lauretis argues that the

slippage between woman as symbol and women as historical subjects of material relations places women both inside and outside the cultural 'technologies' of gender. This liminal position grants a potential for insight that was previously historically unachievable:

The subject that I see emerging from current writings and debates within feminism is one that is at the same time inside and outside the ideology of gender and conscious of being so, conscious of that two fold pull, of that division, that double vision. (1987: 6)

This double vision of 'woman' offers the chance for feminists to reconceptualise this marker which both bestows and denies essence. Judith Butler celebrates this potential as liberating:

The category of woman does not become useless through deconstruction, but becomes one whose uses are no longer reified as 'referents' and which stand a chance of being opened up, indeed of coming to signify in ways that none of us can predict in advance. (1993: 29)

There is, she argues, great energy to be generated by the fact that both 'woman' and 'women' are not terms which can be defined and closed. They have 'anti-descriptivist' properties which make them a 'permanent site of contest ... there can be no closure on this category and ... for politically significant reasons, there never ought to be' (1993: 221). The destabilisation of political categories does not spell an end to feminist politics, but women simply have to face the 'difficult labor of forging a future from resources inevitably impure' (1993: 241).

The positions rehearsed above are made possible by the fact that post-structuralism has made evident the disruptive potential of the culturally repressed feminine term. However, feminists do not receive this as a gift from the hands of great male thinkers. It is now being forcefully argued that the turn to 'woman' in theoretical discourse is integrally related to the gradual revival of feminist thinking in the twentieth century. The works of Simone de Beauvoir on woman as other and Virginia Woolf on women and writing, to take two famous examples, are rarely quoted by male theorists. However, their ideas were widely debated within the women's movement and it is claimed that this represented the beginning of an epistemological shift, the resonances of which are evident in later poststructuralist writing. Linda Curti argues that it is the responsibility of feminists to claim these genealogical connections because the 'postmodern weakening of the unitary, universal subject may have been brought about by the very existence of female and feminist thought' (1998: 10).

When viewed in this light the contested space of 'woman' becomes more evidently connected to women's efforts to construct radical social visions. It also becomes apparent that claims to an identity which is always provisional and resists determination can be allied to a politics which is just as 'real' as those based upon universalised appeals to essence or experience. Feminist poststructuralists would argue that that 'woman' defined in binary opposition to the male subject (either on the basis of essence, embodiment or experience), may merely serve as a mirror image incapable of upsetting the terms of the prevailing social and cultural order. If this is the case, a move away from concepts of woman defined by sexual difference (i.e. in relation to man) towards the more elusive idea that the female subject is a site of otherness may be just as viable a political mythology as those which have prevailed in the past (see Braidotti, 1991: 262–264). Judith Butler argues that:

> The deconstruction of identity is not the deconstruction of politics; rather it establishes as political the very terms through which identity is articulated. This kind of critique brings into question the foundationalist frame in which feminism as an identity politics has been articulated. The internal paradox of this foundationalism is that it presumes, fixes and constrains the very 'subjects' that it hopes to represent and liberate ... If identities were no longer fixed as the premises of a political syllogism, a new politics would surely emerge from the ruins of the old. (1990: 148)

The matter of bodies

It is now more generally accepted that the slippage between 'woman' and 'real women' does not imply the abandonment of a feminist political agenda. However, many feminists continue to harbour unease that a focus upon 'woman' as other, as that which defies signification, is part of a shift away from the robust materialism which characterised early second-wave feminist thinking. Whether in its essentialist or socialist forms, the bodies of women, working and loving, suffering and bearing children, served as the uniting focus of a heterogeneous movement. Poststructuralism appeared to threaten this straightforward understanding of the body as primary matter. Indeed for many poststructuralists the notion of the body as a prelinguistic given is an illusion perpetuated by a cultural order which first creates and then regulates and disciplines the body. The appearance of the body as primal conceals its secondary creation as a result of the splitting apart of rational and material existence. The body becomes what is left over when the essence of human nature is removed. Matter functions as 'what is cast out from philosophical propriety in order to sustain and secure the borders' (Butler, 1993: 31).

These analyses have proved highly creative in exploring such diverse issues as sexuality, femininity, health, the construction of penal systems and aesthetics. It is now commonplace to see inverted commas around the word 'body', indicating that what is being signified is not a natural given but a site of cultural contestation. Simon Williams and Gillian Bendelow, in their attempts to construct sociology of the lived body, point to the problems that now exist in coming to meaningful understandings of the term. They state 'the body is both everywhere and nowhere in social theory today' (1998: 1). What is disturbing in this proliferation of the uses of the word is that 'the body' is somehow dissipated and may even seem to disappear in the multiplicity of roles it is called upon to perform, as:

a fleshly organic entity and a natural symbol of society; the primordial basis of our being-in-the-world and the discursive product of disciplinary technologies of power/knowledge; an ongoing structure of lived experience and the foundational basis of rational consciousness; the wellspring of human emotionality and the site of numerous 'cyborg' couplings; a physical basis for personhood and identity and the basis from which social institutions, organisations and structures are forged. (1998: 2)

In this ambivalent situation, religious feminists have been particularly vociferous in maintaining the overriding claims of the body. These function as the 'difference in common' (Thistlethwaite, 1989: 125) uniting women of different ethnicities and sexualities against the bodily violence they all experience. At the same time as maintaining the importance of women's flesh and women's pain, however, religious feminists have found the female body to be their most valuable symbolic resource for revisioning spirituality (see, for example, Raphael, 1996). There has been a recognition that male-centred religious systems are patterned upon a male morphology (i.e. they are symbolic systems in which metaphors drawn from male embodiment are predominant) and the female body has been employed as an alternative source of sacred metaphors – *that is as a space of imagined transformation.*

What religious feminists have perhaps been slow to concede is that this work of symbolic reconstruction clearly demonstrates how the female body exceeds the frame in which it has been placed. To require the body to serve as the material foundation and moral guarantor of the feminist project is to insist that it remain simple, pure and uncontaminated by other essences. However, this is to confine it within impossible boundaries. The body overflows into the matter of texts, of language and sacred traditions. While this certainly results in the problems of complexity and ambiguity described above it also allows for exciting re-evaluations of women's embodied existence. No longer can those aspects of women's lives that have been concerned with reproduction, desire and the 'private realm' of bodily existence be regarded as timeless, natural or given – fit to be celebrated by feminists with circle dances and essential oils, but archaic, archetypal and impervious to change.[71] The body must not be cast out from politics in the same way as it has been cast out from philosophy, and the practice of religious feminists in continually re-symbolising the female form is an important practical acknowledgement of this imperative.

---

71 'Only culture, the mind and reason, social production, the state and society are understood as having a dynamic and developmental character. The body and its passions, reproduction, the family ... are often conceived of as timeless and unvarying aspects of nature. This way of conceptualising human history is deeply complicit in claims such as "women have no history" and "reproduction involves the mere repetition of life" ' (Moira Gatens, in Williams and Bendelow 1998: 114).

Writing and reading

Authors and authority

In the previous pages I have argued that poststructuralism's 'denaturalisation' of the key terms in feminist discourse (women's experience, women's identity, women's bodies) does not imply an abandonment of politics. Those who are, and always were, unconvinced by feminist claims may welcome the opportunity to declare that the deconstruction of these terms has demonstrated the naivety of feminist analyses and moved us into a postfeminist era. However, those of us who remain convinced of the necessity of pursuing feminist visions merely find ourselves in a more ambiguous, one might even claim a more 'real', world where we pursue Butler's challenge to assume the political labour of 'forging a future from resources inevitably impure' (1993: 241).

The issues outlined above demonstrate how difficult it has been for religious feminists to engage with poststructuralism because of their fear of losing the moral authority accorded by the rhetoric of the political real. However, the specific concern of this book is religious feminists' engagement with women's literature, and here poststructuralism forces consideration of yet more difficult problems.

Two essays written in the late 1960s by Roland Barthes (1977 [1968]) and Michel Foucault (1979 [1969]) with the provocative titles, 'The Death of the Author' and 'What Is an Author?', issued a challenge to Western theory to consider the key role the concept of authorship plays in defining the origins, meaning and limits of texts and in structuring reading as the passive reception of an author's work. Foucault's essay ends with a question intended to provoke an examination of the relation between authorship and authority, 'What difference does it make who is speaking?' (1979: 160).

This apparently casual dismissal of the significance of authorship caused deep offence to English speaking feminist critics when the work of Barthes and Foucault became more widely accessible in the late 1970s and 1980s. Some feminists detected in poststructuralism's announcement of the death of the author a conspiracy to render the newly rediscovered contribution of women writers to the literary tradition invisible again (see, for example Battersby, 1989: 209). In response to Foucault's 'What difference does it make?', Nancy Miller angrily asserted that this 'sovereign indifference' masks an assault on the emerging cultural visibility of women and is thus one of the masks behind which patriarchy hides its resistance to female power.

> The authorizing function of its own discourse authorizes the 'end of woman' without consulting her. What matter who's speaking? I would answer it matters, for example, to women who have lost and still routinely lose their proper name in marriage, and whose signature is not worth the paper it is written on: women for whom the signature by virtue of its power in the world of circulation is not immaterial. Only those who have it can play with not having it. (Miller, 1991: 68)

Any woman reader who has experienced the excitement and intimacy of an encounter with a female author through her texts can understand the passion of these feminist critiques. However, it is important to make clear that what Barthes and Foucault were contesting was not the work of writers in the material production of texts but rather the notion that the author is the authoritative source of meaning.

Poststructuralist thinkers have identified this assumption as the supporting mythology of Western philosophy (see, for example, Derrida, 1978: 91). Just as the author's identity and intention are held to be transparently present within the text, so is the ordering power of the divine logos taken to be evident in a world that can be empirically known and rationally controlled. It is this assumption that meaning and power originate from one pure source that is at issue. The human author as origin and guarantor of meaning thus serves as a model for the divine logos and it is this understanding of authorial power against which Barthes and Foucault raised their standards. Gayatri Spivak argues that the death of the author is not to be equated with the extinction of writers or writing, subjects or agents, but rather with the author,

who is not only taken to be the authority for the meaning of the text but also, when possessed of that authority, possessed by that fact of 'moral or legal supremacy, the power to influence the conduct or action of others'; and, when authorising, 'giving legal force to making legally valid'. (in Eagleton, 1996: 65)

If the authority of authors is being challenged on this basis, then surely feminists should welcome this assault on logocentric power? It creates space to revision the relation between readers and writers and to understand the creation of meaning (or the meaning of creation) as dialogical work. However, while many women are happy to see the sources of male authority being challenged, the 'female author' has a special claim upon feminist loyalties. The gynocritical movement invested heavily in its endeavour to restore to women a genealogy of creative mothers and the literary future, it was argued, depended upon remembering the women authors of the past. However, poststructuralism threatened more than the newly constructed female literary tradition. Gynocriticism's interest in the 'female author' was based upon the prior assumption that texts written by women displayed a distinctive character confirmed by the living link between the woman author and her textual productions. Women's specificity could not be defended if this link were severed for 'it is the author who guarantees the presence of this difference by her womanhood' (Weedon, 1987: 154). Moreover, as women had expressed themselves both primarily and principally through literary (rather than philosophical or political) activity, this literature was an indispensable resource when developing identity politics. If an author was a woman, or more specifically a particular type of woman, then her writing might be sorted and sifted for the patterns of distinction necessary to establish the existence of her authentic voice:

The concept of authorship which guarantees most feminist readings of black, white and lesbian women's writing is shared with liberal-humanist criticism. The author is the speaking, full, self present subject producing the text from her own knowledge of the world and she is the guarantee of its truth. (Weedon, 1987: 162)

But not only was the woman author a necessary 'fiction' in the construction of distinct identities, like her male counterpart she had a theological role to play.

In chapters 2 and 3 we saw how an awareness that women's specificity had not been given voice in the sacred traditions of male-centred religions led religious feminists to turn to women's writing as an alternative source of spiritual insight. Because the canonised sacred texts of these religious traditions came to be seen as 'male writing' there developed a corresponding tendency to view books *written by women authors* as supplying for women what men receive from 'their' scriptures and holy books. But should religious feminists have been more reflective concerning our desire to read women's literature as sacred text?

Sacred texts and religious reading

In an important essay published in 1985, the North American theologian Robert Detweiler asked, 'What Is a Sacred Text?' He argued that when members of a community privilege texts as sacred they begin to read them differently from other writing, 'They will feel more constrained in their interpretation of the sacred text because it ... commands reverence and restricts a free play of response' (1985: 214). He then went on to discuss the requirements that sacred texts should be authorised and interpreted according to certain conventions and argued that questions of intercommunal power quickly become apparent when sacred texts are put into play in communal life.

In her early work, Carol Christ spoke of feminist readers 'requiring' exemplary literature appropriate for sustaining women in their political and spiritual quests (1980: 40). Few religious feminists since then have been quite so forthright in their judgement that certain types of literature are more suitable than others for inspiring reflection. However, it remains a fact that the literature of heroic struggle is preferred to the love-story, that forms of realism[72] are preferred to fantasy, content predominates over form, etc. Furthermore, an unwritten convention appears to require that the author's moral status[73] must justify serious attention being paid to her work. While it would be an oversimplification to describe the textual choices made by religious feminists in these areas as a process of canonisation, it is clearly the case that not all literature written by women is judged to be an equally valid creative resource. We must ask what issues of power are being negotiated in this process of textual choice. How

---

72 Spiritual/magical realism is acceptable particularly when written by women from non-dominant groups.

73 Ethnic identity, marginal social location or a public commitment to feminist politics are the significant markers of a writer's authoritative status.

is it that certain works of literature have assumed such importance for religious feminists, and what has been lost in the process of selecting and interpreting literature in a manner that 'restricts the free play of response'? Van Heijst's accusation that religious feminists are reading for recognition of their own core values and 'wish to see their meanings (theological or feminist themes) endorsed in the literary text' (1995: 256) cannot be easily refuted.

Detweiler made another important observation in his essay which is also relevant to our discussion of the forms of literature preferred by religious feminists. He argued that for a believer sacred texts mediate 'some divine reality and hence connect her to that reality' (1985: 221). Sacred texts are 'evocative of a divine presence' (1985: 223) and Detweiler asserted that the reader is brought to expect that an encounter with the text will generate personal transformation, disclose hidden meaning and make possible a glimpse of God: 'an ultimate goal of a sacred text is to create an epiphany' (1985: 222). When literature is required to perform these functions for religious feminists the disclosure of the sacred is expected to be deeply connected to women's embodied experience, identity affirming, politically empowering and ultimately benevolent. Although the literary text may not necessarily explicitly refer to a deity, the sustaining power or spiritual values it mediates are expected to affirm women in their processes of personal/political development. A divine encounter which does not have these nurturing qualities is not regarded as authentic. In the early days of feminist theological scholarship Ruether made an affirmation of the full humanity of women a test of the validity of all theological truth claims[74] and this critical principle remains as significant today as it was twenty years ago. While such a perspective has functioned as an important tool for the critique of misogynist theological systems, the assumption that God is good, and nice, and a girl, is certainly a domestication of the divine. If women's literature as sacred text is expected to reflect our own best features back to us then it is functioning as a gilded mirror rather than a burning bush.

Perhaps the above discussion enables us to understand other unspoken reasons why poststructuralist reading strategies have been eschewed by religious feminists. When women's literature is functioning as sacred text it is necessary to constrain interpretative possibilities, and these restrictions are based upon the power relations within the reading community. Poststructuralism, particularly deconstruction, makes evident the power relations negotiated within and through texts and effectively challenges the conventions that hold dominant interpretations in place. Similarly, poststructuralism as a discourse of alterity, or a poesis of trauma, reflects upon loss, absence, absolute otherness. The epiphany of darkness

---

74 'Theologically speaking, whatever diminishes or denies the full humanity of women must be presumed not to reflect the divine or an authentic relation to the divine, or to reflect the authentic nature of things, or to be the message or work of an authentic redeemer or a community of redemption' (Ruether, 1983: 19).

it mediates may generate massive energy but it is not easily conducted to create light and warmth. Its incomprehensible speech cannot be easily incorporated into the pragmatic, optimistic, progressive and publicly orientated discourse which has been established within feminist theology.

In *Breaking the Fall: Religious Readings of Contemporary Fiction* (1989), Detweiler builds upon and moves beyond his essay on sacred texts. In this later work he criticises the dominant traditions of literary readings within theology. Theologians have 'tended to assume that the authority behind their project ... would somehow, eventually, crystallize into definitive readings, aspects of a truthful vision about the nature of things' (1989: xii). These theological readings function to bolster authorised truths and institutional power. In contrast to these reading practices he imagines communities of 'religious readers' who are brought together in recognition that their reading/writing work will generate multiple interpretations but be sustained by a reverent awareness of what literary texts may embody – namely pain, desire and worship. 'The writing and reading community especially as a liminal entity, could nurture a respect for the incomprehensibility of form and a reverence for mystery' (1989: xiv).

In presenting this vision Detweiler is responding to the cultural crisis mediated through poststructuralism – particularly as this is articulated in the work of Jean-François Lyotard (Detweiler, 1989: 61). Lyotard's insistence upon the ethical imperative to avoid synthesising or totalising interpretations is interpreted by Detweiler as a theological challenge.

It is truly our business as [Lyotard] states, 'not to supply reality but to invent allusions to the conceivable which cannot be presented' – and this is precisely what *religious writing and reading* as I have sought to redescribe them can do: the *communitas* is drawn together by the need to celebrate the conceivable but unpresentable, and its narratives act as the allusions that Lyotard calls for. (1989: 62, my emphasis)

The notion of 'religious reading' that Detweiler introduces here has provoked a fruitful debate (see, for example, Jasper and Ledbetter, 1994b). The vision of an open community that is capable of fostering the 'literary energies of doubting, of aporia and of paradox' (Bruce, 1994: 95) is an attractive alternative to the image of a closed group centred upon regulated readings of sacred text/s.[75]

David Jasper, in particular, has been keen to assert that religious reading represents a political challenge to the status quo. Attempts to subordinate literature to philosophy or theology always have conservative outcomes, he argues (1995). They represent attempts to consolidate a cultural order rather than look beyond it. Furthermore, they tend to supplement the magisterial power of interpretative

75 Detweiler argues that the community of readers is religious 'in its very openness to others, its willingness to adapt; its readiness to entertain the new ... These are characteristics contrary to what most religious institutions have championed. These tend to be closed, restrictive, defensive and prescriptive – in short what the dominant interpretative tradition has also been' (Detweiler, 1989: 35).

authorities. In contrast, Jasper argues, religious readings takes place on the liminal borders of faith communities where established traditions confront what they cannot assimilate. Religious reading is an activity practised on the margins where the political terror/promise of the unknown is anticipated (Jasper and Ledbetter, 1994b: 1–2).

Detweiler, and the scholars who have welcomed his invitation to explore the potential of religious reading, are practitioners who use the insights of poststructuralism to explore religious issues through a practical engagement with specific literary texts. Religious reading can be observed in these dialogical encounters rather than through a precisely formulated set of 'rules for engagement' with literature. This gives the work a fresh, dynamic and unsystematic quality. The openness, inclusivity and political commitment expressed in the work of Detweiler, Jasper and others appear to point to a possible way forward for religious feminists who are seeking to consider, alongside reading strategies which have proved creative in the past, new ways of reading which will keep us open to change. However, while the scholars who advocate religious reading have been careful to signal respect for feminist theory and women's writing, there has been little use of these sources as a significant resource.[76]

It is now time to consider what a 'feminist religious reading' might achieve. This would entail reading with awareness of what women poststructuralist writers (as well as the male theorists who are more usually consulted) can contribute to our understanding of the religious significance of engaging with literary texts. It will be a new venture to engage with the work of Kristeva, Irigaray and Cixous in this way. Much has been written about the significance of their thinking for literary theory. Less has been written concerning their importance for theological thinking. Hardly anything has been written which brings together these two areas of concern. However, when we take the relationship between literature and theology as a hermeneutical key to their work we will uncover many new insights in their writing that have been neglected in the past. Their work also offers rich potential both to 'en-gender' religious reading and to recover for religious feminism the ambivalent challenge of the literary imagination.

---

76 Both Detweiler and Jasper do state that feminist criticism has made a very important contribution to scholarship. Nevertheless they rarely engage with the work of feminist poststructuralist theorists.

PART II

Feminist religious reading

CHAPTER 5

Julia Kristeva and journeys to the end of night

Revolution in language

Dialogue across borders

I begin my explorations of the work of women poststructuralist writers with a new reading of Julia Kristeva. Within the academy, Kristeva is best known for bringing an unorthodox Lacanian perspective to the psychoanalytic study of cultural forms. What is less commonly recognised is that the entire trajectory of her writing career has been plotted between the twin poles of literature and theology. On occasions she has explored the sharp forces of repulsion between them – at other times she has demonstrated the strong convergences and attractions drawing them closely together. Furthermore, her research has been dominated by the concern to trace the significance of the feminine, of the repressed maternal sphere and the female body, for the contrasting public worlds of theology and artistic production. For these reasons her work is particularly pertinent to the concerns of this book, which in turn represents an excellent opportunity to study Kristeva's work through a new and particularly illuminating lens. In this chapter I will undertake a close reading of her oeuvre which will display how she has taken the gendered distinctions between the realms of literature and theology and reshaped them in distinctive and provocative ways. I will argue that, as she herself has described her work as a lifelong quest to see how far literature can take us in wrestling with the unspeakable mysteries of existence (2000: 112), the literary and theological questions she wrestles with should now be foregrounded in our engagement with her work.

As Kristeva has frequently affirmed, her intellectual journey owes much to the personal circumstances of her life. She grew up in communist Eastern Europe and migrated to France in the mid-1960s at a crucial point of radical upheaval in political and intellectual structures. She has passed most of her life as an alien, seeking to understand the relation between personal estrangement and the desire for a primal home.

When she was a child growing up in Bulgaria, Kristeva's parents sought to interest her in the study of literature and the French language as a means of communication with a world less bounded than her own. They also sought to nurture a spirit of religious devotion which, Kristeva perceived, enabled them to make an imaginary transcendence of circumstances. While understanding the significance of this 'freedom' Kristeva found herself unable to subscribe to her parents' beliefs. She interpreted religious faith as a retreat into the archaic comforts of past epochs in European civilisation. Nevertheless, despite her early rejection of Christianity, Kristeva recognised that, alongside artistic production, religion played an important role in securing a space beyond social regulation:

The experience in Bulgaria permitted me at once to live in an extremely closed environment … and at the same time to find the small spaces of freedom, which include for example the arts, the interest in foreign languages, even religion. (1996d: 49)

When she grew older Kristeva's interest in literature and religion was further stimulated by her study of Mikhail Bakhtin. His work was materialist enough to appeal to the progressive sympathies she held in her early twenties. Kristeva has, in fact, never repudiated the materialism of her own intellectual formation in Eastern Europe, although she now expresses this through psychoanalytic rather than socialist categories. Bakhtin offered her a compelling model of culture as a complex conversation in which differing social groups pursued their own distinctive themes. This dialogical understanding of the social order was accompanied by a vision of language and subjectivity constituted through conversational relations with others. Identity and agency were achieved through these social processes rather than originating from an interior space within.

What is particularly significant about Bakhtin's imprint on Kristeva is that he identified literature (particularly the novel) and religion as privileged sites in which dialogical cultural relations could be discerned. In novelistic writing many voices are able to form and dispute the ordering of the social world. In religious rituals and their unravelling in carnival, Bakhtin identified the construction of social regulation and its carnivalesque contestation by the common people. Kristeva was particularly interested in the link Bakhtin makes between literary form and social relations:

Bakhtin accounts for what happens in the literary forms of Rabelais and Dostoevsky but did not disconnect these formal aspects from the surrounding history and ethics. He looked at the aesthetics of the carnival in relation to the church and so on. I was interested in how *he already considered form as part of historical and moral issues*. (1996a: 149, my emphasis)

By emphasising the significance of literary form here Kristeva is arguing that the manner in which a literary text is 'embodied' represents as significant a social dynamic as its content. This concept, unfamiliar to many English-speaking feminists, is one which has played a major role in the development of Kristeva's work.

Bakhtin's thinking gave Kristeva the theoretical tools she needed to critique the ahistorical individualism of the linguistic theories she encountered upon arrival in France, and she earned early recognition, along with other Eastern Europeans, by introducing Bakhtin's work to a wider audience. However, despite her integration into Parisian intellectual life, Kristeva felt a profound sense of displacement. She was now a foreigner and the experience of being 'not at home' presented her with a new academic agenda. She was sympathetically drawn to study how the infant takes its place in the conversation of culture and was particularly interested in how early experiences related to the acquisition of language continue to impact upon adult subjectivity. As Anderson has written, 'she sought to understand how the child remains within the adult consciousness as a stranger within' (1997: 215).

An encounter with the nascent feminist movement further stimulated her thinking and caused Kristeva to revisit the materialist epistemology of her Bulgarian education. Not only were social relations crucial to an understanding of cultural forms but the body had to be acknowledged as the mater-ial home of language. Kristeva began to investigate the role of the mother in the infant's transformation into a speaking subject. Of her debt to feminism Kristeva writes, 'I was very interested in the questions they were asking: the specificity of the feminine, the mother's influence on her child's development into an independent being, language acquisition, the child's dependency upon the mother, the mother's role in language and symbolic processing, the nature of women's writing and women's art' (1996c: 7).

The symbolic, the imaginary and the real

Kristeva's arrival in France coincided with the publication of Lacan's *Écrits* (1973 [1966]). Their impact upon Kristeva was immense. Lacanian psychoanalysis appeared to offer the means of linking her various concerns into a coherent project. Initially Lacan's thinking was a significant resource, among others, through which she sought to make the connections between the body, subjectivity and language. Increasingly Lacan's threefold orders of the *real*, the *imaginary* and the *symbolic* came to structure her analysis of Western culture. Their status in her work is revelatory.

The Trinity itself, that crown jewel of theological sophistication evokes, beyond its specific content and by virtue of the very logic of its articulation the intricate intertwining of the three aspects of psychic life: the symbolic, the imaginary and the real. (1987a: 43)

Because these theoretical terms are so important for an understanding of her thinking it is important to spend some time clarifying their meaning for Lacan before examining the transformation they undergo in Kristeva's work.

If Lacan's account of the development of subjectivity were to be described chronologically, the infant enjoying unity with the mother (or, more specifically, undifferentiated from elements in the mother's body) in the realm of the *real* must make a journey of separation from this fearful, ecstatic union. The child must experience a precarious and painful process of separation. The first step towards this is entry into the *imaginary order* through the 'mirror stage'. In this process the child confronts a (social) image beyond itself which it both recognises as its reflection and identifies with as an ideal ego. This identification, however, is ironically predicated upon misrecognition, for the coherent and bounded subject which confronts the child in the image does not correspond to the still inchoate and amorphous infant which has yet to gain control over its fragmented parts.

This mirage, however, does serve to initiate a tear in the previously seamless bond with the mother and this prepares the way for the child's entry into the *symbolic* order through the Oedipal crisis. Lacan maintains the importance that Freud placed in this drama through which the subject is confronted with its own lack. In Lacan's retracing of this archetypal event, castration is the constitutive fact of human life. What propels the subject into language and culture is primordial loss.

Already a split and divided subject the infant must come to concede direct relationality with the other is impossible. The mother/child dyad is fractured by the intervention of the phallus, not a biological penis but the token both of the mother's desire and the father's law. In contrast to full presence of the real the symbolic order offers language which appears to fill the lack caused by loss of the mother.[77]

Lacan presents an image of the subject which is lacking, desiring and possessing only an ironic cohesion based upon illusion. The entry into language has been achieved at the loss of primordial completeness. Moreover 'mastery' over the real is never fully achieved and Lacan describes how the paternal law, the social and moral order are organised to prevent the subject from entering into the dangerous and desired proximity of the 'maternal Thing'.

While it is easiest to follow Lacan's meditations upon the real, the imaginary and the symbolic by reading them through a developmental account, this is potentially misleading. The processes of loss, desire and symbolisation are in fact constitutive of subjectivity throughout human existence. Similarly, any straightforwardly developmental account of Lacan must also confront the greatest irony of all. Even the 'maternal Thing' has no existence as a definable point of origin. Its monumental impact lies in the trauma of its loss. It can never be enjoyed because it has no existence other than through its absence. The real and imaginary stages are in fact constituted by the rupture with the symbolic and thus owe their existence to that which comes after them. As Eugenie Georgaca states:

77 David Crownfield offers this description of the substitutionary processes through which the subject becomes inscribed within the symbolic order: 'Blocked by the father (not by any behaviour of the father, but by the function, the position, the very existence of the role of the father) from total possession of mother's desire, the child is forced to substitute other gratifications, other objects of desire, other roles to play or places to play them. This positional logic of substitution, of representing one thing by another, of displacing desire along a chain of representatives, is the foundation of the formal order of language, of what Lacan calls the symbolic order' (1992b: xiii).

The Thing is the lost object, but an object that never was there. It is an object that has been constructed by the introduction of language as that which is excluded from it. (Georgaca, 1995: 13)

Within Lacan's schema the real is the limit of language, and the play of signification is radically separated from the jouissance which compels its movement. To quote Georgaca again:

The real is the limit of our experience, that which the symbolic constantly bangs itself against but cannot penetrate, tame, fend off or assimilate. The real is that radical otherness that haunts human existence. (1995: 16)

Even such a brief résumé of Lacanian thinking reveals its grave problems for feminists. While Lacanians insist that his theoretical categories are cultural rather than biological, it is difficult to concede a radical separation between the penis and the phallus. Feminists might object equally to the subjection of the body to the symbolic order and the pre-eminent significance given to the 'phallus'.[78] However, I also hope that, even in a brief account, the powerful 'poetic' attraction of Lacan's thinking may also be perceived. As a complex, engrossing narrative of loss and desire it claims an important place in the modernist tradition. It powerfully evokes nostalgia for completeness while also requiring an acceptance of the inevitability of fragmentation. It names the human desire for restored plenitude as the force which drives history while insisting that the quest is based upon a primeval repression. Its appeal to a generation of intellectuals sick for change and yet fearing the blind force of mass political movements is evident. As Lacan articulates the human condition there can be no hope of casting off the chains forged within the symbolic order. What is achieved is not healing or restitution but the satisfaction of recognising illusion.

Lacan's evocative and tragic images have influenced all Kristeva's writing. However, in her earliest works (*Desire in Language*, 1980; *Revolution in Poetic Language*, 1984), his thinking is used alongside insights drawn from the Russian formalists and Bakhtin to present an optimistic reinterpretation of the relationship between the real and the symbolic which holds open the possibility not only of wry understanding but also social change.

Semiotic and symbolic

Kristeva's starting point for revising Lacanian thinking is her interest in the mother's body and its influence in promoting the development of subjectivity

---

78 Mitchell and Rose summarise these objections thus: 'The demands against Lacan therefore collapse two different levels of objection – that the body should be mediated by language and that the privileged term of that mediation be male' (1982: 56). Similarly, although both 'women' and 'men' are constructed within the symbolic order (one becomes a man or a woman inside language), it is hard to set aside the profound cultural associations that link women to the real and the unconscious or to avoid the conclusion that Lacan is perpetuating the traditional homology made between woman, death, absence and lack in many religious traditions (see Jonte-Pace, 1992: 6–7).

into the imaginary and symbolic orders. In renaming this 'maternal' sphere the 'semiotic', and stating that she does so because this term implies 'distinctive mark, trace index, precursory sign, proof, engraved or written sign, imprint, trace figuration' (1984: 25), she indicates a greater possibility of a complementary relation between this order and the paternal symbolic than can be inferred from Lacan.

> For him the real is a hole, a void, but I think that in a number of experiences with which psychoanalysis is concerned – most noticeably the narcissistic structure, the experience of melancholia or of catastrophic suffering and so on – the appearance of the real is not necessarily a void. It is accompanied by a number of psychic inscriptions that are of the order of the semiotic. Thus perhaps the notion of the semiotic allows us to speak of the real without simply saying that it's emptiness or a blank. (1996b: 23)

The semiotic inscribes itself upon the subject primarily through the fluctuating experiences of physical impulses, energy discharges and drives orientated and structured around the mother's body. Kristeva refers to the maternal space in which this semiotic structuring occurs as the *chora*, recalling Plato's famous description of the womb-like cave, 'the *chora* is a womb or nurse in which elements are without identity and without reason. The *chora* is a place of chaos' (Kristeva, in Oliver, 1993c: 46).

However, although the *chora* is the place of nameless meetings between the undifferentiated bodies of mother and child, these encounters are more than shadow dances; they are integral to the signifying process. Kristeva writes that although 'deprived of unity identity or deity the *chora* is nevertheless subject to a regulating process ... which is different from that of symbolic law but nevertheless effectuates discontinuities by temporally articulating them and then starting over again and again' (1984: 26). The initial impress of the maternal body is thus experienced in what Kristeva names 'semiotic operations' (1980: 134): the rhythms, intonations and muscular contractions dependent upon the body's drives. While heterogeneous to language it incubates the signifying disposition; thus though prior to the rupture that generates meaning the semiotic is yet 'always in sight of it or in either a negative or surplus relationship to it' (1980: 133).

It can thus be seen that, while Lacan envisages the real as circumscribed by the retroactive power of the symbolic and thus only able to exert a destructive or chaotic eruption within it, Kristeva can conceive of a continuing relation between the maternal and paternal realms within the *subject in process*. This is because the disjunctures necessary to inculcate signifying disposition are already experienced within the semiotic. It is possible for her to posit such a relationship because although the semiotic lies beyond the father's law it contains its own 'order'. Oliver states:

> Before it enters the Symbolic and encounters the No/Name of the Father, the infant has already lived with maternal regulation, the mother's 'no'. The mother regulates the material processes of the infant's body. She oversees what goes into and comes out of the infant's body. She alters the relationship between her own body and the infant's accordingly …
>
> The bodily relation that ensures the child's survival also sets up the child's entrance into the Symbolic … the semiotic *chora* is both the space that supports the Symbolic and an essential element of signification. (1993c: 46)

Kristeva's 'materialism' can be clearly seen in this insistence that the body has found its way into language. 'The mother's body is therefore what mediates the symbolic law organising social relations' (Kristeva, 1984: 27). The barrier separating the semiotic from the symbolic is presented as a traversable boundary (1984: 51). It is a feature of the breadth of Kristeva's early speculations about the influence of the semiotic that she is able within the space of a few pages (for example, 1980: 132–135) to speak of its impact upon the earliest babbling of infants, psychotic discourse and the heteroglossia of contemporary culture. Within culture *religion* and *art* have the particular functions of mediating the semiotic in ways that can either confirm or destabilise the social order.

Theology, literature and the 'thetic break'

To understand Kristeva's thinking about religion and literature in the light of her developing interest in psychoanalysis it is necessary to return to the threshold where the semiotic and the symbolic both meet and are separated. As I have argued, Kristeva suggests that it is the mother's body which functions as the infant's primordial other and begins to imprint upon the child the dispositions that are necessary for its entry into the social world. There is a process of rejection, or separation, experienced within the body which eventually culminates in what Kristeva terms the *thetic break*. Through this the child makes its entrance into the symbolic order. As in the Lacanian schema, however, this developmental account is potentially misleading. In fact it is the thetic break which constitutes the semiotic *both as* a place beyond language and as an essential part of the signifying process.

> It exists in practice only within the symbolic and requires the symbolic break to obtain the complex articulation we associate with it in musical and poetic practices. In other words, symbolisation makes possible the complexity of this semiotic combinatorial system, which only theory can isolate as preliminary. (1984: 68)

The thetic break, which structures the semiotic and positions it in relation to the symbolic, is the founding moment not only of subjectivity but also of civilisation. Confirming psychoanalytical insights, structural anthropology points to the prohibition of incest as the beginning of social organisation. This encoding of the traumas of thetic rupture continues to be rehearsed in religious and artistic practices. These two means of culturally mediating the semiotic have, however, very different functions.

In Kristeva's early writing the religious impulse, principally focused in sacrifice, serves to police the boundary between the semiotic and the symbolic. It regulates the dangerous eruptions of chaos and violence in the social order by ascribing them a ritual place: 'sacrifice assigns jouissance its productive limit' (Kristeva, 1984: 78). Religion also provides the means of transgressing its own forms; carnivalesque anarchy operates as a floodgate in societies in which the control of the symbolic order is most severely felt. In times of social chaos and change the religious systems seek to build bulwarks to defend society against the dangerous incursion of the semiotic. To fulfil these functions religion must draw very close to the power it curtails, and often employs mystical and artistic means to sublimate the impress of the semiotic. At these points the regulating power of religion is particularly vulnerable to its own dependency upon the forces it seeks to harness.

Poetic language and mimesis may appear as an argument complicitous with dogma – we are familiar with religion's use of them – but they may also set in motion what dogma represses. In so doing, they no longer act as instinctual floodgates within the enclosure of the sacred and become instead protesters against its posturing. And thus, its complexity unfolded by its practices, the signifying process joins the social revolution. (1984: 61)

In contrast to religion, which seeks to secure the thetic break, art is the means of revealing the permeability of this boundary and facilitating the flow of jouissance into the symbolic order. Kristeva ascribes a salvific role to the artist, who is a voyager between worlds. Artists carry 'death' as a consequence of their willingness to cross the thetic divide (1984: 70). They are, nevertheless, able to bring rebirth to cultures which are subject to the excessive domination of 'paternal' authority. Music and painting are artistic vehicles through which the semiotic is mediated. For example, Kristeva discerns in Giotto's use of vivid colour in religious painting a 'chromatic joy' which 'discreetly enters the theological signified distorting and doing violence to it without relinquishing it. This joy evokes the carnivalesque excesses of the masses ... which came to light later, through literary art' (1980: 224).

Poetic language

It is with this 'literary art' that Kristeva is particularly engaged. In her early work she gives most attention to the innovative linguistic constructions of modernist literature: the 'poetic language' which shatters conventional communicative forms. Kristeva argues that it is not the signifying function of this language that gives it revolutionary potential but rather its anarchic form which accomplishes a fracturing of the symbolic by allowing the repressed rhythms and impulses of the semiotic back into signification. In artistic practices the semiotic – the precondition of the symbolic – is revealed as that which also threatens the symbolic with destruction. For Kristeva this linguistic function is of the strongest political significance:

poetic language in its most disruptive form (unreadable for meaning, dangerous for the subject) shows the constraints of a civilisation dominated by transcendental rationality. Consequently it is a means of overriding this constraint ...

This means that if [the] poetic economy has always born witness to crises and impossibilities of transcendental symbolics in our times it is coupled with crises of social institutions (state, family, religion), and, more profoundly a turning point in the relationship of man [sic] to meaning. (1980: 140)

Herein lies the revolutionary function of the artist: not to criticise, or to campaign for some new social vision, but to assault the signifying system upon which the father's law is based. As Lechte comments, 'the ethical function of a text has nothing to do with ideological purity but with a semiotic process which "pluralises", pulverises, musicates all ossified forms' (1990: 139). In her early texts Kristeva expresses the optimistic belief that since the end of the nineteenth century, despite the rise in totalitarianism, poetic language has born its own witness to the coming of a new era. Avant-garde linguistic forms are the inevitable companions of crises within social institutions and bear witness to 'the moment of their mutation, evolution, revolution, or disarray' (1980: 124).

There is no doubt that in positing a beyond of language Kristeva has made a significant intervention in poststructuralist thought. Lacan viewed eruptions of the real into the symbolic as essentially meaningless and Kristeva contradicts this assumption. In making this theoretical move she is also engaged in an implicit dialogue with Derrida (whose work she encountered shortly after arriving in Paris). Kristeva alleges that Derridean deconstruction operates entirely within the realm of the symbolic system which, when perceived as a totality, may be disturbed from within but not radically challenged from without. Kristeva claims that because Derrida explores the field of 'signification' rather than 'subjectivity' he can theorise the dynamics of 'différance' but may not express the energy of separation, rupture and negativity experienced in assuming a speaking position while also being constituted by the 'beyond' of language − a beyond which confronts both the individual and the symbolic order with the promise of death and rebirth.[79] She writes:

The grammatological deluge of meaning gives up on the subject and must remain ignorant not only of its functioning as social practice, but also of his [sic] chances for experiencing jouissance or being put to death. (1984: 142)

Kristeva's admirers have argued that her theoretical analysis, incorporating breaks, negativity and rejection experienced through the body, is fundamentally different from one based upon a play of différance (see, for example, Oliver, 1993c: 42–43). It allows revolutionary disjunctures to be imagined. Because of this, Georgaca writes, Kristeva's early work has important political implications:

79 Such judgements would be more difficult to defend in relation to Derrida's later work.

If difference and heterogeneity [are] confined only within the frame of language as signifying then one cannot foresee any alternative beyond minor changes in linguistic and discursive configurations. For radical change to be conceived, something radically heterogeneous yet potentially constructive has to be theorised. (1995: 28)

Kristeva has achieved a new model of the subject in her insistence that the thetic rupture is not a once and for all separation between the maternal and paternal spheres; 'As a traversable boundary the thetic is completely different from an imaginary castration ... imposed once and for all, perpetuating the well-ordered signifier' (1984: 51). The influence of Bakhtin is evident here. His insistence upon the material nature of communication and its dialogical and carnivalesque qualities is the inspiration for her vision of subjectivity (and culture) as fragmented and yet potentially able to sustain a vital discourse. Moreover, Bakhtin makes literature the privileged window into the dialogic and heralds the birth of the novel as a witness to a revolutionary moment in the unfolding of culture. Kristeva embraces this social and historical approach to literary texts and supplements it through her own introduction of psychoanalytic concerns. Literature can be analysed to reveal the tensions, amorous play and fragile interactions between the semiotic and symbolic orders – both within the 'subject in process' and in social forms in transition.

The embrace, in Kristeva's early writing, of the positive potential that can be discerned within the semiotic invites a rethinking of subjectivity in defiance of the coherent and bounded humanist model (1980: 23). It is also an invitation to engage in new forms of ethical thinking – what she later comes to describe as *herethics*. Recognition of the 'other' within implies a relation to alterity that is prior to the law, prior to the imposed regulation of mutual obligation which at some point always constructs a boundary around those to whom ethical duty is owed. This is an ethical relation which originates within the maternal sphere and incorporates, rather than excludes, jouissance and the presence of death.

Women and the avant-garde

It would appear from the above statements that Kristeva's achievement has been of great significance, that she has predicated upon her journeys into the realm of the semiotic the possibility of new political beginnings and ethical understandings which are in marked contrast to patriarchal visions. However, the fact that these are based upon a new understanding of the relation to the 'mother' does not mean that they are implicitly celebratory of women. In fact the opposite is rather the case.

It is necessary to remember, and Kristeva's later work makes this very clear, that the 'maternal' semiotic is not merely a delightful, creative realm of blissful jouissance. It is also the place where forms disintegrate, the realm of horror, abjection and death. Moreover, there is always a temptation to extend the meaning of 'maternal' into mother and into woman. This is a temptation to which Kristeva increasingly succumbs. However, in her early writing she quite explicitly makes clear that the semiotic is not to be interpreted as a quality, affinity or sensitivity especially pertaining to women as they exist within the symbolic. Because it is beyond language it is also beyond the gendered subject positions ascribed within the social domain. Kristeva's maternal function is therefore to be seen neither as 'female' nor as 'personal' but rather as the point of contact with the unsymbolisable. It is of course tempting, and almost unavoidable, to seek to give the mother a name and predicate upon her nurturing intention, but that is to deny the radical alterity of the maternal to the world of paternal nomination.

We recognise on the one hand that biology jolts us by means of unsymbolized instinctual drives and that this phenomenon excludes social intercourse ... On the other hand we immediately deny it; we say there can be no escape, for mamma is there ...

Through a body destined to insure reproduction of the species, the woman subject ... more a *filter* than anyone else – a thoroughfare, a threshold where 'nature' confronts 'culture'. To imagine that there is *someone* in that filter – such is the source of religious mystifications, the font that nourishes them. (1980: 239)

Nevertheless, the fact that the semiotic does not correspond to cultural constructions of femininity does not mean that women and men enjoy a similar relation to the beyond of language. Kristeva's thinking here is far from straightforward. At times she appears to suggest that a woman's relationship to her body gives her a particular role of an outsider within culture: she is a potential dissident or subversive. This perspective appears implicit in such passages by Kristeva as the following:

A woman is trapped within the frontiers of her body and even of her species, and consequently always feels *exiled* both by the general clichés that make up a common consensus and by the very powers of generalisation intrinsic to language. (1986b: 296)

However, in the same piece of work Kristeva goes on to speak of the problems that women experience in creative writing. Their more tenuous location within the symbolic order makes them less likely than men to be able to survive the dangers of mediating the semiotic. Those who represent the revolution promised through poetic language are most likely to be men. Women authors are forlorn creatures who suffer as they speak. It is a particular irony, since Kristeva has now become a writer of fiction herself, that she has consistently favoured the revolutionary art of men. This fact is neither coincidental nor insignificant but relates directly to Kristeva's understanding of the Oedipal struggle and the powerful attachment the female subject must make to the phallus to become a 'speaking' subject.

A man can imagine an all powerful, though always insignificant, mother in order to 'legitimise' himself; to make himself known, to lean on her and be guided by her through the social labyrinth ... For a woman as soon as the father is not calling the tune and language is being torn apart by rhythm, no mother can serve as an axis for the sacred or for farce.

If she tries to provide it herself, the result is so-called female homosexuality, identification with the virility, or a tight rein on the least pre-Oedipal pleasure. And if no paternal legitimation comes along to dam up the inexhaustible non-symbolized drive, she collapses in psychosis or suicide. (1986a: 158)

But perhaps the fact that Kristeva believes women are less likely to be avant-garde poets need not depress feminist critics unduly. It is certainly the case that the work of male modernist writers has been the most celebrated within the academy. However, we are increasingly aware of the significant contribution women have made to the traditions of literature favoured by Kristeva.[80] We can also be confident that the work of women writers in genres other than those that interest her have made considerable social impact. The negative opinions Kristeva expresses concerning women writers are ones that will be contested by feminist religious readers. The challenge then facing us will be whether we can profit from the powerful images through which Kristeva affirms 'the indelible association of women's bodies with language, whether in texts written by women or by men' (Humm, 1994: 103) while remaining aware that the 'semiotic' itself has the status of a metaphorical construction justified by the need to speak what lies beyond language? Is it possible to imagine, alongside Kristeva, the maternal function (or space, or body, or boundary, or prohibition) as a radical site of alterity upon whose monumental power in abasement both subjectivity and society are founded, while retaining an awareness of the ambivalence of her project? Does this offer another way of framing literature as feminine that has productive political potential and, on this basis, are we prepared to accompany Kristeva in her quest to discern how far literature can take us in wrestling with the darkest mysteries of existence (2000: 112).

The journey will become increasingly uncomfortable as Kristeva pursues this challenge in the second phase of her career. In this new phase Kristeva's thinking is profoundly disquieting and yet, arguably, at its most powerful. Her famous trilogy *Powers of Horror* (1982), *Tales of Love* (1987b) and *Black Sun* (1989) shows her tracing the impress of the 'maternal' upon three classic sites of psychoanalytic interest: *abjection*, *love* and *melancholy*. These texts exemplify Kristeva's continuing concern to display how the repression (murder) of the mother offers the key to interpreting psycho-social traumas via the liminal insights of art and religion.

Abjection, love and melancholy

Approaches to the abject
Powers of Horror: An Essay in Abjection (1982) begins by invoking the familiar nausea that all children have in relation to some loathed food item which is often in a state between liquid and solid, hot and cold (like the thin skin of warmed milk).

80 See, for example, Bonnie Kime Scott's (1990) excellent anthology of modernist literature written by women.

She then moves on to explore the deep cultural need to make ritual or ethical boundaries between the clean and the unclean, good and evil, the living and the dead.[81] For Kristeva the compulsion experienced to separate oneself from a dreaded object, which nevertheless fascinates and compels, prompts the analyst to explore, 'our earliest attempts to release the hold of maternal entity' (1982: 13). Maintaining that this experience is universal, Kristeva insists there are both individual and cultural instances in which the maternal hold is so powerful that the strongest force must be expended to achieve release into the social/symbolic order. It is in such cases, where the thetic break is at its weakest, that the 'powers of horror' become most active. In what Kristeva terms 'borderline' psychological cases the subject returns obsessively to the 'abject', motivated by a fascination that braves the dangers of annihilation.

But devotees of the abject ... do not cease looking within what flows from the other's 'innermost being' for the desirable and terrifying nourishing and murderous, fascinating and abject inside of the maternal body ... the advent of one's own identity demands a law that mutilates whereas jouissance demands an *abjection* from which identity becomes absent. (1982: 54)

As in individual 'borderline' cases, Kristeva argues that in cultures where fear of defilement and ritual impurity are most active, paradoxically, the renunciation of the maternal is least secure.

In societies where it occurs, ritualization of defilement is accompanied by a strong concern for separating the sexes, and this means giving men rights over women. The latter, apparently put in the position of passive objects, are none the less felt to be wily powers, 'baleful schemers' from whom rightful beneficiaries must protect themselves ... That other sex, the feminine, becomes synonymous with a radical evil that is to be suppressed. (1982: 70)

Kristeva argues that a study of ancient Jewish religion reveals how paternal anxiety, manifest in dietary and behavioural regulation, transforms itself into an ethics of purity and impurity based upon a horror (abjection) of maternal power. However, the religion of the lawgiver, of the father/creator, is formed through the necessity of overcoming its origins in Near Eastern traditions which celebrate maternal deities. Kristeva believes Jewish monotheism wears 'like a lining, the mark of maternal, feminine, or pagan substance' (1982: 186).

Christianity, drawing upon this heritage, further internalises its own roots in abjection. Henceforth abjection is 'no longer exterior it is permanent and comes from within' (1982: 118). The journey has been made from pollution to sin – sin linked inevitably by the theological imagination with its half-remembered inheritance in the desire for the body of the mother. 'The brimming flesh of sin belongs, of course, to both sexes; but its root and basic representation is nothing other than feminine temptation' (1982: 126).

81 Kristeva is much indebted to the work of the anthropologist Mary Douglas (1966) in formulating these ideas.

A trajectory of separation intended to secure the paternal symbolic cannot but lead to ever more desperate attempts to abject the maternal, but the flight from jouissance and extinction issue in a perverted reinscription of her power.

Mother and death, both abominated, abjected, slyly build a victimising and persecuting machine at the cost of which I become subject of the Symbolic as well as Other of the Abject. (1982: 112)

Religion and the law are ultimately compelled to reinscribe sacred horror, which they had sought to push aside by 'purifying, systemising, thinking' (1982: 210). Once again it is art, in this case literature, in which horror can be expressed in a way that is cathartic, revealing the bloody sacrifices that are inherent in our subjective and social beginnings:

The aesthetic task – a descent into the foundations of the symbolic construct – amounts to retracing the fragile limits of the speaking being, closest to its dawn … 'subject' and 'object' push each other away, confront each other, collapse, and start again – inseparable, contaminated, condemned, at the boundary of what is assimilable, thinkable: abject. Great modern literature unfolds over that terrain: Dostoevsky, Lautreamont, Proust, Artaud, Kafka, Céline. (1982: 18)

The writers who most adequately accomplish this 'purifying' task, however, do not only use the rhythms of poetic language to introduce the 'music' of the semiotic into the symbolic. There has been a change since Kristeva wrote her early essays and *Revolution in Poetic Language*. This time the inscription of violence, pornography and representations of death is taken as a means of expressing abjection. 'Because it occupies such a place, because it here decks itself out in the sacred powers of horror literature may also involve not an ultimate resistance to but an unveiling of the abject' (1982: 208). The artists who achieve these effects may be fascists and 'haters' of the mother. Although Kristeva has revealed the ancient matricide encoded in religious horror she cannot bring herself to view literature's embodiment of hatred of the other as 'abominable' in the same way. She cannot herself resist performing the religious function of purifying and absolving this 'nocturnal power'.

What has been accomplished in *Powers of Horror* is an unstated conflation between the maternal real and women. If women are abjected in the literary text, if strangers are hated, this in some way encodes the archaic birth of subjectivity. Braidotti sees this move as tactical and inevitable. 'In what may seem a sort of conceptual slippage, but which is in fact a deliberate strategy, women become assimilated to Woman, as a sign for the feminine … No attempt is made to theorise this slippage' (1991: 231). Kristeva, like Lacan, is haunted by her bodily symbolics. As Marilyn Edelstein argues, the materiality of metaphor cannot be avoided:

To read Kristeva's use of the maternal as more metaphorical than biological presents at least the same problems that many feminists find in separating Lacan's notion of the phallus from the actual penis. Can metaphors be separated from their roots? (Edelstein, 1992: 42)

Speaking of love

Tales of Love (1987b), is described by Lechte as a book of 'intimidating diversity' (1990: 167). It follows upon *Powers of Horror* as an exploration of the ground that must be traversed between the abject mother and the ideal father. The work is undeniably complex and the inclusion of material written over a period of quite some years contributes to the sense of this being a more fragmented text than others she has produced. Nevertheless, familiar Kristevan themes are discernible and aid navigation through the chapters.

As in all her work, Kristeva places individual psychic development alongside her analysis of culture. In her frame, the achievement of subjectivity is always a cultural moment. In this case the personal development of the capacity to love (seen as analogous to attaining a healthy responsive subjectivity) is viewed alongside the mythological tales of love that Western culture has fashioned both to secure social peace and to transcend the terrors of collective loss. Both these mechanisms Kristeva believes to be under threat in a world where subjects are frustrated from imaginary identification with an idea which draws them beyond the annihilating pleasures associated with the maternal sphere.

What is required for loving to be possible is a place of fantasy, a psychic space, 'playful and sublimatory' (1987b: 46): a shadow land between the symbolic and the real. In her earlier work the binary poles of the semiotic and the symbolic exercise powerful forces of attraction and repulsion. In *Tales of Love* Kristeva turns her attention to what she had previously somewhat neglected, the third term in Lacan's trinity – the imaginary or mirror stage.

> The experience of love indissolubly ties together the *symbolic* (what is forbidden, distinguishable, thinkable) the *imaginary* (what the Self imagines in order to sustain and expand itself), and the *real* (that impossible domain where affects aspire to everything and there is no-one to take account of the fact that I am only a part). (1987b: 7)

The importance of this mediating stage is set out in the first section of the book. In this she uses Freud's concept of the *'imaginary father in individual prehistory'* to describe an ambiguous but benign influence that draws the child away from union with the mother. This initial step into idealisation is a move towards the symbolic order but may not straightforwardly be associated with the austere forces of paternal authority; the mother's desire is a fundamental part of the energy the child draws upon to make its journey (see Weir, 1993: 79–91). It is clear that for Kristeva, in the looking-glass world of primary identification, both the mother and father move beyond the ascribed territories of their influence and meet in the amatory space where love is born. Father/mother/self? It is impossible to define the actors in this romantic drama because they subsume each other's roles.

He or I – who is the agent? Or even is it he or is it she? The immanence of its transcendence, as well as the instability of our borders before the setting of my image as 'my own' turn the murky source ... from which narcissism will flow into a dynamics of confusion and delight. (1987b: 43)

What should be noted in this delightful confusion, however, is that the trajectory the healthy subject follows is from the maternal to the paternal sphere. The dynamics of love include the forces of abjection and the proper place of the maternal depends paradoxically on the sovereignty of the father's law. This is made clear in Kristeva's interpretation of two paradigmatic expressions of love encoded in religious tradition: the Song of Songs and the cult of the Virgin Mary.

Kristeva's essay on the Song of Songs is a celebration of the meeting of different spheres. 'While it radically opposes the sexes it still ties their real and symbolic communities together' (1987b: 93). It is also an accolade to the 'precocious yet fragile triumph of heterosexuality tinged with impossibility' (1987b: 60). While the Song may be seen as a tribute to the significance of the erotic in personal development it is also the memorial to a significant cultural moment. Its achievement is incomprehensible without awareness of the powerful tensions surrounding the development of paternal monotheism within a context of a religious pluralism in which the mother goddess still exercised enormous influence.[82]

However, this uncharacteristically enthusiastic response to female initiative should not blind the reader to the fact that the Song's authority is centred in the male lover and paternal divine. According to Kristeva the regal lover represents the masculine divine and what the Song celebrates is the splendour of 'love under the husband's rule' (1987b: 99). It is the success of patriarchal religion in incorporating the dark and dancing female lover that ensures its influence beyond the boundaries of ancient Israel and into the heart of the twentieth century. This energy is at work in the delicate synthesis of rejection and reconciliation with the flesh achieved by Christianity and can be observed again in paradigmatic form in the cult of the Virgin Mary.

Kristeva's extraordinary 'Stabat Mater' lies at the heart of *Tales of Love* and perhaps also at the heart of her philosophy. The text is divided and must be read in two separate columns down each page. A discussion of the significance of

---

82 Kristeva states that the ability of Judaism to acknowledge at its centre a drama that ties together God and desire secures its growing influence and prepares the ground for the coming religion of love and incarnation upon which Western culture is founded. The figure of the Shulamite woman Kristeva takes to be of particular significance in the narrative. Her restless search for her elusive regal partner, whose transcendence/absence confers upon her the space in which to love, becomes the prototype of the quest of the modern Western subject. 'Limpid intense, divided, quick, upright, suffering, hoping, the wife – a woman – is the first common individual who, on account of her love, becomes the first subject in the modern sense of the term. Divided, sick and yet sovereign' (1987b: 100).

Mary in theological understanding and popular devotion (in one column) is placed alongside an account, both personal and archetypal, of the experience of motherhood (in the other). The text is split also as a metaphor. It represents the wound of divided subjectivity, the opening of woman to receive the other, and it also echoes the divide between the symbolic and the semiotic which marks Kristeva's writing. While there is an implicit dialogue between the two sides of the text there are also points at which they are in tension.

In her account of Marian devotion Kristeva presents an immensely powerful image of a popular religious movement secularised by the church which has secured a space for idealisation in which both men and women are able to compensate for maternal loss and enter into relation with the symbolic.

This is because the Virgin represents the semiotic order – the order of bodily drives and their rhythms which is associated with the mother – and reconciles this with the symbolic order under God the Father. (Weir, 1993: 81)

This process is ambivalent for, while securing social peace and allowing the 'return of the repressed in monotheism' (Kristeva, 1987b: 250), it does so at the cost of alienation, particularly for women, who may be led to repudiate their relationship to other women through identifying with the feminine ideal.

On the 'other' side of the text Kristeva evolves her own experiences centred around the birth of her son. Pregnancy and motherhood are offered as windows to alterity. The maternal experience is one through which the woman can enjoy in her own motherhood a reconciliation with her mother, that impossible thing, a love with her mother which restores jouissance and makes a woman complete. It is also an experience that is the most complete model for 'herethics'. In maternity the woman opens herself up both to her own mother and to the child that she must separate from to love. This is the divided subject beatified:

Recovered childhood, dreamed peace restored, in sparks, flash of cells, instant of laughter, smiles in the blackness of dreams, at night opaque joy that roots me in her bed, my mother's, and projects him, a son, a butterfly soaking up dew from her hand, there, nearby, in the night. Alone: she, I and he. (Kristeva, 1987b: 247)

This extract is an example of Kristeva at her most brilliant and most disturbing. For what space, apart from psychosis, is there for a woman who refuses the heterosexual embrace which offers her maternity? Moreover, the evocation of maternal grandeur may be profound, but it is also nostalgic.

While celebrating its former power Kristeva believes that the idealisation of motherhood is collapsing. The space the Virgin won for a discourse on motherhood is threatened and, deprived of a locus for veneration within the symbolic, the mechanisms leading to maternal 'abjection' may be dangerously unchecked. 'The image of the Virgin – the woman whose entire body is an emptiness through which the paternal word is conveyed – had remarkably subsumed the maternal "abject". Lacking that safety lock feminine abjection imposed itself upon social representation' (1987b: 374). As this cult of imaginary love vanishes from culture once again it is (male) writers and artists who, in sometimes violent and obscene attempts to portray the unspeakable maternal, 'travel to the end of night' (1987b: 371) in pursuit of what has been lost.

Picasso's women, and those of De Kooning, like Bataille's *My Mother* represent the wild wager to omit nothing concerning that death-Mother, to catch hold of frontally or obliquely, but to catch her just the same within the grid of their work. (1987b: 371)

What the artist strives half consciously to achieve, the analyst (the last priest) may contrive within the analytic relation. Kristeva believes it is not the task of psychoanalysis to repair the father, and soothe the mother in order that a safe home may be made (imagined) for the child. Rather it is to understand the crisis caused by the failure of the amatory relation: the loss of space for idealisation. It is to allow those whose erotic development has been thwarted to be heard, written and spoken of, to turn them into writers themselves:

Help them, then, to speak and write themselves in unstable, open, undecidable spaces … trigger a discourse where his own 'emptiness' and her own 'out of placeness' become essential elements, indispensable 'characters' if you will of a *work in progress*. What is at stake is turning the crisis into a *work in progress*. (1987b: 300)

The analyst here assumes religious and artistic functions, transcending both. The analysand is offered a love language through analysis. This is an imaginative and creative work. Analysis 'is a flight of metaphors – it is literature' (1987b: 3).

The future of mourning

Kristeva's preference for border territory beyond emigration and immigration controls places her own writing in the tradition of modernist literature. The writer, whose status is that of traveller and observer, offers her commentary upon this interrupted journey. Kristeva begins *Black Sun* (1989) by assuming a frequently rehearsed melancholy narrative role.

On the frontiers of life and death, occasionally I have the arrogant feeling of being witness to the meaninglessness of Being, of revealing the absurdity of bonds and beings. (1989: 4)

There is no chance of escaping the depressing contours of the by now familiar scene on which her focus falls.

Talking about depression will again lead up into the marshy land of the Narcissus myth. This time however, we shall not encounter the bright and fragile amatory idealisation; on the contrary we shall see the shadow cast on the fragile self, hardly dissociable from the other, precisely by the *loss* of that essential other. The shadow of despair. (1989: 5)

Powers of Horror and *Tales of Love* cast light upon the processes by which the prearious dissociation from the maternal sphere is achieved in psychic and cultural life. *Black Sun* explores what happens when these mechanisms fail, when the separation does not happen. Refusing to accept the loss of the mother (and the comforts of language) the melancholic subject carries the sense of being deprived of some supreme, though unrepresentable, good which no compensation can appease.

> The depressed narcissist mourns not an Object but the Thing. Let me posit the 'Thing' as the real that does not lend itself to signification, the centre of attraction and repulsion, seat of sexuality from which the object of desire will become separated.
>
> Of this Nerval provides a dazzling metaphor that suggests an insistence without presence, a light without representation: the Thing is an imagined sun, bright and black at the same time. (1989: 13)

Because this 'goodness' lies buried within (it must do so and necessarily defy objectification) the wounds of loss provoke sadness but without the possibility of recovery through mourning.[83] Once again, as a prescription against melancholia, religion and art provide sublimatory means of surviving the awful dangers of the journey away from the 'maternal' embrace. The genius of Christianity, for Kristeva, is that it sets separation at the 'very heart of the absolute subject Christ' and represents this Passion as the condition of resurrection, thus bringing 'to consciousness the essential dramas that are internal to the becoming of every subject. It thus endows itself with tremendous cathartic power' (1989: 132).

Through Christianity, Western culture has found a way to bring 'death' into the realm of symbolic and to allow 'nonrepresentable catastrophic anguish' (1989: 133) a space bound by the triumphant resurrection of the father's word. Similarly, poetic language, with its semiotic affinity, draws close to the entombed mother:

> How can one approach the place I have referred to? Sublimation is an attempt to do so: through melody, rhythm, semantic polyvalency, the so-called poetic form, which decomposes and recomposes signs, is the sole 'container' seemingly able to secure an uncertain but adequate hold over the Thing. (1989: 14)

When means are found to contemplate the ghastly face of death some sort of healing is achieved. The celebrated heart of *Dark Sun* is Kristeva's profound meditation on *The Corpse of Christ in the Tomb* by Hans Holbein the younger. The isolation, passivity and stillness of the image, which promises no resurrection, which is shut inside with no hope of escape and painted with a 'realism' that forbids symbolic elaboration, come as close as can be imagined to an artistic mediation of the real. Holbein paints a pattern 'of man subject to death, man embracing Death, absorbing it into his very being integrating not as a condition for glory or a consequence of a sinful nature but as the ultimate essence of his desacralized reality, which is the foundation of a new dignity' (1989: 118–119).

That Holbein's work is able to achieve this melancholic vision is not due

---

83 The melancholic is not deprived of speech as such but radically asserts the inability of the symbolic to replace the desired Thing. They become foreigners in their mother tongue because of an unwillingness to concede a replacement for the mother.

to the effects of his personal circumstances or temperament. Kristeva always images religion and art as the analysable discourses of culture. Working amid the traumatic events of the reformation Holbein bears witness in his paintings to "*a melancholy moment*" (an actual or imaginary loss of meaning, an actual or imaginary despair, an actual or imaginary razing of symbolic values, including the value of life)' (1989: 128). While Holbein was able to 'overcome melancholy latency whilst keeping its trace' (1989: 128), our own age, subject to traumas of unprecedented dimensions, struggles to find a means to mourn and thus escape its tragedy. Lechte, summarising Kristeva's concern, argues 'never has reality been more cataclysmic but never has there been such a poverty of symbolic means for coping with it' (1990: 193).

Kristeva illustrates her argument with reference to the coldly horrifying novels of Marguerite Duras, in which the madness of the twentieth century is charted. The protagonists do not contemplate death but identify with it, absorb it and are assimilated into it: 'Because of that mourning becomes impossible' (1989: 333). Once again Kristeva is expressing her belief that the female author does not possess the cathartic power of her male counterpart. She writes more on Duras than on any other woman writer,[84] and yet concludes that she may better be termed a sorceress than an artist. Her work succeeds because she has made her own problems of melancholia a 'symptom of our generation':

Her work is personal, but it also joins with the depression that we know. But I consider that it is not cathartic but, let's say, an echo, a connivance with depression. Catharsis supposes that we leave depression, while I sense that these books plunge us into depression and do not give us a way out of it. (1996d: 54)

In her analysis of Duras art itself enters the madness and Kristeva can only offer, in lieu of other comforts, the suggestion that in the complex whirlwind of post-modernism 'the very transparency and humdrum nature of our grief may lead to the carnival resurrection of comedy through the heartrending distraction of parody' (1989: 259).

Black Sun, the last of Kristeva's trilogy, is also the most conservative. Her work has taken a progressively greater turn towards the clinical as her interest in Lacanian theory and psychoanalytic practice superseded the varied appropriation of a variety of theoretical tools in her early writing. This gives these texts from her second phase an extremely powerful internal coherence. However, whereas once she could speak of concepts like the semiotic as theoretical suppositions justified by the need for description, she later uses arguments about the relations between maternal and paternal realms in an increasingly empirical style (see, for example, the chapters 'Life and Death of Speech' and 'Illustrations of Feminine Depression'). The clinical turn in her work is accompanied by a growing tendency to pathologise subjectivities and identities which do not display 'normal' adjustment

84   In this period. In later work she revisits women authors (see Kristeva 2004).

to the symbolic law. It becomes increasingly difficult to place inverted commas around her use of the term 'perversity'; and such comments as 'The homosexual is a delightful, melancholy person when he does not engage in sadistic passion with another man' (1989: 27) are profoundly disquieting.

Both *Tales of Love* and *Black Sun* identify current cultural crises with the failure adequately to master maternal power through sublimating and subjecting its energies. The former revolutionary appears to mourn the decline of patriarchal religion's ability to set the maternal within bounds. Correspondences between fascism, nuclear destruction and the deathly visage of the mother are strongly implied but weakly justified (for example, 1989: 221–225). Ziarek comments upon the distance Kristeva has travelled:

The encounter with the maternal is no longer even ambivalent but seems to be accomplished entirely in negative terms as a psychosis of the subject and a crisis of the symbolic order. Kristeva herself occupies a defensive position and accepts violence as the only possible response to the mother: 'matricide is our vital necessity, the *sine qua non* condition of individuation'. The ethos of this position only confirms the primacy of identity and its violence in Western metaphysics. (1993: 75)

Revolt and the sacred

The foreign writer

Black Sun encodes a crisis in subjectivity and the social order which appears overwhelming. Following her own logic of catharsis it is not unreasonable to suggest that Kristeva's nostalgia for the comforts of religion, her ambivalent relation with her own mother and her cynicism concerning social change are 'symbolised' within the text. This process seems to have enabled her to move on to a new phase in her writing. This is evidenced in a renewed interest in politics, or as Kristeva would be more likely to describe it, ethics. If religion no longer possesses the power to sacralise the bonds of the social order a new way of living alongside others must be sought:

I want to create new connections, not to isolate myself but to explore with other people. This requires another relationship to social bonds, another morality that is different from religious morality. (1996c: 8)

Kristeva seeks this new morality through creating works designed to reach a wider audience. In a surprising move, considering her derogatory reflections on women authors, Kristeva has turned to writing fiction herself. She explains this development as a personal journey away from potentially destructive melancholy (1996h: 270). Fiction gives her a psychic space and has also become an important way of extending her skills as an analyst. She has grasped the opportunity to become a 'character' to herself and this gives her greater awareness of the intertwining of her own narrative with those of her patients.

I believed that working on the novel would allow me to continue listening to my patients in a way that was attentive, inventive, and receptive to them and to their symptoms. This type of fiction eases the rebirth of the analyst and an awakening of the unconscious that ventures beyond sublimation and revitalises the potential of interpretation. (1996e: 252–253)

It is also Kristeva's hope that the novel genre will allow her to reach a new public who would not read theoretical works. She intends that her fiction will help create the collective imaginary space for projection, sublimation and healing that contemporary culture has lost (1996g: 241).

In Kristeva's second novel, The Old Man and theWolves (1993a), these intertwining aims can be clearly observed. The work provides Kristeva herself with a sublimatory space in which to mourn both the death of her father and her own state of permanent exile: 'standing on a dividing line: as a bone between two cavities, a boat between two waves'(1993a: 17).

The story, in which she is clearly a character, is offered as an amatory gift to her readers in order that they might use it to explore their own *subjectivity in process*:

Since you were born to die, the words most suitable for those two unavoidable extremes, as for all that happens in between, is a story, made and unmade at the same time as what you believe to be yourself. (1993a: 66)

It is also intended to make visible the banal and commonplace appearance of violence in contemporary society. It is set in a decaying metropolis which could be located in any country but particularly evokes the state of Eastern Europe after the decline of communism. The inhabitants of the town are turning into wolves and it is the 'Old Man' (a teacher/father figure) who discerns this process and repeatedly attempts to warn others of its consequences.

Kristeva makes clear that she sees the metamorphosis of people into beasts as a consequence of the dangerous decay of contemporary civilisation: 'People lose both their form and their content when they live on a watershed between two eras' (1993a: 31). The imaginary space safeguarded by a benign paternal influence has been lost and 'when there is no father the wolves prowl' (1993a: 140). While such comments as these betray some of the nostalgia shown in Black Sun it should be recognised that it is the 'imaginary father in individual prehistory' that Kristeva is evoking here: the liminal figure who stands between the maternal and paternal realms. Uncharacteristically, she makes her female detective the inheritor of this crucial role. This woman detective (like the woman writer, as Kristeva lately concedes, 1996h: 270) has a particularly significant role to play. Having a subjectivity formed on the edge of chaos she understands the wolves. She has a wolf's senses with which to combat their power.

A female wolf who knows what's behind it all and is prepared to talk about it …
    I turn my key with the alert assurance of a detective.
    Expect no quarter. I hate the wolves, and now I've got their measure. (1993a: 183)

As well as seeking a wider audience through fiction Kristeva has sought to write in a more accessible style about specific social problems. *Strangers to Ourselves*, (1991) attempts to discover a way of renewing 'morality in social bonds' in response to the growing expression of racial hostility in France. This work was to bring Kristeva into contact with the mainstream of French political life at the crucial point of transition in relationships between Eastern and Western Europe. The process of living with the stranger is predicated on the familiar Kristevan theme of the recognition of alterity within:

Strangely the foreigner lives within us: he [sic] is the hidden face of our identity, the space that wrecks our abode, the time in which understanding, affinity founder. (1991: 1)

Kristeva presents an overview of the development of the concept of the 'foreigner' within Western culture. Once again significance is bestowed upon religious means of incorporating the stranger. Both the Christian and Hebrew traditions drew strength from the incorporation of strangers within. 'Foreign-ness and incest [are] at the root of David's house' (1991: 75). Literature also incorporates the energy of the alien. For example, in romanticism's obsessions with outlaws, monsters and the uncanny the stranger is given a dramatic role in passing judgement upon social life. In each epoch the stranger plays a role that is essential for the regeneration of community.

In contemporary France, Kristeva suggests, the 'violence of the problem set by the foreigner today is probably due to the crises undergone by religious and ethical constructs' (1991: 2). In other words, the foreigner is the target of passions unleashed by social upheavals. They may also inspire the rebirth of love, an ethical concern that saves a culture which would otherwise 'die of cynicism or stock market deals' (1991: 40). However, for this to happen, the stranger must point the culture towards its own internal heterogeneity and the alterity at the heart of every subject. Psychoanalysis has provided the conceptual framework within which this recognition can develop: 'Freud does not speak of foreigners: he teaches us to detect foreignness in ourselves' (1991: 191). Kristeva believes it offers the opportunity for a new bodily ethics fashioned in the knowledge of death and desire:

Psychoanalysis is experienced as a journey into the strangeness of the other and oneself towards an ethic of respect for the irreconcilable. How could one tolerate a foreigner if one did not know one was a stranger to oneself? And to think it has taken such a long time for that small truth ... to enlighten the people of our time! Will it allow them to put up with one another as irreducible because they are desiring, desirable mortal and death bearing? (1991: 182).

Children in the garden

What is noticeable in *Strangers to Ourselves* is Kristeva's return to the political and optimistic interpretations of the impress of the maternal upon culture which so inspired *Revolution in Poetic Language*. There are few technical references to psychoanalytic theory but underlying the whole text is the vision of creative dialogue between the maternal and paternal spheres: between the householder and the welcome guest. Meetings balance wanderings, and in the offering of shared food Kristeva presents an image of a Eucharist which deflects violence away from both the stranger and the host (1991: 11). The positive spirit of this encounter is preserved in her subsequent volume of essays, *New Maladies of the Soul* (1995).

This begins by asserting that psychoanalysis promises a new ethics which 'will allow change and surprise, which will allow life' (1995: 4). This ethical approach will build upon the fundamental religious perception that the desire for the mother and the need to separate from her are the twin poles of the psychic life. Kristeva offers her opinion that this provides the key to interpreting the Bible's sacred insights:

In my view the fulcrum of this biblical process can be located in its particular conception of the maternal: the maternal is a promised land if you are willing to leave it; the maternal is delight as well as murder, an inescapable 'abject' whose awareness haunts you, or which may very well be the constitutive double of your own awareness. (1995: 120)

The analyst must 'cling to the Bible's vigour of logic and love' (1995: 125) by offering symbolic means of sustaining psychic space while not underestimating the significance of the maternal real. In doing so, they have much to gain from 'listening' to the achievements of great writers who have found ways of mediating the semiotic in their texts. She turns again to Joyce whose work 'displays a connivance with the themes of incarnation and transubstantiation' (1995: 16), arguing that his writing is faithful to the impulses which were once enshrined in religion and now need to be re-formed in culture. In his modernist prose:

An image which is about to topple over into flesh *and meaning* is coagulated within language. The themes of Ulysses are a perfect illustration of this incandescence of imaginary space, whose two sided nature (body and signification) and 'transcorporality' cause it to challenge the place of the sacred. Was this not Joyce's ultimate ambition? (1995: 187)

In all her work Kristeva travels through, crosses and recrosses the frontiers of, religion, psychoanalysis and literature. But in this later phase she has gone beyond the sense that one realm surpasses another. She is also more willing, at this point in her journey, to admit the provisionality and weaknesses of psychoanalytic theory (see Kristeva, 1996f: 91) and the significance of religious mechanisms in mediating the sacred. She now presents an ethics which is manifested in the religious impulse, made symbolisable through psychoanalysis and communicable through art.

In another work from this later period, *Proust and the Sense of Time* (1993b), she celebrates Proust's attempts as a 'stranger' within culture (a gay man who suffered from a painful illness) to use fiction as a means of psychic healing. She is haunted by his simple phrase, 'ideas come to us as the successor of griefs'

119

(1993b: 77–83) and perceives in his use of 'time' a project to create an imagined space in which what has been lost can be revisited.

Proust uses time as his intermediary in the search ... for an embodied imagination: that is to say, for a space where words and their dark unconscious manifestations contribute to the weaving of the world's unbroken flesh of which I is part. I as a writer; I as a reader; I living, loving, dying. (1993b: 5)

Kristeva recalls Victor Hugo's phrase, 'The grass must grow and children have to die' (in Kristeva, 1993b: 10), but reads in Proust's remembrance a celebration of an impossible meeting of the opposing realms of natality and mortality, a carnival of children picnicking among the tombstones. She argues that the space of Proust's book is like a déjeuner sur l'herbe. It has the paradoxical ability to bring the taste of death to the picnic and also to,

transform the graveyard of the dead children into a pleasure garden, dedicated to the ambiguous, loving, vengeful memory of a mother who always loved excessively and not enough – and made you into a child who is still dying perhaps, but who has the chance of ultimate resurrection and maturity in the luxuriant grass of the book. (1993b: 10)[85]

Literature as woman's form

We have traced the development in Kristeva's thinking from an interest in revolutionary linguistic practices to a concern with the dangerous irruptions of horror and despair into culture and, more latterly, a concern with the ethics of alterity and the cultivation of cultural spaces in which the life of the spirit might be renewed. In her most recent work (2000, 2001) Kristeva markedly affirms the earliest insights of Revolution in Poetic Language concerning the significance of religion and art in mediating necessary social change. However, she is concerned that there is a withering of the roots of revolt in our culture which prompts 'an urgent return to the resources of the aesthetic heritage' (2000: 7).

In this recent text the common jouissance of literature and religion is affirmed. Kristeva argues that it is wrong to interpret the religious impulse, according to our current experiences of fundamentalism, as that which regulates the feminine in a regime of purity (2000: 26). While it is the work of the priest to curb the disruptive power of the maternal realm but the primary impulse of religion lies in revolt, and religious and artistic rebels both draw upon the power of the sacred 'in a magnificent parallel history' (2000: 2). However, in a cultural context in which religious (and political) mechanisms for revolt are in crisis, it is literature which must bear revolt into a culture in which solitude and disillusionment are experienced in unprecedented forms.

Looking back on the last thirty years of her own work, Kristeva describes it as a quest to see how far literature could probe and penetrate this cultural crisis,

---

85 Literature is vital to this 'chance of resurrection' and it is necessary to maintain faith in its power. 'Belief in art? In reading? But whom do we read? Still the cult of art might ... offer an abiding guarantee of the life of the psyche' (1993b: 90).

'to see how far literature could go as a journey to the end of night, the end of the limit of meaning' (2000: 112). This journey to the end of night is not undertaken to restore what has been lost (the cult of ancient Greece, or the cult of the cathedral), but rather as a gesture of faith in the vitality of the imaginary, which is the frail but living source of new social configurations. In this important new work literature is evoked in mystical terms as 'thought of the impossible, or perhaps, literature as a-thought' (2000: 113)

It is interesting that at the heart of this discussion of literature's sacred role Kristeva makes a direct comparison between 'literary utterance and poetic statement with the feminine' (2000: 111), a theme she picks up once again in an exchange of letters with Catherine Clément published as *The Feminine and the Sacred* (Clément and Kristeva, 2001). Here Kristeva makes the suggestion that the body of woman might enable us to reconceive the sacred and allow its energy back into our lives. It is in the female body – always positioned between nature and culture, the sensory and the nameable – that the sacred is incarnated. Women might thus be in the best placed to reinscribe the sacred 'not as the religious need for protection and omnipotence that institutions exploit but the jouissance of that cleavage – of that power/powerlessness – of that exquisite lapse' (Clément and Kristeva, 2001: 26–27). Here we have the female body itself as 'literature'. In 'the future which is upon us', she speculates, women embody the mysterious signs of the communication between 'body and thought, biology and memory, life and meaning' (Clément and Kristeva, 2001: 178) which testifies that human life remains permeable to the sacred despite the attempts of religious regimes to purge away the trace of the flesh from the temples and holy books.

Sweet milk at midnight

This chapter has charted Kristeva's journey from revolutionary optimism, through a melancholy moment and towards a renewed conviction of the necessity of revolt. I have shown how Kristeva has been occupied throughout this passage in exploring the relations between literature, religion and the feminine, but I have made clear that her journey has taken her in very different directions from those followed by religious feminists whose work was discussed in chapters 2 and 3.

Up till now few religious feminists have taken up Kristeva's thinking as a significant resource. Well-founded suspicions concerning the gendered terms of Lacanian critical theory have been sufficient to discourage most of us from engaging with work that often appears deeply complicit with the powers of horror ranged against women. However, I wish to argue that Kristeva does, nevertheless, have a great deal to offer the feminist religious reader.

What is evident from the earliest texts is the huge significance Kristeva accords to literature. While religious feminists have been quick to celebrate the female author or to sacralise particular texts there has been little recognition of the importance of literature per se. Perhaps because literature is so deeply intertwined in the discourses of feminist theology, we have lost the sense that literature occupies a special place within culture. This is the space of the not true, the not complete, the not normal. Literature is where language does not behave in a regular manner and where communication is both intensified and broken. Because of these characteristics literature has come to signify more than a defined body of texts. It is an oppositional term regarded as a precious resource in a culture which is powerfully regulated. In Kristeva's vocabulary, literature becomes the language of revolt.

The advantage for religious feminists in according literature such a significant status may not be immediately apparent. We currently use extracts from literature as an adornment to our own oppositional discourses caring little about the wider frame in which literature and theology are situated. However, my argument has been throughout that feminist theology must be open to the challenge of what lies beyond its own borders if it is to maintain a radical and transforming presence. Feminist theology needs the challenges of literature to sustain its creativity and vigour in an epoch that is now quite different from that in which it first emerged.

'Literature', in the manner described above, may also be disturbing to some religious feminists because it refers to a space occupied by both men and women. Up until now it is the work of women writers which has been used by feminist theologians, and those women have been strategically isolated from the literary/cultural traditions and networks out of which they have constructed their work.[86] A number of women writers have protested against this cloistering.[87] While Kristeva's early comments on female authorship (before she assumed this identity herself) are straightforwardly unhelpful, I believe that her conversations with the literary and artistic work of men do demonstrate a powerful resource in challenging the dominant symbolic. Feminist theologians do not need to preserve their virginity, and intercourse with male partners is not always sleeping with the enemy.

Following Kristeva even further into her analysis of literature as a language of revolt that challenges the 'paternal symbolic', religious feminists may be perturbed by Kristeva's clear focus upon literary form rather than content. Particularly in her early work Kristeva reverses the customary reading practices of English-speaking cultures and focuses her attention upon the manner in which art is embodied rather than the message it conveys. I have argued that this may have lead Kristeva to lend tacit approval to images of fascistic violence and misogyny that the majority of feminists would consider powerfully destructive. However, it is important to recognise that the concern of feminist theologians to approve the acceptable content of literary texts written by women has resulted

---

86 Unless these networks and associations can be claimed as a women's tradition based on women's experience.

87 See pp. 46–47.

in an almost total denial of the significance of form. And form matters. Some of the most important writing done by women was created with an awareness of the importance of speaking in a new way that shatters conventions, and in the company of fellow artists experimenting in similar fashion.

To take an important example: the work of Virginia Woolf may appear useful to religious feminists because she has a history of political and sexual activism and because her work can be sifted for images of the female divine crafted from her readings in anthropology and ancient history. It may seem less apparent why we should attend to her more difficult texts or why those which trace the interior meanderings of upper-middle-class characters are worth our attention. And yet there may be more theological significance in her attempts to break open the novelistic form and experiment with new versions of the authorial voice, as she does in *Mrs Dalloway* (1925) or *The Waves* (1931), than in her espousal of emancipatory causes. In works such as these she resists the narrative closure that is so prominent in theological discourse and offers a challenging way of reconceptualising the relation of an author to her voices that has direct implications for the way we conceive divine creativity.

An appreciation of the theological significance of literary form will enrich feminist theology by restoring to us the work of women authors currently disregarded because their work is difficult, awkward or strange. It will also encourage us to stray beyond the novel into poetry and the dramatic arts. While it is neither likely or desirable that the content of literary texts will cease to engage religious feminists, we have much to gain from cultivating an awareness of and sensitivity to literary form. Not to do so would result in much of the genius of women's literary creativity being lost to us.

Kristeva's work thus challenges religious feminists to develop a renewed awareness of literary culture and a deeper understanding that feminist theology, like all theology, exists in constant tension with the creative arts. Literature, in Kristeva's terms, includes works written by women and men which are together placed in opposition to the logocentric authority of the paternal symbolic. She thus repeats the familiar gesture, performed by Eliot and others, of characterising literature as a feminine resource. But although she reiterates this conventional binary schema she does so in a new and challenging way. Kristeva's discovery/ invention of the semiotic is the means by which she links literature to women's bodies in a profoundly creative move. As Anna Smith writes, 'That language can have a *body*, even if it exposes its subject to psychosis, opens literature to a different kind of reality: a place of negativity and jouissance, where everything is put into play' (Smith: 1996: 108). A question immediately arises, however, as to how the concept of the semiotic is to be received.

For some feminists convinced of the truth of psychoanalytic theory, the semiotic has the status of a defensible hypothesis concerning the nature of subjectivity and the cultural order. For others, and here I include myself, it has the status of an image which displays the dangerous power of the symbolic order (regime) and allows us to imagine the possibility of things beyond language. This image persuasively captures the violence of the cultural order and reveals how essential gender is to the maintenance of power. As the creation of gender lies at the archaic genesis of culture, the semiotic appropriately portrays the feminine as that which must be radically excluded and can never be overcome. All that subverts the symbolic order is of the semiotic and thus literature becomes intimately associated with what is ultimately feminine – the body of woman.

I have described the semiotic as an image – perhaps icon would be a better term. It is an artistic creation which mediates sacred power: a dark Madonna, the Virgin of the 'Stabat Mater' which haunts Christian art. It reminds us of how we are intimately formed by that which both nourishes and destroys us. It enables us to contemplate how the flesh cradles the word – weeping. This icon enables us to gaze upon death and darkness and to inhabit our own tragedy. In this iconic sense literature, by mediating the semiotic, presents us with all that culture must exclude, those things which overwhelm subjective discreteness: jouissance, the satiety of completeness, the full presence of the other. It also incarnates those things we most dread: death, dismemberment and the uncanny. And all of these things are symbolisable through the female body.

Finally, the image of the semiotic enables Kristeva to imagine a subversive force at the heart of the symbolic. Nothing is as discrete or stable as it seems, and in the later texts Kristeva is keen to argue that religion itself is not simply to be identified with the fundamentalist form that the symbolic has assumed in our time. Faith and desire, mysticism and ecstasy are so close as to whisper together on the pillow and if, as Kristeva asserts, in these days the religious impulse for revolt is weakened then the sacred powers of the semiotic are its guardians through literature as 'thought of the impossible' (2000: 113).

In the next chapter I will consider Luce Irigaray's project to move beyond current cultural forms to a symbolic system in which the specificity of the feminine, rather than the abysmal power of the maternal, is celebrated. Kristeva does not take this path. She leaves us with the 'Stabat Mater' and with the vision that an impossible love between the symbolic and the semiotic will make an imaginary space inhabitable for us in the body and the green grass of the text. This is the mother's bed in which we drink sweet milk at midnight. We are forever children playing among the stone tablets.

CHAPTER 6

Luce Irigaray and the threshold of the divine

The symbolic has annihilated women

Openings and pointers

I have argued that the significance Kristeva accords to literature as a political and spiritual force is challenging to feminist religious readers, and that the semiotic is a deeply resonant image that does display many of the salient features of the social order and is worth struggling with despite its ambivalence. However, despite my largely sympathetic reading of Kristeva's oeuvre, I am aware that her work does not result in a radical reconceptualisation of the masculine and feminine spheres. On the contrary, the masculine symbolic remains the sphere of reason, law, doctrine, language, social and subjective coherence. The semiotic is positioned as powerful and necessary for cultural regeneration but also remains chaotic, fearful, sexual and deathly. While Kristeva does argue that renewed mutuality between the symbolic and the semiotic is an urgent social necessity this does not entail any revisioning of the archaic distinctions between the paternal and maternal realms. It is these gendered partners which gave birth to culture and which together parent subjectivity in each person. It is an ancient drama endlessly repeated.

The problem this raises for feminists is that, in Kristeva's opinion, it is not fruitful to contest the terms upon which the masculine and feminine spheres are constituted in relation to each other but rather to ensure that each is appropriately honoured. And yet many feminists are persuaded that the indelible association that is made between women and all that is marginal to culture cannot be disassociated from questions of social inequality. While Kristeva is arguing for a renewed appreciation of the feminine sphere, other women have conceived a more radical project. Their aim is not to deny the significance of gender but to make a reconceptualisation of sexual difference the key to changing the world.

In this chapter I shall explore this alternative strategy as it is expressed in the work of Luce Irigaray. However, as the concern of this book is the relation between literature, theology and feminism so my task is not only to elucidate Irigaray's thinking on sexual difference but also to demonstrate its significance

125

for feminist religious readers. This raises particular challenges. Whereas Kristeva writes extensively on literature and theology, Irigaray's work (while frequently described as literary and theological) does not contain the many direct references to the two disciplines previously encountered. Thus it will frequently be necessary to extrapolate positions from Irigaray's work rather than offer a direct exegesis of her texts. Such is the style of Irigaray's writing that this is a necessary move when engaging with her work in relation to most spheres of feminist concern. As Jantzen has stated, Irigaray's work on religion (and I would add literature) is not presented in systematic form but rather 'at the level of openings and pointers to further thought' (1998: 121). Following these openings and pointers I shall focus upon three main areas of particular interest. First, I shall outline the analysis Irigaray offers of how the masculine sphere of philosophy/theology is constituted in a relationship of dominance over the feminine sphere. Of great importance here is the way Irigaray teaches us to become deconstructive readers/writers of our own tradition. Second, I shall argue that Irigaray's project of transforming the masculine cultural order through the nurturing of a feminine imaginary necessitates a re-evaluation of the cultural and theological significance of women's creative writing. Third, I will suggest that Irigaray's reflections on the sensible transcendental point to an understanding of the divine economy which aids us in reconceptualising the threshold that exists between literature and theology and how these gendered partners might together stand as heralds of a divine epiphany in our time.

The history of erasure

Luce Irigaray was born in Belgium but has spent her adult life working in France. Her earliest work was in the field of linguistics where she began to investigate how gender identity was manifest in the subject positions men and women adopted in everyday speech. A significant turn in her academic career took place in 1974 when the publication of her most famous work, *The Speculum of the Othe Woman*, resulted in her estrangement from the influential Lacanian community and the loss of her lecturing position in the Department of Psychoanalysis at the University of Vincennes. After this break Irigaray continued her research and served as a Director of the Centre National de la Récherche Scientifique in Paris. The work of an empirical researcher into gender and linguistic practice was pursued in tandem with the unorthodox reflections upon psychoanalysis, philosophy and theology for which she is better known.

The narrative of Irigaray's expulsion from her lecturing position can be seen as a parabolic representation of the thesis of *Speculum*. This is that the symbolic order functions continually to silence women and annihilate their cultural specificity. The symbolic is described in Lacanian terms on p. 99. However, Irigaray does not limit herself to conventional psychoanalytic categories when conceptualising the symbolic. For her this is the whole cultural sphere dominated by the Name of the Father, which finds its paramount expression in theological and philosophical discourses.[88] The two are fundamentally linked, for the philosophical tradition has its roots in 'religious discourse [which] serves as the linchpin of the Western symbolic' (Jantzen, 1998: 12). It is critical to Irigaray's argument that contemporary logocentric discourses, such as existentialism and psychoanalysis, continue to repeat the ancient gesture of representing what is masculine as divine.

In *Speculum*, Irigaray sets out to display the mechanisms through which the feminine is eclipsed and the masculine assumes its godly status. Her aim is to display how woman functions in the symbolic order as 'the mute outside that sustains all systemacity and still silent ground that nourishes all foundations' (1985a: 365). She makes this perspective evident not by using the critical conventions of the discipline but by offering the tradition to the reader again to be read differently. She creates a bricolage of quotations, rhetorical interventions and intertextual edits which sustain the form of philosophical discourse but render it strange. Such a strategy is deeply undermining, without being merely a negation, of the work she critiques. The reader is compelled to inhabit familiar texts in a new way. Work that was formerly monological becomes conversational and unfamiliar; female tones are heard at the heart of the tradition – as if the silent stones from which it had been formed had begun to speak.

The order in which the work is presented is as significant as its unconventional content. It is structured as a journey through the Western symbolic order, beginning with contemporary psychoanalytic theory and journeying towards the depths of Plato's cavern. This is a retracing of Kore's (the daughter stolen from her mother according to Greek myth) journey to the centre of darkness and reverses the familiar paradigm of the ascent of man, who leaves the base world of flesh and desire to achieve enlightenment.

In the work's first essay she interrupts Freud's discourses on female sexuality and displays how the 'old man' has been seduced by an older reverie, the dream of symmetry. He has thus 'failed to notice' the specificity of the female in his construction of desire. The difficult trajectory he prescribes in relation to the 'achievement' of femininity is based on the presumption that the little girl is identical in her fascinations and bodily obsessions to the little boy. He eradicates the specificity of the feminine, marking the girl child as castrated. This castration is, for Freud, a necessary wounding which will bind female eroticism to masculine gratification.

---

88 Tina Chanter states that to write philosophy 'is to speak the voice of universality, to seek for ultimate causes behind appearances, to account for why "reality" is the way it is, to unify, synthesise and systematize' (1995: 141). Like Derrida, Irigaray regards the unacknowledged violence of the philosophical system as the exclusion of difference, and for her the most significant difference which philosophy seeks to annihilate is sexual difference.

He does not want her to be anything but his *daughter*, whose gratifying fantasies of seduction it is his task to interpret, and who must be initiated into, and curbed by, the 'reasonable' discourse of his (sexual) law. Or else he wants her to be *his mother*, whose erotic reveries he would take some pleasure in hearing, whose most secret intimacy he would finally gain access to. (1985a: 129)

Although *Speculum* does not offer an explicit critique of Lacan's elaboration upon Freud, the frequent 'specular' images are implicit recollections of his theories. Irigaray implies that the male analyses of subjectivity it contains can be compared to a (boy) child gazing in the mirror. He concentrates only upon the reflection of himself and not the matrix (mother) which supports him. This judgement particularly refers to the manner in which Lacanian theory banishes the m/other from representation but requires her presence in absence to sustain the symbolic order (1985a: 133–151). As we have noted this was enough to provoke Irigaray's expulsion from Lacanian circles.

The critique of psychoanalytic theory is repeated in her analysis of the foundational texts of Western philosophy. For example, Plato's allegorical fable of the emergence from the cave of illusion to the full light of truth is presented in *Speculum* as a journey away from material origins. But it is the sensual substance of the first home that supports the ascension to the intelligible, and Irigaray delights in showing that Plato's descriptions of its features (veils, walls and curtains) are images recalling the female body. These material contours, however, are forgotten in the journey towards the paternal Idea which needs no material clothing, no imperfect images or supports, but is registered upon the opaque surface of the soul.

Eclipse of the mother, of the place (of) becoming, whose non-representation or even disavowal upholds the absolute being attributed to the father. He no longer has any foundation, he is beyond all beginnings. Between these two abysses – nothing/being – language makes its way, once the mother has been emptied out. (1985a: 307)

Between her excursions into Freud and the historical traditions of philosophy, Irigaray includes a short and powerful essay upon mysticism at the centre of her text. Mysticism is unique in being a discourse of transcendence spoken by women (1985a: 191). Irigaray is familiar with the Belgian traditions of powerful women mystics living independent lives and making audacious speculations on the divine. This brief gaze in the 'burning mirror' points to themes which will emerge as significant in her later work – particularly the body inflamed with the passion of the divine: 'Now the abyss opens down into my own self and I am no longer cut in two opposing directions of sheer elevation to the sky and sheer fall into the depths' (1985a: 200). In its location, at the heart of the book, the essay serves to contrast the mystic's body which 'shines with the light of glory that radiates it' (1985a: 197) with the separation that is made between the sensible and the intelligible in the philosophical tradition. Irigaray is reaching for an

association of word and matter that has been forbidden from Plato to Lacan.

A fling with philosophy

In discussing Irigaray's strategy in *Speculum*, Elizabeth Weed quotes Barthes: 'An intellectual cannot directly attack the powers that be, but he [sic] can inject new styles of discourse to make things change' (1994: 79). Like Derrida's, Irigaray's 'cure' is homeopathic, operating within that she seeks to contest (Whitford, 1994a: 17).

When she takes on the critical texts of the Western canon, it is those texts – Freud, Nietzsche, Marx, Hegel, Plato and so on – that supply the language, that is to say the conceptual economies of her writing. She always cites, usually without attribution, and often ventriloquizes. For her, taking on a writer means more than intertextuality; it means inhabiting his text. She does not write on Heidegger, she writes Heidegger. (Weed, 1994: 83–84)

Irigaray's strange complicity with, and subversion of, philosophical discourse is also a refusal to become its passive victim. Although philosophy has committed violence against woman, the trace of origins cannot be obscured. Male thinkers might imagine they have banished woman from their discourse but their efforts are unsuccessful. She remains 'the elemental substrate of life, existing beyond all forms, all limit, all skin, and of heaven, visible beyond the horizon' (Irigaray, 1993b: 46). Irigaray thus makes the annihilation of woman in (philosophical) texts appear as a male fantasy or dream. Male discourse is inverted and instead of enjoying the status of dispassionate rationality it is revealed as unstable language produced by a crazed desire for domination. The position of woman is reconfigured as reasonable and authentically powerful. Because she speaks from a position of authority the woman has no need to return male violence. Irigaray can afford to be bemused and playful as well as angry. The philosophers are contradicted but they are also teased and fondled. There is no question of an end to dialogue or to separation from the guilty ones.

The discursive position established in *Speculum* is carried forward into Irigaray's later work in which she continues to enter into the fantasies of male philosophers concerning women and to 'role play' within them. For example, when addressing Nietzsche, she speaks as mummy to his naughty boy:

So remember the liquid ground. And taste the saliva in your mouth also – notice her familiar presence during your silence, how she is forgotten when you speak. Or again: how you stop speaking when you drink. And how necessary that is for you!

These fluids softly mark the time. And there is no need to knock, just listen to hear the music with very small ears. (1991a: 37)

To Levinas she plays the part of abandoned bride and complains her lover has withdrawn his affections from her female form and despised her caress. He no longer considers her the image of heaven, but uses her to cook his meals and receive his mechanical lovemaking while he devotes his energies to higher pursuits. Playing the part of philosopher's wife is Irigaray's way of demonstrating the debt of philosophy to the female form by representing this through the debt philosophers owe to the women whose lives they devour.

> She is brought into a world that is not her own so that the male lover may enjoy himself and gain strength for his voyage towards an autistic transcendence. In his quest for a God who is already inscribed but voiceless, does she permit him not to constitute the ethical site of lovemaking? A seducer who is seduced by the gravity of the Other but approaches the female other carelessly, he takes her light to illuminate his path. Without regard for what shines and glistens between them. (1993a: 209–210)

There is no doubt of the pleasure Irigaray takes from her 'fling' with philosophy. There is game-playing going on but it is also serious work. Irigaray has adopted a mimetic strategy in choosing to speak with the voices that have been culturally assigned to women. She refers to this deconstructive technique as the use of 'nuptial tools' for although the women lack *a tool* they are able to 're-utilize its marks on her, in her' (1985b: 150). It is necessary to recycle these marks of men upon women's bodies. The discursive regime which has defined women cannot be simply dismantled. Going backwards and going through the history of women's erasure is an ironic acknowledgement of the fact that the first place women can begin to find their own symbolic representation is in the traces of their image in culture. It is necessary to inhabit these forms because they are the ones in which woman has been located, 'in the little structured margins of a dominant ideology, as waste, or excess' (1985b: 30). The project of self-naming begins when women begin to speak out of these silent places in recognisably female tones.

A tremendous amount of energy is expended in this task of ventriloquising from the mute spaces within the philosophical/theological tradition. And it is a process that must be undertaken again and again while this discourse continues to exercise its violent power over women. Irigaray writes that she situates herself in the borders of culture and moves in and out like a partisan. This is a guerrilla fighter's reading strategy. There is no decisive battle in the open air but a constant struggle in the undergrowth to reclaim the beloved territory. This imagery accurately reflects the situation of religious feminists engaging with established traditions. It is a context in which small skirmishes are the expression of our resistance. Irigaray does not deny the crucial significance of this struggle with tradition, however; she encourages us to look beyond it. If the symbolic order has annihilated women then what is required is a new order. She reaches towards this through envisioning a process of social transformation as women achieve their own voice and language.

Imagining a new language

Sexuate culture

In the work of Kristeva the masculine symbolic (in which theology is located) is pictured in creative tension with the feminine semiotic (made manifest through literature). Irigaray eschews this path. The symbolic as currently constituted has no feminine equal. Its violent power has obliterated female specificity. The first task therefore is to use the deconstructive techniques we have examined to reveal the true nature of the symbolic. These second is to nurture the birth of a new symbolic order.

My account of Irigaray's engagement with philosophy reveals many similarities with Derrida's project of unmasking the phallogocentrism of Western culture through attending to the repressed feminine term in our binary symbolic system. It is Irigaray's goal to transform the symbolic that distinguishes the way she and Derrida situate themselves within the feminine sphere. Some feminist theorists have criticised Derridean deconstruction on the grounds that Derrida is so enthralled by the tradition he critiques and so thrilled by the possibility of cross-dressing that he is content to play the kept woman of the master discourse.[89]

Although Irigaray moves in a similar way to Derrida when she assumes the role of the philosopher's wife (1985b: 150–152), she is, at the same time, seeking to nurture the birth of a new language. This work is facilitated by her fluid position between the two major poles of contemporary critical theory. Irigaray moves between deconstruction and psychoanalysis – replicating their performances while remaining sceptical as to the assumptions underlying their theoretical methods: 'For isn't it the method that has always led us astray … from the woman's path?' (1985b: 150). There is, however, an alternative interpretation of the term 'method' as 'detour, fraud, artifice', one which, ironically, leads women back to themselves – and this is the route she follows.

Thus Irigaray assumes deconstruction's veils and traces to accomplish her disruption of the philosophical tradition. She also draws upon psychoanalysis, which links language to the body and insists upon the potential of radical breaks, separations and rebirths within the speaking subject – while revealing that the body of this discourse is still marked as masculine. Her painstaking 'woman's path' through the tradition is also a means of transcending its limits. Both deconstruction and psychoanalysis have claimed the feminine in order to establish their own sacred territories beyond the limits of the law. Irigaray mimes

89 For example, Margaret Whitford writes: 'In a sense he wants to make his position impregnable, ultimately undecidable, ultimately "feminine". Deconstruction enables him to speak indefinitely, to hold the floor. As has often been pointed out, he masters feminist discourse by speaking about it. In a sense it is useless to try and prove him wrong (where is he?), and to agree with him changes nothing. It is, as Rosi Braidotti once put it cogently, a "passage a vide"- that is to say a mechanism like an engine turning over but not in gear, so that the motor is not driving anything' (Whitford, 1991a: 130).

deconstruction and psychoanalytic theory in order to claim back what they appear to promise and in fact deny – the specificity of the female and her need for clothing, a home, a body within language.

In order to make their own place, Irigaray claims, women need a new sexuate culture in which their specificity is recognised and honoured. In a famous interview, 'Woman's Exile', Irigaray stated that her vision was nothing less than the creation of a *feminine language* 'adequate for the body, sex, the imagination (imaginary) of women' (1990: 80). After her complex manoeuvres through the undergrowth of philosophy and psychoanalysis some of her critics appear disappointed at the apparent naivety and utopian nature of this project. Irigaray has been interpreted as, and consequently ridiculed for, suggesting a separatist strategy that would leave women permanently babbling beyond the discourses of power. Alternatively, she has been derided for not understanding the sophistication of the theories she critiques and reinstating an essentialism which deconstruction and psychoanalysis had effectively challenged.[90]

Upon closer inspection, however, it appears that Irigaray's project for creating a new language is rooted in everyday social practice – while also reaching beyond this towards a new horizon. In fact Irigaray had been deeply engaged in exploring the linguistic practice of contemporary culture at the same time as constructing her visionary philosophical interventions. Her research career has involved the painstaking study of the way men and women use language in conventional social contexts. Her investigations, based on the detailed analysis of hundreds of hours of taped interviews, have presented compelling evidence that there are significant differences between the ways men and women speak the same language. However, this empirical research has brought just as much condemnation as her theoretical writings. The conclusion that men and women differ fundamentally in their linguistic repertoires is profoundly threatening to a cultural order based upon notions of unitary human identity.

To prove that discourse has a sex amounts to a show of force, and its outcome is challenged even when the most rigorous and scientific standards of proof are followed. (Irigaray, 1993a: 133–134)

Irigaray's research on the everyday display 'sexed discourse' in everyday speech belongs alongside her textual analysis of the meta-discourses of Western culture as both point to the effacement of the female subject and the difficulty women have in representing their own agency and identity within the current symbolic order. Moving beyond a situation in which women are both effaced and self effacing in language is regarded by Irigaray as a political necessity rather than a utopian ideal: 'above all we must not wait passively for language to progress. Issues of discourse and of language can be deliberately used to attain greater cultural maturity, more social justice' (1993c: 32).

90 A full discussion of these issues may be found in the opening chapter of Tina Chanter's book *Ethics of Eros: Irigaray's Rewriting of the Philosophers* (1995: 1–46).

Irigaray presents many practical suggestions as to how this 'change in language' might be achieved. These range widely from the consideration of sexuate civil laws (i.e. laws that recognise the differential cultural, social and embodied contexts of women and men) to the production of icons of female sociality in artistic and cultural life. Two related themes emerge as particularly significant in this practical agenda for social change. The first is the need to create visible representations of the mother/daughter bond, which is systematically expunged by patriarchal representations of human relations: 'to find, rediscover, invent the words, the sentences that speak of the most ancient and current relationship we know – the relationship to the mother's body, to our body' (1993b: 18). The second is to reclaim a genealogy of women. One that has roots both in blood and the celebration of generative acts of creativity:

If we are not to become accomplices in the murder of the mother we also need to assert that there is a genealogy of women. Each of us has a female family tree: we have a mother, a maternal grandmother and great-grandmothers, we have daughters ... Let us not forget, moreover, that we already have a history, that certain women despite all the cultural obstacles, have made their mark upon history and all too often have been forgotten by us. (1993c: 19)

It is in passages such as these that Irigaray comes closest to expressing similar concerns to those displayed by the gynocritical movement in the Anglo-American tradition. However, her approval of the creation of a female tradition and her common sense 'shopping lists' of required ingredients for the creation of a sexuate culture (see particularly *Je, Tu, Nous: Toward a Culture of Difference*, 1993c) are accompanied by the exploration of a new imaginary/symbolic idiom based upon the female body. The new language women require is one that must be adequate for the body, sex, the imagination (imaginary) of women (1990: 80).

Imaginary reason
Irigaray's invocation of the feminine imaginary represents a significant contribution to contemporary feminist theory. It challenges women to view culture as a dynamic theatre of transforming possibilities rather than a dark tableau representing the exclusion and abjection of the feminine. In conceiving of this image, Irigaray brings into association a number of the key themes already examined in this text – but employs them to a new and radical effect which has particular significance in relation to literature and theology.

First, in referring to imagination in the context of a critique of Western metaphysics, Irigaray draws upon the very familiar binary/hierarchical distinction made between reason and imagination. Imagination stands as reason's other and is closely associated with dreams, visions, fantasies and the ecstasy of the body. By situating her essay on mysticism at the heart of *Speculum*, Irigaray is affirming the significance of those cultural spaces which have been marked feminine.

However, her intention is not to achieve a new balance between the differing poles of culture (as we might characterise Kristeva's project). We should not conceive the female imaginary as an eternal consort or partner to male reason as if they constituted an established and inviolable couple. Irigaray's project all along has been to demonstrate that philosophy has masqueraded as a rational discourse but is in fact a projection or fantasy of male desire that requires the subordination of the feminine. As Michelle Le Doeff (2002 [1980]) has demonstrated, the root metaphors of philosophical discourse betray a gendered apprehension of the world which is predicated upon male experience. What appears to us in the form of reason is the product of an amorphous world of myths, dreams and metaphors that reflect men's ways of being in the world. A female imaginary stands in contention with this as a potential source of an alternative apprehension of the world (language). This new language will reveal the voice of the universal as the voice of mastery but is to be seen as no less coherent, ethical or 'rational' because of this.

Clearly the female imaginary as the generative resource out of which a new symbolic order is emerging cannot be viewed clearly at the moment because it has been eclipsed by the dominance of (masculine) reason. However, a feminist awareness of this situation prompts the active search for 'new tools, new symbols, new resources of language' (Jantzen, 1998: 98). Our imaginative work is calling this resource into being. Pamela Anderson (1998) has argued that traditional cultural myths can be reappropriated and revisioned by women as a resource for creating a new culture. This is certainly the case, but it is also evident that the creative work of women in all artistic fields is a crucial resource. Literary critics (e.g. Yaeger, 1989, and Stockton, 1994) have convincingly argued that women's cultural interventions form the 'imaginary' resources which have sustained the feminist movement. Virginia Woolf is not alone in her conviction that the world began to change when women began to write.

Imaginary space

A second important contribution to Irigaray's thinking on the imaginary comes from her engagement with Lacanian theory, in which the imaginary is presented as a liminal space but one that precipitates the subject into the symbolic order (see pp. 98–99). If this imaginary is itself based upon the annihilation of the feminine (as Irigaray implies in *Speculum*) then the symbolic has also been so constructed – condemning women to perpetual alienation within language. A feminine imaginary can be conceived of as a liminal space in which female subjectivity and a feminine culture (symbolic) are formed in a manner which would affirm rather than deny the specificity and significance of women.

This vision, which represents a significant deviation from Lacanian thought, has been seized upon by Grace Jantzen (1998), who explores the social consequences of a cultural symbolic constructed 'in the West under the domination of the phallus, a masculinist imaginary which renders the becoming of the woman subject, if not wholly impossible, at least fraught with ambiguity' (1998: 121). Jantzen argues that the masculinist imaginary is constituted through phallic representations of isolation, independence and mastery, and it has produced a symbolic order that is dangerous not only for women but for all people. It is now necessary to 'disrupt the symbolic, displacing its masculinity structures by a new imaginary not based on the Name of the Father but on new ways of conceiving being which enable women to be subjects as women' (1998: 12).

Jantzen argues that, while the male imaginary and symbolic orders are fixated upon personal identity and the challenges of mortality, it is possible to imagine the emergence of a culture in which natality and the bonds between 'natals' are acknowledged and affirmed. She also argues that as there has always been assumed to be a direct link between the highest values of the male symbolic order and the divine so the cultivation of the female imaginary will entail the projection of new images of the divine which are necessary for the full achievement of female subjectivity. This is a major theme within Irigaray's later writing as we shall see below. For feminist religious readers it presents a challenge to discern within women's writing apprehensions of a world to come and a divine which do not merely reflect back to us the form women currently wear within the symbolic order but inspire us in the process of 'becoming divine'.

Imagined bodies

While Irigaray strays far from Lacanian orthodoxy in positing the imaginary as a resource for women-becoming-subjects, she retains the link that psychoanalysis makes between culture and embodiment. She also develops this insight in very different ways to the fathers of the discipline. The symbolic re-presentation of the female body is a third significant feature of the feminine imaginary. Mary Douglas (1966) has demonstrated how our profoundest metaphors for interpreting communal life are derived from the human body. However, in the current order the metaphors through which we construct our social world are largely drawn from the male body. Irigaray interprets this as a male morphology in which 'love of sameness is transformed, transmuted into an architecture [of the] world' (1993a: 100). The dominating symbol of the phallus, visible and identifiable, sustains a chain of connections which establish both unity and coherence and divide the self-same from the other. This symbolic economy makes possible a cultural logic of substitution, exchange and sacrifice which is foundational to Western culture and deeply inscribed within its metaphysics. It destroys forcibly an alternative economy of mutuality, dialogue and meeting.

The one of form, of the individual, of the (male) sexual organ, of the proper name, of the proper meaning ... supplants, while separating and dividing, that contact of at least two (lips) which keep woman in touch with herself. (Irigaray, 1985b: 26)

Irigaray's image of two vaginal lips which forever touch, caress, are one-self and two-separate, is an important device for critiquing a symbolic economy based upon the phallus: 'Whence the mystery that woman represents in a culture claiming to count everything ... *She is neither one nor two*' (1985b: 26). It affirms women's active sexual agency in a positive way, contradicting the notion that the female body has no sex. The caress of the two lips may be further celebrated as an affirmation of love between women; the press of the mother and the daughter, an evocation of lesbian desire and the political discourse generated 'when our lips speak together' (see Irigaray, 1985b: 205–218).

Recent scholarship (e.g. Moore, 1996) has drawn attention to the hypermasculinity through which God is 'embodied' in the Jewish and Christian traditions. Irigaray's intention in offering an alternative morphology is to challenge not only the political institutions of the masculine symbolic but also the sacred heart of the tradition. She acknowledges the archaic horror aroused within the monotheistic traditions by attempts to image God as have a woman's body, 'wearing a visible hole' (Irigaray, in Whitford, 1991b: 184). In her early essay on mysticism she had touched this sensitive spot by imagining the woman mystic observing in her beloved wounds and gashes of blood. These fleshly lips are like her own lips and the wounds are a space in which to shelter, 'Ecstasy is there in that glorious slit where she curls up as if in her nest' (Irigaray 1985a: 200). In later writing she employs other images drawn from female embodiment to present a divine emerging from a source undreamed of before – the female sex (1993a: 18).

In all her work Irigaray challenges the conventions of philosophical discourse, but in envisioning the imaginary resources of the female body it reaches its profoundest and most poetic level. Her 'flight of metaphors' is literary: it can be read as literature. However, as it is part of Irigaray's authorial technique frequently to assume the 'voice' of woman coming into speech, a voice not heard before, she does not connect her own literary creativity to that of other women writers who have also developed a female morphology and employed this as a means of transcending social and religious conventions. Feminist critics following Irigaray have sought to demonstrate that an embodied feminine imaginary exists within women's literature (e.g. Stockton, 1994, Walton, 2002) and that this is a powerful resource that should be identified and celebrated by women readers. Feminist religious readers who have engaged with Irigaray will be sensitised to the subversive potential of a feminine morphology in deconstructing the phallic symbolic and will return to read their favourite women authors in a new light. They will also be challenged by Irigaray's audacious claim that God can be discovered at the heart of this work of symbolic upheaval, and that a new advent is taking place as we read, as we write and as we speak.

To summarise Irigaray's project thus far, she seeks to demonstrate how women have been effaced within culture/language from the beginnings of philosophical discourse *and* from the point of their initial acquisition of a language they can speak only through self-effacement. However, this journey backwards into history and subjectivity is undertaken with the intention of transforming the current context. This will be achieved through the embracing of sexual difference – which is as universally coded as it is unrecognised. Women must regather the fragments of themselves which are dispersed into culture and begin the painstaking work of re-membering their bodies, genealogies and mother's love. The project is rooted in the mundane work of small affirmative gestures aimed at creating sexuate culture in civil life. It also reaches beyond these in its creative efforts to shift the social imagination through the construction of new symbolic structures. A female imaginary is envisioned which will become generative of such structures. In the process something will be revealed that has not yet been seen: what Irigaray names a 'sensible transcendent'.

The heralding of this epiphany is Irigaray's most powerful gesture. She has begun the quest for what Braidotti describes as the 'sensible transcendental foundation for a female process of becoming subject' (1994: 112). This is a project of reconnecting the flesh and spirit. It is a work which women who remain within sacred traditions which have deprived them of identity might find particularly helpful. By going backwards into the core of our traditions and learning to speak the parts we have been assigned differently, Irigaray appears to suggest that women altar-dwellers might become witnesses to a new advent. Stockton writes:

As if she could rewind a tape of broken glass, Irigaray asks us to hear fractures and the relics of obliteration spun backwards into filaments, crystal residues of organic reality. And yet, most significantly for spiritual materialism, desire is a search that can never go back without seeking 'beyond'. (1994: 42)

The beyond we are seeking is one which is promised in our creative and imaginative excursions towards what is both female and sacred.

The threshold of the divine

Thresholds of vision
There are a number of ways in which Irigaray's references to the sensible transcendental can be interpreted, and her own dialogical/intertextual style forbids their synthesis into one definition; they multiply in meaning with reference to each other. Commentators are often tempted to privilege one aspect of this evocative image over others according to their political priorities, and few do justice to the range of meanings it conveys. As yet the concept awaits a full appropriation within feminist theology. Sadly a full exploration of the richness of the term lies beyond the scope of this work. I shall focus instead upon a particularly important feature of the image which is important for re-visioning the relations between literature and theology. This is the notion of the 'threshold' which appears in various forms in all Irigaray's meditations upon the sensible transcendental.

By bringing together the two terms sensible and transcendental, Irigaray has created a trope which represents her whole project in one condensed and memorable image. We may think of the sensible transcendental as confronting a symbolic regime which has, from Plato to Lacan, sought intelligibility through the repudiation of material origins. We can also understand it as a way of evoking the female imaginary which is grounded in women's physical and social location but provides the means to move beyond these. The trope also names the divine in a form that affirms the material and spiritual aspirations of women who are becoming subjects. Here Irigaray is deeply indebted to Feuerbach in her insistence that women need a divine horizon through which they can contemplate their deepest essence, and against which they can measure, define and project themselves. This horizon raises them from a state of immersion in immanence (an absorption in cultural symbols that render them invisible as subjects) and provides a secure shelter for their own becoming.

As long as woman lacks a divine made in her image she cannot establish her subjectivity or achieve a goal of her own. She lacks an ideal that would be her goal or path in becoming. (1993b: 63)

In all these cases the expression affirms the continuing significance of two associated but differing realms which may be brought into connection but never merged. The sensible does not become the new transcendent; the female imaginary sustains a liminal space between body and language; the divine which will sustain women's subjectivity is not only imminent but also beyond us.

The threshold of the female sex

As well as being a trope which memorably identifies Irigaray's radical project, we can also think of the sensible transcendent as a means of imaging the divine through the symbolisation of the female body. I have already demonstrated that Irigaray employed her image of the two lips speaking to challenge a phallic symbolic based upon singularity and identity. However, her intention is also to engage in the 'remaking of immanence and transcendence, notably through this threshold which has never been examined as such: the female sex' (1993a: 18). Women's bodies, Irigaray contends, are in themselves places of meeting and separation. If we return to the famous image of the two lips speaking we may now notice a very significant negative feature of the image: the space between the lips, the gap that is never closed. Stockton writes,

It is the lack of closure between her lips – 'woman's-nothing- to-see' that forms 'two lips in continuous contact', a nearness made possible by a space, a lack, a gap that invests in 'woman's slit' – a dangerous expenditure. Nonetheless, castration, by this alternative logic of loss, converts to (auto)erotic pleasure. (1994: 31)

Irigaray does not contradict the idea that women are constructed around an absence, but rather assumes castration to brilliant new effect. The two lips remind us of a touching that could not be closer but is never a fusion. A threshold always remains between woman and woman, woman and man, the body and the sign, the sensible and the transcendent, the human and the divine. In her early work the two lips function as the principal image of this space between. In later writings other images become more significant – particularly the placenta and the phallus.

The placenta allows Irigaray to reflect upon a threshold within the body which allows an ethical exchange between the mother and foetus (1993c: 41). It protects both by maintaining the space between them. However, although the placenta is a helpful metaphor, because women have traditionally been represented by maternal imagery Irigaray seeks other bodily symbols to convey the significance of the threshold of the sensible transcendental. 'Their divinity does not depend upon the fact they can be mothers but upon their female identity, of which the half open lips are an affirmative expression' (1993c: 111). In later writings she prefers to use the metaphor of the mucous or mucosity. Whitford presents a number of reasons why Irigaray finds this symbol such a powerful device for representing the unthought threshold of the divine:

(a) it cannot be seen in the flat mirror, it is interior; (b) therefore it is more accessible to touch than to sight; (c) it is essential to the act of love, i.e. to exchange between the sexes; (d) it is always partly open (entrouvert); (e) it cannot be reduced to the maternal-feminine and the production of children; (f) it is not a part object, like the penis; it cannot be separated from the body … (g) it is neither solid nor fluid; (h) it is not stable it expands, but not in a shape; (i) it cannot be swallowed (incorporated) or spat out; (j) it corresponds both to sexuality and to speech (the two pairs of lips). So, suggests Irigaray, what is unthought, and what we need to think, is the relationship of the mucous to the divine, for 'this mucous in its touching, in its properties, would hinder the transcendence of a God foreign to the flesh, of a God of immutable and stable truth'. (1991a: 163)

The mucous enables lovers to join in love because it keeps them apart. It also provides a passage between inside and out. Without such a passageway body and soul, sexuality and spirituality are divided and God can find no entry (1993a: 15).

These are meditations intended to be both shocking and subversive, but Irigaray is not unaware of the mischief involved in linking God Almighty to the stringy stickiness of women's sex. We are offered a carnival divine, streaming beyond its source and serving love, respiration and song: 'welcoming and festive because the God Nietzsche talked about is dead' (1993a: 110). Those who despise the mucous and its properties will not find the rhythm for the act of love but be restricted to jerky pokings. Those who engage with it will be smeared by its *trace*; sticky lips and sticky fingers. Those who seek to understand it like a *tool* for use will be confounded. In these images Heidegger and Derrida are teased.

Irigaray summons God to return through this most unlikely medium. Once again she is recalling in her own writing the erotic nature of the mystical encounter   139 with the divine. In the mucosity of night-time loving, God is embraced. The mystic knows God then as her best lover 'since he separates her from herself only by the space of her jouissance where she finds Him/herself' (1985a: 201).

Love for the other

Feminists have delighted in the creativity and humour of Irigaray's morphology, but there are other equally significant ways of representing the sensible transcendent within her work that are more challenging for us in that they take us into territory other feminist scholars have regarded as alien and unfriendly. The love between men and women and the old religious images of love between heaven and earth are revisited as sacred thresholds of massive significance to women.

Drawing upon the work of Emmanuel Levinas, Irigaray takes the image of male and female in erotic encounter as a means of symbolising the encounter with alterity. In his early work Levinas takes the image of the (female) beloved as a means of representing the mysterious and sacred other who is passionately desired (see, for example, Levinas, 1985: 68). In the embrace across an ambivalent, equivocal and erotic threshold (Levinas, in Chanter, 1995: 205) the sensible and transcendent, sacred and profane meet. This image is one to which Irigaray is profoundly indebted but it is marginalised in Levinas' later work. The philosopher becomes perturbed by the nature of the association it implies between the divine and human and the confusion it may lead to between the longing for the other and human need, desire, 'concupiscence'. Irigaray regards this changed perspective as a failure on Levinas' part. He has lost the key to paradise. 'The threshold is still missing. The point of access to the most mucous part of the dwelling' (1993a: 204). If he had really regarded the female as autonomous other rather than as his beloved he would not have feared her as a passive creature binding him to his earthly desires but rather respected the 'irreducible nonsubstitutionality' (Irigaray, 1991b: 185) of sexual difference, which is capable of drawing him into an encounter with the divine Other. Relegating the female beloved to the realm of carnality, Irigaray argues, is 'to risk the suppression of alterity both the God's and the other's. Thereby dissolving any possibility of access to transcendence (1993a: 217). In response to Levinas' betrayal, Irigaray assumes the voice of the female lover affirming her autonomous desire and conviction that relations between living human beings offer a 'privileged approach to God' (1993a: 186). The female lover keeps watch over the threshold, maintaining faith in her lover's eventual return and the passionate reunion between them. This longed for encounter does not, however, imply a union between lovers. A space must always remain within intimacy as the threshold or passage for the divine in the relationship (1993a: 14). Only by remaining different to each other can the lovers perceive in their close embrace 'something insurmountable, a mystery' (1996: 104). When this distance is maintained the reconciled couple stand as a miraculous sign of a fecundity of pleasure which will renew the world.

Love between worlds

The image of an advent or parousia which will renew the world is one which Irigaray borrows from biblical tradition. The scriptures and theological monuments of Western culture are reinhabited by female forms within her texts, and the Christian religion is read as revelatory of the sensible transcendent forever seeking a threshold between worlds. The incarnation is a paradigm of this process (1991a: 182), but in masculine form it remains an incomplete symbol of redemption. A third era is looked for after the era of the Father and the Son. In this the Son passionately seeks his female counterpart, who is no longer despised but longed for as daughter and bride.

This event is announced in the gospel itself: the female, the women partake not in the last supper but in the Pentecost, and it is they who discover and announce the resurrection. This seems to say that the body of man can return to life when woman no longer forgets that she has a share in the spirit. In this way her transfiguration would take place ...

She must be longed for, loved, valued as a daughter. An other morning, a new parousia that necessarily accompanies the coming of an ethical God.

He respects the difference between him and her, in cosmic and aesthetic generation and creation. Sharing the heaven and the earth in all their elements, potencies, acts. (1993a: 149–150)

It is clear how such a vision springs from Irigaray's own concerns with the becoming of woman, but such ideas as this have very early counterparts in the writings of Christian Gnostic groups. They have resurfaced in the marginal and heretical teachings of pneumatic movements throughout the centuries (see Ruether, 1983: 127–138). Like mysticism, the prophetic longings of such groups can be most clearly discerned on the boundaries of the religious community. Irigaray asks why such visions are despised. Why has hope for the parousia been held to belong to the immature and popular religiosity of those far from an understanding of the truth? What parousia speaks of is 'a bridge in the present between the past and the future' (1993a: 147). Such a bridge must be made in order to prepare for the 'wedding and the festival of the world' (1993a: 149). And Irigaray borrows further from these marginalised traditions by visioning this bridge as already one of ceaseless traffic. Although man and woman have yet to find their place in the new age, the annunciation has already taken place. Spanning ancient divisions and moving between the thresholds are a multitude of angels. Irigaray uses these creatures to represent mediation between flesh and spirit, between male and female, between human and divine, between space and time:

These swift angelic messengers, who transgress all enclosures in their speed, tell of the passage between the envelope of God and that of the world as micro- or macrocosm. They proclaim such a journey can be made by the body of man, and above all the body of woman. They represent and tell of another incarnation, another parousia of the body. (1993a: 16)

141

The threshold of literature and theology

The reconstruction of space, time and God through the threshold of the female sex constitutes a huge agenda for the feminist theologian. The aims of this text are more modest, however: the concept of the 'threshold' has much to offer the feminist religious reader. Quite apart from the fact that Irigaray's meditations on the sensible transcendental can themselves be classed as mystical and visionary 'literature', her insistence that there is a threshold, or space for meeting, within the divine economy is a helpful contribution to understanding the relation between literature and theology.

I have argued that literature has been gendered female in relation to theology by male critics, theologians, poststructuralist writers and religious feminists. This convention, while originating in the binary and hierarchical traditions of Western culture, has the potential to be reappropriated for radical ends and many feminists have exploited this possibility. However, when placing 'female' literature at odds with male theology, the dangerous tendency has been to turn women's literature into alternative sacred text or better theology. The 'literary' nature of women's writing, and its affinity with literature written by men, are sacrificed in this process, and the beginnings of canonisation and authorisation appear in the work of feminist theologians.

If, alternatively, we conceive of literature meeting with theology at a sacred threshold we can retain a sense that a distinction always endures between them that cannot be breached. And yet the threshold is a place of communion as well as separation. Despite the fact that the threshold is never abolished (literature remains literature) it remains a place of meeting as well as a boundary. The threshold is where touching happens, where lovers embrace and ever reach towards each other. Whitford writes:

Love is the vehicle which permits a passage between, the passage to and fro between sensible and intelligible, mortal and immortal, above and below, immanent and transcendent. Instead of an abyss or an enclosure which defines an inside and an outside there should be a threshold and the possibility of a permanent passage in and out, to and fro. (1991a: 164)[91]

Irigaray offers us 'openings and pointers' towards imagining a love relation between literature and theology which is based upon the fact of their difference rather than an assumed complementarity between them. In our time we may imagine literature speaking as the female lover who has much to protest about in the masterly pretensions of her male partner. However, she looks beyond this to the potential that in their 'carnal' loving something mysterious, profound and life giving is made manifest: a power of becoming which is divine.

---

91 Irigaray here maintains a similar position to that of Kristeva. Whereas Lacan and others forbid the possibility of communication between separated spheres, these boundaries are refigured as places of communicative possibility for the feminine.

Divine writing

In this chapter I have argued that, despite the fact that Irigaray, unlike other post-structuralist writers, does not devote energy and attention to discussing literature, her work has great significance for religious feminists seeking new reading strategies and new means of understanding the relations between literature and theology.

First of all she returns us to the religious traditions in which we have been formed, encouraging us not to abandon the ruins but to make the stones speak. Irigaray encourages us to be deconstructive readers, cultural partisans within theology, but there is no requirement to separate ourselves from male-centred traditions. We are rather to engage with them continually in a passionate dialogue. The resources that will sustain us in this task come from the work of resistance itself. As we recover the traces of the feminine which the symbolic has sought to eradicate we are also beginning to claim our specificity and to build a culture in which sexual difference is acknowledged. We may describe this process as the nurturing of a female imaginary, and women's literature has a crucial role to play in this process. This is because works of imagination have functioned as reason's other in Western culture but also because in the liminal space of the imaginary a new symbolic can begin to take shape. The creation of a female morphology within women's creative writing is crucial to this process. Not only does this challenge the phallic symbolic with images of mutuality and communication. It also offers a means of reconceptualising the divine through the threshold of the female sex.

Second, and most controversially, Irigaray's meditations upon the sensible transcendental cause us to reflect upon a new social order in which love is the relation between masculine and feminine spheres. Neither partner is eradicated in this erotic embrace, as a sacred space always exists between masculine and feminine spheres. In this relation the couple stand as a sign of divine hope for the future.

Finally, I have argued that this threshold provides a helpful metaphor for reconceptualising the relations between literature and theology. I have also stated that the fruitfulness of this approach lies in the stress upon alterity rather than complementarity – which places it at odds with the traditional terms of engagement explored in chapter 1. The lovers are not 'made for each other' but rather to be 'other to each other'. There is no synthesis or 'consummation' here, but each requires the other to gain access to transcendence.

CHAPTER 7

Hélène Cixous and the mysteries that beat in the heart of the world

Writing the body

A 'religious writer'

In my reflections upon the work of Kristeva and Irigaray I have sought to make evident the way in which both contribute to new understandings of the relation between literary creativity and the sacred which are resonant for the feminist religious reader. It is this sustained emphasis upon the relations between literature and theology which distinguishes my interrogation of their work from the many other commentaries offered elsewhere. For the work of Kristeva and Irigaray has been ingested, digested and redigested in feminist scholarship. Although many feminist theologians still display cautious reserve in relation to poststructuralist theory, the work of these women is gradually gaining its place in the theoretical compendium of religious feminists. Of particular significance in this development is the way in which Kristeva and Irigaray have been used in recent attempts to construct a feminist philosophy of religion (see Anderson, 1998 and Jantzen, 1998).

While the names Kristeva and Irigaray are now increasingly appearing in the bibliographies and footnotes of works in feminist theology, this is not yet the case in relation to the work of Hélène Cixous. Although she was initially placed alongside Kristeva and Irigaray in the 'holy trinity' of French feminism (see Leonard and Adkins, 1996) she has not achieved among us the wide recognition given to her more famous contemporaries. This may be due in part to the very negative view of Cixous presented in Toril Moi's highly influential *Sexual/Textual Politics* (1985), which introduced 'French feminism' to many English-speaking readers. Moi characterised Cixous as a shallow and flawed woman who, while capable of brilliant rhetoric, was a highly unsuitable feminist icon. Moi's judgement that Cixous' flamboyant writing was 'flawed as much by its lack of reference to recognisable social structures as its biologism' (1985: 126) was not subjected to critical appraisal at a time when very few of her works were available in translation. Although many of Cixous' books are now published in English by mainstream publishing houses, definitive judgements continue to be made upon her without reference to work published after the mid-1970s.[92]

Another reason for the lack of engagement may be the fact that, although Cixous has held influential university positions and founded the first European doctorate in Women's Studies at the University of Paris VIII,[93] she is also a writer and dramatist. Her play *La Ville Parjure* received France's Prix de la Critique Dramatique as the best play of the year in 1994. Graham Ward, an otherwise enthusiastic reader of Cixous' work, justified his decision not to include her thinking in his edited collection, *The Postmodern God*, on the grounds that she is a practitioner rather than a theorist (Ward, 1997b: xxxiv). Certainly all her writing is deeply metaphorical and its poetic form does not lend itself to easy appropriation into the sorts of debates which are most common within the academy. In conversation with Mirelle Calle-Gruber, Cixous reflects that 'the texts of mine which are put into circulation are often the texts that can be easily circulated and appropriated ... but the situation produces errors in evaluation: because to have an upright position analogous to that of a theoretician is not my intention' (Cixous, 1997: 7).

Cixous' unusual position as an academic critic/poet has made the reception of her work problematic. However the very factors that have made her reception in 'an upright position' difficult suggest that it will be of interest to the feminist religious reader, and there are additional reasons why it might become a very significant resource indeed.

Although Kristeva and Irigaray both point to literature and the creative imagination as important sites of political struggle, they do not emerge as 'readers' rooted in the work of other women. They can be criticised as championing an ideal of feminine intervention in the symbolic order but less interested in what other women are actually performing through their cultural work. Cixous, on the other hand, is deeply embedded in the reading relationships she enjoys with other authors and, significantly for this book, engages with them in a manner that challenges the received understandings of authorship and reading which have always undergirded theological reasoning.

Second, it could be argued that the faith Kristeva and Irigaray place in the power of 'imaginary' resources to challenge oppressive social structures is rhetorically highly appealing but practically suspect. Kristeva is ultimately a grim realist. Irigaray, on the other hand, is a utopian thinker who deliberately turns her face away from present sufferings towards a new dawn. Both perspectives

---

92 For example, Michelle Boulous Walker, in her very important book *Philosophy and the Female Body* (1998), forms judgements about Cixous and the maternal relation which are based upon texts written in 1975. Of these texts Cixous says they were 'inspired by the urgency of a moment in the general discourse concerning "sexual difference" ... I would never have thought when I began writing, that one day I would finding myself making strategic and even military gestures: Constructing a camp with lines of defence!' (Cixous, 1997: 5).

93 Successive right-wing governments have attempted to close this doctoral programme down but public support has ensured its survival.

are unlikely fully to satisfy feminists concerned with the claims of the political real (as discussed in chapter 4) who may raise serious objections to their work. Cixous shares the same hope/faith in writing as Kristeva and Irigaray but is more open to questioning whether the 'divine' energy it generates can effectively challenge the forces of oppression in society. When I ask myself why I consider literature to be so important for religious feminists I find Cixous' honest struggle with the principle that creative writing should be accountable to political practice extremely helpful. She wrestles with the (likely) possibility that there might be more effective routes to the achievement of justice than reading/writing, demonstrating an ironic self-awareness that is largely absent from the work of Kristeva and Irigaray. Furthermore, the sense of moral ambiguity she discerns in feminist reading practices is one which it is essential to foreground in debate if we are to move away from the assumptions of female virtue and innocence which have structured our engagements with women's literature in the past.

Third, Cixous' later work takes up the theological question discussed at the end of chapter 1 – namely, how can literature become for us the bearer of our pain in the face of God? The question 'how can suffering speak?' reverberates throughout her work and she pursues it in conversational relation to the 'literature of testimony' inscribed in the work of Lispector, Celan, Hillesum, Blanchot and others. Her work in this area leads her to acknowledge that her feminist politics do not promise a resolution to the darkest mysteries. Thus she declares that politics leads her to faith and faith leads her to cast her lot with those who do not deny 'the mysteries that beat in the heart of the world' (1989: 1). She further states that she is a religious writer who has never written without Dieu, despite the fact that she has frequently been informed that Dieu is not a feminist (1998b: 150).[94] Cixous' work is thus a precious resource to those of us who are seeking an encounter with literature that deepens our sense of wonder and strangeness and pain – rather than one that confirms us in our convictions and comforts us in our sorrows.

Finally, in all Cixous' work we are called upon to wrestle with the relationship between women and writing. This subject was explored in early works of gynocriticism (see pp. 50–52) in which the difficulties women experienced claiming authorship and receiving recognition for their creative work were a major concern. Cixous acknowledges these problems but moves beyond them in trying to reimagine women's writing. She employs the conventions of poststructuralism (particularly deconstruction) to picture 'feminine' writing in opposition to the 'masculine' logos. But her re-visioning is not merely a rhetorical gesture. As a woman writer herself she sets out to affirm alternative authorial strategies that express the 'feminine libidinal economy' of writing. These experiments are

---

94 This is not to imply that Cixous has an uncritical approach to religion, particularly in its impact upon women, or that she subscribes to an orthodox understanding of the divine.

spiritual exercises which eventually lead her to affirm the mystical vocation of the author to put the metaphor in the place of suffering. In this last stage of her work very powerful female imagery is developed to describe writing which mediates between life and death. In these later works the love between mother and child stands as a metaphor for writing as a divine force that is overwhelming.

Writing belongs to women

Cixous was born in 1937 in Oran, Algeria. Both her parents were Jewish. Her father's family had followed the trajectory of Jewish migration from Spain to North Africa and were Spanish and French speaking. Her mother's family were from Northern Europe and German was Cixous' mother tongue. As well as personal bereavements Cixous' childhood was marked by war, occupation and struggles against colonialism. She married at eighteen[95] and migrated to France, where she completed her education and began research on the works of James Joyce. She met Jacques Derrida in 1962 and, by the mid-1960s, was immersed in French literary and cultural circles. Although active in the radical movements of 1968 she also successfully defended her doctoral thesis in that year, and in 1969 she was appointed Chair in English Literature at Paris VIII University, where she has continued to teach throughout her career.

Although Cixous has been a prolific writer, her two best known works in translation are still her early polemical essays 'The Laugh of the Medusa' (1990a [1975]) and 'Sorties: Out and Out: Attacks/Ways Out / Forays' (1989a [1975]). In these texts she begins to address the relation of writing to women and to admit that in the past writing has functioned as a tool of the 'phallogocentric' regime:

Nearly the entire history of writing is confounded with the history of reason of which it is at once the effect, the support and one of the privileged alibis. (1990a: 320)

As a challenge to this historical writing Cixous announces the emergence of 'a new insurgent writing'. (1989a: 106) that comes from women who have turned their sexual energy and connectedness to other women into language. Out of the ferment of the women's movement Cixous declares that this writing has revolutionary potential:

A feminine text cannot fail to be volcanic; as it is written it brings about an upheaval of the old property crust; carrier of masculine investments; there's no other way. There's no room for her if she's not a he. If she's a her-she-it in order to smash everything – to shatter the framework of institutions, to blow up the law, to break up the 'truth' with laughter. (1990a: 326)

For Cixous' women's writing is a 'volcanic force' because it carries traces of a feminine libidinal economy, an economy of the gift that is not fixated around

---

95 There were three children born during Cixous' marriage but one died as an infant. Her later thinking on writing 'as child' may owe much to this bereavement.

the phallus but will disseminate itself in the manner of women who are used to expenditure, bodily births and separations.

And there is a link between the economy of femininity – the open and extravagant subjectivity, that relationship to the other in which the gift doesn't calculate its influence – and the possibility of love; and a link between this 'libido of the other' and writing. (1989a: 109)

The idea that women can practise a different form of writing if they explore their bodies as material systems of knowledge (for Cixous the body is never a natural presocial given) is one that has remained important throughout her writing life. However, even in these early works, she is beginning to suggest that there is a deep affinity between the 'feminine libidinal economy' and writing itself. She is already claiming that writing belongs to women: 'I will say: today, writing is woman's' (1989a: 105).

In marking this continuity between writing and the feminine Cixous is deeply indebted to Derrida who was a personal friend and intellectual soul-mate for many years.[96] Derrida took the 'primacy' of writing as a means to unravel logocentric authority. Undermining the 'natural' authority of speech, writing reveals the conditions under which meaning is produced and simultaneously undermined. In this sense, as Gayatri Spivak states, 'Writing no longer refers to the production of prose and verse but to that mechanism which fractures knowing ... whose origin and end are necessarily absent' (1987: 147). Because of its association with repressed difference, writing is a feminine gesture. Cixous assumes Derrida's barely submerged mythology of writing as a female revolt against authority. Women's writing is a volcanic force, to shatter the framework of institutions, to blow up the law, to break up the truth with laughter. She incarnates this feminine writing in the symbolic figure of the woman who writes her body.

This is a figure who emerges in many forms throughout Cixous' work. In the early texts she is wild and sexy. Cixous takes Derrida's articulation of the excessive nature of writing and refers it back to women's capacities for multiple pleasures. Excess for Derrida can, at times, appear darkly threatening but Cixous celebrates its disruptive power.

Whereas in Derrida excess as that which cannot be recuperated in a system of conceptual oppositions is not necessarily on the side of abundance, Cixous, closer to Bataille, writes of excess as effusion, eros, poetry, drunkenness, and laughter [which] exceeds dialectics and negativity but never appears. (Conley, 1991: 28)

---

96 Each had a great admiration for the other's work. On the back cover of Cixous' *The First Days of the Year* (1998a) Derrida stated his belief that Cixous is 'the greatest writer in what I shall call, if I may, my language French. And I weigh my words saying this, for a very great writer must be a poet-thinker, very much a poet and a very thinking poet.'

As well as claiming writing as feminine, Cixous makes an early identification between writing and literature. In her developing symbolics, if the Book of the Law is 'male' then the books outside the law are somehow female and participate in the revolutionary insurgence of writing. Literature has been 'working at this subversive activity ... for a long time' (1994b: 32). Literature in this frame is radically intertextual and multi-authored. It resists genres and definitions, and Cixous will give her later work an indeterminate quality by experimenting in the construction of fictive criticism and citational literature. The 'religious writing' to which she aspires is not to be found in any particular text or type of creative work but is to be understood as an energy source (in her work it is to be compared with the unconscious, desire or the dangerous memories of marginalised people). It enables the reader/author to sense the potential of escape from the power of the 'Proper'; signifying the full presence and authority of logocentrism. Beyond this realm is the place of No one. This is a heterogeneous, strange, potentially female sphere outside the limits of what currently exists.

Life without limit the whole of life: this is what will be in question in these texts ... the possibility of limitlessness.
  What happens in this non-place where the word 'fiction' only names in order to inscribe the blurred and shifting lines of that adventure beyond genres and oppositions ... where desire is not a dream, where in the plureal, the other place to come announces itself. (1994b: 28)

Cixous presents writing as a sublime force; 'the passageway, the entrance, the exit, the dwelling place of the other in me' (1989a: 109). It carries the writer towards the other but not beyond the body. Cixous talks about the force of writing as a gradual climax emanating from the inside. It is grounded in the flesh and wells up as a light radiating from the body's core. It streams outwards making everything fertile: 'It doesn't plant it spawns. And I see that she looks very closely at this light and she sees it has the veins and nerves of matter' (1989a: 109). We can see how an alternative libidinal economy is in play in this metaphor. It is the female body's depths, not the masculine body's visible contours, which are employed to describe writing. 'Not the shaft. The vessel' (1989a: 109). These depths, Cixous argues, have been too long confined to silence.
  Just as Cixous found in Derrida a helpful mythology linking women and writing, so in Lacan she finds a useful narrative which represents the confinement of the female body to muteness. According to Lacan women enjoy a supplementary 'jouissance' to that of men which comes through their differential connection to the maternal realm beyond language. Neither this jouissance, nor the maternal connection which is its source, can be spoken. As they are beyond language, Lacan asserts, what woman experiences, she cannot express.
  Cixous takes Lacan's theories as a modern account of an ancient horror. In contradiction to his theory she asserts that women's jouissance is coming into

149

writing and women are drawing the strength to write from the deepest, oldest and loveliest connection:

> In woman there is always, more or less, something of 'the mother' repairing and feeding, resisting separation, a force that does not let itself be cut off ... the part of you that puts space between yourself and pushes you to inscribe your woman's style in language. Voice: milk that could go on forever. Found again. The lost mother/bitter lost. Eternity is voice mixed with milk. (1989a: 111)

Cixous' writing on female jouissance and the relation with the mother is a deliberate mis-reading and disinterpretation of Lacan. She is well aware, of course, that a theoretical distinction is to be made between jouissance and women's orgasmic pleasure; between the unspeakable archaic maternal and women who are mothers – but she resists this separation. Although Lacan's prohibitions must be 'written over' he is correct in his awareness of the force that forbids the articulation of women's knowledge. To write the body is to break the most ancient taboos. You shall not eat this fruit. You shall not journey within to the place of the dead.

Mindful of this, Cixous uses images that recall flesh and sweetness – apples, pomegranates, Eve and Persephone – to describe the transgressive work of writing the body. These are appropriate because, she believes, the female body has been feared as the site of encounter with what is repressed/forbidden and yet most desired. Furthermore, she implies that the body's tremendous force is now seeking form. What has been inexpressible is taking shape, and something that was beyond language is now demanding to be written. The body is the inexpressible which seeks a shape; beyond language it demands to be written.[97]

The Roots of Writing

Cixous' first articulations of the power of feminine writing and the force of writing the body are rhetorical interventions intended to attack powerful cultural conventions head on. Unfortunately, they have often been interpreted literally as a turn away from politics towards language – a move Cixous decisively rejects:

> I don't think the revolution is going to happen through language either. But there is no revolution without a conscious grasp – without there being people who get up and begin to yell. (1991: 131)

97 Cixous writes: 'A bright force. Not a god; it doesn't come from the heavens but from an inconceivable region, inside me but unknown, at a great depth, as if there could be inside my body ... another space, limitless ... That's the enigma. One morning it all explodes. My body knows, deep in there, one of its panicky cosmic adventures. I have volcanoes in my terrains. But no lava: what wants to flow is breath. And not just any way. The breathing wants a form. "Write me!" One day it begs me another day it threatens. "Are you going to write me or not?" It could have said to me: "Paint me." I've tried. But the nature of its passion demanded the form that stops the least, that encloses the least, the body without a frame, without skin, without walls the flesh that doesn't dry, that doesn't stiffen, that doesn't clot the wild blood that wants to stream through it forever' (1987: 450).

If not to be interpreted literally, however, 'writing the body' is, for Cixous, much more than a rhetorical device. It is also a distinctive creative practice which she has sought to develop in her long apprenticeship as a writer. Although 'The Laugh of the Medusa' and 'Sorties' are joyful and feisty works, it quickly becomes apparent that 'writing the body' is not only to be understood as defiant excess but as an immense responsibility and painful compulsion. Like mystical vision this writing appears both entirely gratuitous and also the product of intense bodily discipline. Cixous struggles to achieve this gift and as she experiments with a number of figures of the 'woman who writes her body'; the circumstances of her own life become writers' material. The story of her own journey to writing is rehearsed and analysed[98] and alchemically transformed in her texts.

The narrative of Cixous as a writer of the body begins with a loss. This is the classic Lacanian location of the entry into language. In psychoanalysis this loss is generally figured as separation from the mother, but because Cixous' father died when she was a small child her own construction of loss is rather different.

With the ferocity of a beast I kept my mother within my sight. Poor calculation. On the chessboard I brooded over the Queen; and it was the King who was taken. (1987: 446)

In the face of this bereavement writing becomes the desire which keeps the lost parent alive: 'I've armed love, with soul and words, to prevent death from winning. Loving, keeping alive: naming' (1987: 446). Although the loss of her father was a personal tragedy it also represents a passage into a world in which parents are always lost, homes are inevitably broken, God is savage and exile is the place in which the writer permanently dwells. Writing is the force that mediates this reality which is denied by logocentric pretensions to order and control.

That Cixous' parents were Jewish and that German was the language of her childhood[99] adds to the sense of perpetual estrangement that she claims has formed her as a writer. She attributes to Jewishness her sense of inhabiting ancient and sacred pages, rather than a country. This is a place to which it is always possible to return when in exile. The idea of belonging in a book rather than a homeland is paralleled by the sense that she belongs as much with the dead as with the living. It is not only her father who haunts her writing but all those others whose lives were cut short. These two powerful sentiments contribute to a contradictory sense of being alive in a book and of its being the book of the dead which is being rewritten in her texts. 'I see Jews passing in the depths of my writing, singing ancient psalms in silence behind my memory' (1979: 34).

The sense of Jewishness is a source of further ambivalence because 'being a woman' has contributed as much to her sense of cultural unhomeliness as

---

98 This is a dangerous device which has brought charges of individualism and elitism upon her. It also risks creating assumptions about authorial functions which are quite the opposite of Cixous' intentions. She warns that '"Author" is a pseudonym that should fool no-one' (1991: 11).

99 Cixous does not write in German.

being Jewish, and she does not wish to privilege one form of 'unbelonging' over another. She occasionally uses the term 'jewoman' to signal a dual sense of estrangement and to describe the particular sense she has that to write from a woman's body is to break the most sacred of taboos. It is to melt women's bracelets and bangles into a form that shatters the tablets of the law. It is to mix the world of flesh and spirit and thus create a graven image. The jewoman who writes also usurps the place of the prophet or patriarch who is the person elected to inscribe the voice of God. Cixous pictures herself as the mouse who might find the strength to scamper up Sinai only to learn that 'a mouse is not a prophet' (1987: 449). She must continually struggle with an uneasy inheritance which bequeaths her writing but continually threatens to remove it from her: 'Writing had spoken to its prophets from a burning bush. But it must have decided that bushes don't dialogue with women' (1987: 452).

Although Cixous has a powerful sense that when a woman writes she 'breaks the law' she also argues that the prohibition creates the jouissance which overwhelms it. This jouissance is experienced in the waves of desire that sweep through the body and explode into writing. Cixous believes that she, and every writer, is born from these passions in a process of 'libidinal education'. The 'story of the writers' soul' is the story of a quest which brings them through many trials and turnings to the point where they find themselves faced with a choice between obedience to the law and the temptation of fruit.

In the story of their discovery of the world, of its joys and its prohibitions, its joys and its laws, always on the trail of the first of all human stories, the story of *Eve and the Apple* … It is the supreme text, the one written through a turning back to the place where one plays to win or lose life. The stakes are extremely simple, it is a question of the apple does one eat it or not? Will one enter into contact with the intimate inside of the fruit or not? (1988: 15)

Writing the other

Living the orange

Although the choice between the law and the fruit appears simple, the minute that the hand is stretched out to grasp what seems lovely, or to write what is intimate and fleshly, many doubts invade the writer. In *To Live the Orange* (1979), Cixous chronicles her own wrestling with these demons.

The orange is a favourite metaphor for Cixous. It is a vivid word linking fruit, flesh, her maternal home (Oran/Oran-je) and writing. To write is to know the orange. To immerse oneself in its flesh. It is an overwhelmingly absorbing and sensuous experience, and a contrast is made between a hunger for this fruit and the need for disciplined action on behalf of suffering women.

In *To Live the Orange* the female author is tormented by insecurity, loneliness and guilt: 'And sometimes reproaching myself for having "religious writing"'

(1979: 12). She wishes to stretch out her hand and grasp the orange, but the phone keeps ringing with urgent messages urging her to take action in support of women in Iran. Orange/Iran – what has priority? If writing is to be fruitful, 'one must have seen life tortured, disfigured, bled, to have heard life cry out in despair' (1998: 98). But one must also have nurtured the capacity to believe that beauty is not completely overwhelmed by sadness. There is an unbearable pressure experienced in this tension. The law appears to require that the orange be set aside because of the evident needs of suffering people, but can these needs be met if faith has been lost?

Under what conditions could a woman say, without dying of shame – what I am only able to write this Monday after three days of suffocating terror 'the love of the orange is political too' – at what cost? (1979: 26)

This question will return throughout her writing life, but at the moment of its utterance Cixous finds a way forward for her own work through a momentous encounter with the work of another woman writer, the Brazilian author Clarice Lispector, 'She put the orange back into the deserted hands of my writing' (1979: 12).

Cixous has conducted an imaginary conversation with Lispector since the late 1970s. She writes of her initial discovery of Lispector's work as a rescue from despair: 'I was alone, at the extremity of my finite being' (1979: 12). Cixous was tormented by guilt that her concern with writing the body was a guilty retreat from reality, and yet she also felt herself to be the only one daring to try and write in a new form. The recognition of another woman struggling to be creative in a manner similar to her own brought relief.

I had turned against my writing: 'What have you in common with women? When your hand no longer even knows anymore how to find a near and realizable orange at rest in the bowl?' Mute I fled the orange, my writing fled the secret voice of the orange ...

I asked: 'What have I in common with women?' From Brazil a voice came to return the lost orange to me, 'The need to go to the sources. The easiness of forgetting the source. The possibility of being saved by a humid voice that has gone to the sources. The need to go further into a birth voice'. (1979: 15–16)

Like all her personal accounts the narrative of this reading encounter can be read on many levels.[100] At one level Lispector stands as practical mentor, spiritual

---

100 Once again Cixous' multi-layered writing has been subject to much criticism. Declarations of loneliness as a woman writer have been a scandal to many of Cixous' critics. Feminists have struggled to create a 'women's tradition' and locate women writers within an extended genealogy of creative mothers. In this context Cixous is judged anti-feminist for acknowledging a feeling of being alone among women. What right does she have to elevate and isolate herself in this way? Or to appear to place herself in the company of Lispector among a small elite band of writers who have managed to make the journey to the inside? Braidotti, for example, writes: 'What is celebrated is glorious feminine creativity – which would presuppose that all women are united by their specific relation to jouissance and to the text – but is, for the moment at least, the privilege of a few women' (1991: 244).

guide and literary friend to Cixous. She is happy to go to the 'school' of Clarice and eagerly desires to learn her craft from another woman. At another level Lispector is much more than just another woman writer, she is the representative of feminine writing which streams beyond individual authorship. The following extract from *To Live the Orange* carries a narrative of a 'reading encounter' with another female writer. It links this with the 'voice' from a far-away home which always recalls the mother. The voice comes from a birth-town; Lispector, like Cixous, lived as an exile in a place of many languages. It becomes the writing of the body; a mystical writing which is jouissance – 'mad/joy':

A woman's voice came to me from far away, like a voice from a birth-town, it brought me insights I had once had, intimate insights, naive and knowing, ancient and fresh like the yellow and violet color of freesias rediscovered, this voice was unknown to me, it reached me on the twelfth of October 1978, it was writing to no one, to all women, to writing, in a foreign tongue, I do not speak it, but my heart understands it, and its silent words in all the veins of my life have translated themselves into mad blood, into joy blood. (1979: 10)

So Cixous responds deeply and reverently to Lispector's power in writing. Her words are divine. 'It seems to us ... that they are strokes of god: but when they come in we see by their smile they are strokes of Clarice' (1979: 110). Beyond this excessive praise of Lispector it is important to identify what it is in Lispector's work that has touched Cixous so deeply.

First, Cixous admires Lispector as another author who reads and is aware not only of the literary tradition in which she stands but also of the way an epoch and a culture presents its questions through poetry, philosophy and theory. Lispector stands within the place where writing streams beyond authorship.

I let myself read in the manner of C.L., her passion read me, and in the burning and humid current of reading, I saw how the texts, both familiar and strange, of Rilke or of Heidegger, or of Derrida, had been already-read, carried along, and answered in the living-writing. (Cixous, in Shiach, 1991: 68)

Second, Cixous finds an alternative economy of language in Lispector's work which enriches her own critique of the 'economy of lack' she ascribes to Lacan. In 'Extreme Fidelity', Cixous meditates upon a powerful passage from Lispector's *The Passion according to G.H.*, the conclusion of which reads:

Ah, my love, don't be afraid of want: it is our greatest destiny. Love is much more fatal than I had thought, love is as inherent as life itself, and we are guaranteed by necessity which will be renewed continuously. Love already is, is always'. (Lispector, in Cixous, 1988: 27)

From her reading of this text Cixous gains a vision of a grateful 'hymn to want' which, she argues, defies the theoreticians of lack. It is the desire for the other, experienced painfully in the body, which is also the only means of partaking in life – through loving it. What is required for this to happen is an immense attention to things as they present themselves in their own being; Heidegger's imprint upon Lispector's writing is acknowledged by Cixous. This is an attention which allows a relationship of thankfulness for the other to exist without overwhelming them. A distance is necessary for this to happen. 'Clarice would say this: hunger is faith' (Cixous, 1988: 24).

Such a hunger-faith, Cixous believes, issues in a particular style of writing. A writing which is marked female because women, she argues, stand in a different relation to loss. Their economy is not dominated by the fear of castration but by the positive 'maternal' experience of the other which departs. Theirs is the 'economy of positive lack: above all let us not be lacking in lack' (1988: 24). Cixous names this form of writing the *style of live water*:

Where thirst itself is that which quenches, since to be thirsty is already to give oneself a drink. The style of live water gives rise to works which are like streams of blood or water, which are full of tears, full of drops of blood or tears transformed into stars. Made of phrases which spill forth dripping in luminous parataxis'. (1988: 25)

The writer whose work is 'live water' assumes a different relationship to her characters and to her readers. She is not their master or controller. Her fidelity to them consists of her attentiveness to their being. 'When Clarice says: "What I write you is this", this orders, gives direction' (Cixous, 1990b: 25). The gift she gives her readers is to be able to place the subject of her narrative in relation to them so that when the writing ceases the relationship between the reader and the writing continues. She is the good mother who does not either abandon or possess the child.

From then on, separation … can take place. She can rest and the world continues. This does not bring about death or absence in the world, since there is I and you and it is. 'What I write you continues'. One should even hear the what-I-write-you-continues in one word. It is what I write you that continues and brings I into continuity. But the I is no longer an author who masters. (1990b: 25)

'One might say that the work of Clarice Lispector is an immense *book of respect, a book of the right distance*', writes Cixous (1988: 19). Having found renewed grounds for faith in a writing of love, she returns again to the question that haunts her: how do I write before the 'orange' in a world of suffering and pain? How do I write the body in a context of violence and oppression? Particularly, how do I write, as Lispector puts it – after the lobster – (neither Lispector or Cixous shrink from bathos), for having once tasted rich food it is impossible to return to the place of those who have not.

What is sought is an authorship that no longer masters and a writing that is so attentive to the particularity of pain that it presents it as minutely and as faithfully as a scribe transcribes the Torah, 'giving the name, the right, the cry to pain' (1989b: 8). However, writing also has the task of offering poetry to the condemned. Its work is to cherish the 'orange', or offer the rose, because how else will those who suffer receive 'the hope that writing offers as a small trembling light' (1989b: 6)?

> To make the present of a living rose, so that the infinite tenderness contained in a rose may through the forty sadnesses reach veiled women without deceiving them, or offending them ...
>
> At the school of Clarice, we learn how to be contemporaneous with a living rose and with concentration camps. (1979: 100)

Such rhetorical gestures as Cixous makes here (the rose/the concentration camp) are in excessive defiance of ethical accounting or political acceptability. What she is presenting is an act of faith, a testimony as to how through the work of Lispector she has learned to 'believe weeping' (1988b: 14) that writing has sacred power. Lispector gives Cixous back the 'orange' and encourages her along the path of writing. For Cixous this is an encounter with the holy. Lispector becomes a figure of one who has reached reconciliation with the *source* and now partakes in her being:

> Her life being so profound that she must have reached, way deep down, what is not a place ... until reaching this depth where the life of a life rejoins Life, the Great Mother – Life. (1979: 60)

Writing the other

Although all of Cixous' work, including her 'autobiographical' writing, is an attempt to transcribe the encounter with the 'other', after the encounter with Lispector reflected in *To Live the Orange* she engages with renewed intensity in a sustained attempt to locate her own writing in the body/place of positive lack. The works which follow are experiments at constructing a writing of love and respect – and the right distance. They offer a number of fictional representations of women writing the body – sketches or studies Cixous uses as she struggles to find an adequate form for the mystical writer.

In *(With) Or the Art of Innocence* (1981) Cixous creates a chorus of female characters to help her write 'the Book of You'. These disperse the author's presence in the text by being both figures for herself and autonomous others who have a power of witnessing what the author cannot. There is wistfulness in the book, a sadness at not achieving the right delicacy of approach to writing and being frustrated rather than empowered by loss. 'I think what is spoken is lost', she writes, 'and what is not spoken is lost differently' (in Salesne, 1988: 117).

Limonade tout était si infini (1982) takes the form of a love letter written in the long unnamed war against women and similar beings. A war raging all around inevitably makes writing difficult, and the text lives more easily with the 'author's' inability to write the 'ultimate', 'free' book. The snatched fragments and the imperfect texts the woman writer manages to create, in spite of the battles, are evidence that paradise can still be achieved in the immediacy of struggle. The justification of writing which Cixous offers is that it gives the strength to believe that Paradise can be re-entered for brief moments – even during a war.

It is in The Book of Promethea (1991) that the sense of having achieved the power of a new perspective on writing is most confidently revealed. This is a joyful, sexy and romping book in which Cixous expresses her thankfulness for the gift of writing given to her by another woman. Writing is a living flame precariously passed from person to person and in this text it is not the author who warms and enlivens her subject but vice versa. Promethea, although the subject of the novel, is described as its creator, and the book is her body. Stylistic devices are deployed to confound the sense of the author as creator of her subject. The narrator ('I' and 'H') has two places in the text and slides between them. And although Cixous describes this as a true story she also insists that the truth comes guaranteed by 'Promethea' rather than herself. The book is Promethea's book in the sense that is her gift of love to the narrator. It comes from the inside. It is the place Cixous thought she had lost access to now triumphantly regained.

Promethea has kindled dreams of fire in me, dreams of abysses. They are terribly dangerous dreams; as long as they are dreams alone one can fool around with dreaming, because afterwards one forgets. But now, ever since I learned how Promethea brings the fire of all dreams to reality, how she climbs back through the shaft of the Red Cows, how she crosses the Chamber of the Mares, how she goes through every epoch of existence reawakening along the walls of memories of times so fragile and so inflammable and comes out in 1982 still carrying in her hands the primitive spark, I feel myself wavering between exultation and terror. Formerly I too sucked satiny coals. Once I burned my tongue (That only happens if someone makes you lose faith.) Ever since I have no longer dared suck red fire; for a long time I lived on electricity. Yes Promethea is her true name. (1991: 24)

The Book of Promethea is a book about writing the body in which lesbian desire allows a deep meeting between author and subject and even a transference between them. Writing and the body are exchanged and confused: hand to mouth, tongue to fire. Yet it is a fragile moment and a brief epiphany.

I am a little afraid for this book. Because it is a book of love. It is a burning bush. Best to plunge in. Once in the fire one is bathed in sweetness. Honestly: here I am, in it. (1991: 3)

From the Scene of the Unconscious to the Scene of History[101]
The satisfaction Cixous believes she has found in her loving writing of Promethea does not sustain her for long. Although The Book of Promethea is a triumphant love story, Cixous still hears the phone ringing with its insistent echo: Orange/Iran. After writing The Book of Promethea she attempted a very different response to this call and focused her energies on exploring the potential of drama, collaborating with the Theatre du Soleil to produce theatrical presentations of historical events in Cambodia and India. What had been learned in other contexts about respect

101 The title of Cixous' important essay published in English in 1989.

for the subject of writing is no longer an intellectual question causing practical unease. It is a test of the writer who claims the body as her territory.

How to write about those who do not write? We should present ourselves this problem … How to grant oneself the project of writing about the Khmers … How to avoid putting my tongue before their tongue? (1989b: 9)

What Cixous creates in these plays is not political theatre in the familiar sense of the word. It is not an attempt to convey a radical message. If it were, some of Cixous' characters would prove very strange instruments for agit-prop and some of her judgements either hopelessly naive or irresponsibly negative. It nevertheless is political writing in a new way – albeit one Cixous has been reaching towards for many years. The aim is to make room for the other to enter. Cixous takes as her model the actor who empties her- or himself in order to allow the other to 'invade and occupy' (1989b: 13). This time the other is not represented a character or individual but is encountered in movements of peoples across the stage of great events. The dramas thus created have an immense weight to carry and an awkward strangeness to read. Cixous, however, believes that in their collaborative staging they present the author/actor/audience with an opportunity to make a journey of political desire: to move from the scene of theatre to the scene of history.

And this project is another illustration of writing the body. 'Actors write with their bodies', Cixous states, 'I do the same type of thing when I write about others' (in MacGillivray, 1994: xli). In the theatre the movements of the soul express themselves in the body. 'Where does tragedy take place? In the body, in the stomach, in the legs, as we know since the Greek tragedies' (in MacGillivray, 1994: xix). What Cixous has also discovered is that the body she is writing is Shakespeare's body. The body of renaissance drama in which the real and symbolic are once again united as 'the body politic in which the organs are factions, nations, individuals in history' (in MacGillivray, 1994: xix). Writing the body for the theatre is to perform on a public stage the dark miracle of reviving the dead. Cixous first wrote because of the pain of individual bereavement. Now she has let the aching loss of whole peoples enter her narratives. Her father returns to her as legion.

He comes back to help me open the book of the theatre. The dead in flesh and blood, this was my childhood dream as I fought against the misery of the unclothed bones. The theatre makes our most archaic desires come true. (1989b: 14)

Cixous' writing for the theatre opened up for her what Catherine MacGillivray describes as a new epic 'genre and a refocused inscription of her political commitment' (1994: xi). This change can be very clearly seen in Cixous' epic prose poem *Manna: to the Mandelstams to the Mandelas* (1994a). This focuses upon the respective relationships between Nelson and Zami (Winnie) Mandela and the Russian poets Osip and Nadezhda Mandelstam. The two women characters,

Zami and Nadezhda, become new ciphers for the woman who writes her body. The text moves between these central figures in an echoing of sounds ('manna', 'amande', 'amandla', 'Mandela', 'Mandelstam') and an echoing of circumstances. Both couples see their love swept up in a tragic tide of historical events. Yet their loving is part of history and has had its impact upon it. Both men are imprisoned (enwombed) and both women are pregnant with loss. Zami carries Nelson's absence 'on her back in the Xhosa way as though absence were their child' (1994a: 67).

In this context jouissance is felt as a bliss that is agony. The inside is no longer figured as nourishing darkness. It is a prison cell, it is hell – but remains womb as well. The fruit is an almond (amande). This represents the mother's nourishment and the man's seed. It binds shell and inside, darkness and light: 'In the bitter kernel the milk seed' (1994a: 241). The hunger of desire no longer feeds itself on the pleasure of writing but upon manna – a strange dry substance long taken as a symbol for language, a food for exiles that is both words and flesh.

Cixous presents Zami's 'writing' as a mystical work. She struggles to compose the permitted letters of exactly five hundred words that send life to Nelson in prison. Using an image drawn from Jewish mysticism, each letter becomes a promise, revelation and deception. In each letter there is 'the music of all spheres – if you are musician enough' (1994a: 230).

The writing of Nadezhda is also presented in mystical imagery. Osip dies in exile but returns to his wife in a dream and recites to her his last poem. She carries it in her body and in her own writing out into the world where it is set free like a flock of birds. The final lines speak a famous mystery.

> Sea gulls rejoicing in their pasture were fluttering and diving, etching
> the water with pale lips and sparkling signs ...
> And nothing will have been lost. (1994a: 254)

Whoever wants to write must be able to read
In following the trajectory of Cixous' creative writing from *To Live the Orange* to *Manna* it is possible to discern a deepening faith. The excessive jouissance of writing becomes transformed into a love/lack:

Writing is in the end only an *anti-oubli* ... of remembering what has never existed, remembering what could disappear, what could be put off limits, killed, scorned, remembering the far off, minimal things, turtles, ants, grandmothers, the good, first and burning passion, women, nomadic peoples, peoples who are exiled little by little, flights of wild ducks. (1989b: 7)

In reflecting upon this spiritual journey, in a number of essays and articles published shortly after *Manna*, Cixous makes very clear that her own journey in writing has been a quest in which a number of 'spiritual guides' (1997: 26) have played significant roles. She owes a peculiar debt to Lispector. But in her own reading, and in the lively atmosphere of her seminar discussions, Cixous has walked alongside other creative writers who have made the passageway to the inside, to the heart of the fruit, in the most appalling historical circumstances.

One of these guides is Etty Hillesum, whose war journals (1998 [1981]) Cixous discovered shortly after their publication in the early 1980s and brought into her seminar discussions. Hillesum was an ecstatic lover of the body, of beauty, of poetry, of God. What is most remarkable and significant to Cixous is that her delight in all of these endured through the Nazi occupation of the Netherlands, her removal to a transit camp and the final journey to Auschwitz. Etty Hillesum packed her volume of Rilke into the small rucksack she carried with her into exile, 'It is the best one can hope from poetry that it will serve in the face of death. Etty read Rilke right up to death' (1989b: 6). Cixous had wondered whether the avowal of life in writing could survive this supreme test. 'I wondered what would become of this in the concentration camp, when there is really every reason, every circumstance to be without hope' (1997: 27). She finds in Hillesum's writing confirmation of her own trembling faith.

The next question Cixous asks is, could this experience itself, Etty on board the packed cattle truck, Stalin's great terrors, the killing fields of Cambodia, could this become poetry? Her readings in Russian literature convince her that it could. She recounts this narrative of the poet Akhmatova — whose first husband was killed and whose second husband and son suffered greatly in exile:

She used to stand in line outside the prisons of Leningrad … suddenly a faceless woman turns back towards her because the woman with no face in front of her tells her: Akhmatova, the great poetess is standing behind you. And the faceless woman asks: could you know how to describe this. Akhmatova responded: yes. She did a little of what Etty Hillesum did with Rilke. Yes, she could know how to describe the indescribable, she would know how to give the gift of recognition to these people who had become faceless as the result of the greatest misery. (1989b: 8)

And if such horrors can become poetry how are we to understand this writing? Paul Celan is the guide Cixous chooses here. Celan does not offer words of hope or encouragement. There is no optimistic story that can be shared of his personal triumph over circumstances, but only the melody he has left us. His poetry in German is music of unbearable beauty to Cixous: [102]

That had to be written. God had provided otherwise a pain would have died unsung … So a Celan had been created for singing, his mouth full of earth under the century's cleaver; under the pickaxe, the only tiny slip of fleshly paper that will succeed in escaping the shovel of the Apocalypse. (1998a: 8–9)

In the company of Hillesum, Akhmatova, Celan and others — always with Lispector — Cixous no longer asks if this love of writing is 'political too'. She has

---

102 That beautiful poetry can emerge from the experience of the Nazi persecution was an issue that deeply troubled Celan himself and with which he wrestled in his later writing. Cixous does not address this problem in depth and it could be argued that she exploits the work of Celan inappropriately because of this.

achieved the confidence to claim the vocation of poets as watchers and witnesses (1997: 6).

The distant, foreign, insufficient witnesses of non witnesses... It seemed to me that we have a duty to act as reverberators by writing the history of this century's pain and sorrow. (1998b: 36)

Activism is necessary, as is stubborn resistance and political wisdom, but to the poet is delegated the responsibility of writing pain in the only way it can be written. The literature of testimony functions through the metamorphosis of art.[103] In response to human agony there can only be either silence or art, because the extremity of another's pain cannot be expressed as if the conventions of the real world remained unchallenged. Of course remaining silent avoids the risk of abusing and misrepresenting the other, and feminist theologians who have learned the hard way not to speak on behalf of others or claim another's experience as their own have been particularly circumspect in recent years. However, the innocence of silence is denied to the watcher who has become a witness. She must always risk the blasphemy of putting the metaphor in the place of suffering.

We must go to Auschwitz or to what remains of the Cambodian charnel-houses and wrap ourselves up in meditation upon these remains. But this is without language, obviously it is done in silence and it isn't art. Once there is art, of whatever kind, there is metaphor and language is already metaphor ... the word placing itself on what would otherwise be only silence and death. This is a huge problem, it is the problem of the poet. Can a poet permit him- or herself, and does she have the strength to speak about that which has been reduced to silence? Wouldn't this be blasphemy? Isn't it a necessity? Isn't this exactly what we must attempt to do, knowing all the while the paradox. Knowing there is a price to be paid on both sides: something is lost but something is safeguarded. This is the question I am always asking myself. My choice has been made, after all I have decided to try to speak about what takes our breath away. Because more than anything else I am suspicious of silence. (in MacGillivray, 1994: xlix-l)

Writing as child

The book of chronicles

Cixous is one of the few women writers to have engaged in public debates as to whether poetry can be written 'after Auschwitz'. The question is itself a scandal and any answer will inevitably be blasphemous, but Cixous takes the risk of breaking the silence with writing. What is surprising is that after having engaged with the biggest questions of all she returns in her later texts to the intimate metaphors of maternity to explore the work of writing. Why should Cixous at this point of her journey now make repeated references to domestic and primal

103 See pp. 31–36.

relations? Why does Cixous in her latest work frequently employ the metaphor of writing as child?

The child image is a ubiquitous one. It is a familiar means of signalling hope in survival and regeneration. It is also commonplace for a book to be seen as its author's baby – a precious work brought to independent existence. Nor is it unusual to describe the author as the 'mother' of 'her' creation. Many male writers have seen themselves in a quasi-maternal relation to their texts (see Walker, 1998: 65). Is Cixous simply employing this well-worn trope to signal that she feels a strong attachment to her writing and hopes that it will contribute to a brighter future? Or is she making a cyclical return to the imagery of her earliest work, in which the maternal relation is presented as a vital source of creativity in women, stimulating them to write with milk-white ink (1989a). Given the deepening vision we have noted it would seem unlikely that any of these comfortable images are what is being put into play here. Cixous has sought to make herself the chronicler of griefs and is now quite well aware that 'sometimes the milk is black' (1993: 78).

As usual when reading Cixous, it is important to understand that this metaphor is one that functions at many levels. First 'writing as child' has to be seen in relation to the personal history with which Cixous always resources her writing. She is elegising her own child lost in infancy, contemplating the mortality of her own mother and celebrating the adult relation with her daughter. 'Garden moments in springtime – my mother, my daughter and I, in the garden we engender ourselves reciprocally' (1998b: 146). These relations are poignant because they are already passing beyond reach. Mother-daughter stories in her recent texts are compounded with small family narratives, photographs, lists of births and deaths in which Cixous tabulates her genealogy in notes like these:

Sarah KLEIN   Died in c.c.
——— COHEN   Liska, Rumania – died in c.c.
1 son, Isodore, married, daughter in Tel Aviv.

Marcus KLEIN   8 years in South Africa, died in c.c.
Married and lived in Velky-Meder, 4–5 children, all died in c.c.

Schamschi KLEIN   Died in c.c.
Olga SCHLESINGER   Died in c.c.
Lived in Tyrnau, 5 daughters, all died in c.c. (Cixous and Gruber, 1997: 194)

What we are presented with in these scraps of memories, photographs and family trees is a vivid tableau in which the living and the dead children are tumbled together in the text as in Cixous' experience. Cixous is trying to locate herself in the book of chronicles, and we can expect that the understanding of writing as child encompasses the sense of a genealogy marked by absence as well as flourishing. These brutal erasures are the birth-marks of writing.

The Changeling Child

The image of writing as child returns us to the central theme of Cixous' work, and that is that writing belongs to the body, but not only to the body in its procreative power. In another extended prose poem, *First Days of the Year* (1998a), Cixous repeats the conflation of womb and tomb to describe her own birth as an author out of her father's death:

The author was born from my ashes. From the incombustible anger amid my ashes. I fell into the secret's tomb …

Fountains, doves, coolness in the midst of flames, come to me. In my womb a birth is gently born. (1998a: 52)

The image of writing born out of ashes is then amplified in curious, funny and violent metaphors in which the author conceives and simultaneously aborts a child, or bears a precious child and then mislays it.

The child cannot be born, does not want to be born. We are stunned at having forgotten a child. What is forgotten? The child in the room next door? How can one forget-expect a baby? … Forgettings baby has not been fed … The idea of going to find the dead child is unfaceable. The face of the dead baby, our hunger, our forgetting. (1998a: 137)

But then if the mother does return, perhaps the child is not dead at all but armed and dangerous? 'The child smiles broadly baring all its teeth' (1998a: 137).

These children that the author bears and loses are strange children, dream children, their begetting is not within the author's control. The author is not a good mother, her teats are quite black (1998: 24), but she cannot prevent her profligate procreation.

[If] on my dress there are traces of birdlime, of sperm, of blond adopted children's diarrhoea. I rip my dress off, if on my dress is one of those children I carry without noticing, one of those tiny green parasites clamped to my white skirt with its ivy fingers, I seek to detach it so as to place it on the ground … There will be enough left all the same, I say, and I rip off my parasited dress. Ah! The babies: at ninety years old I will still find some stuck to my wall. (1998a: 66)

These are surreal pictures that Cixous does not attempt to cleanse but presents still damp from the womb/tomb. Their abnormalites are what is most compelling. They strip away the romance from the maternal relation and present a disturbing picture of the author and her texts. As well as strange images drawn from her own dreams and nightmares Cixous employs archetypal images of the strange child from literature, religion and everyday life to deepen her reflections on this theme.

The folk image of the changeling, or foundling, is explored. This is the child who is always much stronger than we are. 'We don't know where they come from. The child adopts us' (1993: 78). This child does not love but is fiercely loved. It is Heathcliff. 'A stiff, black, withdrawn, silent savage who looks on love with an appalling look' (1998b: 89). Cixous uses the metaphor of the cruel seduction of the foundling to describe the strange process of exchange between the author and writing which is equivalent to that between the parent and the stranger-child. In conventional terms the parent creates the child who remains dependent upon the continuing existence of its carer to survive. In this reverse economy the child creates the parent who is in terror at the abysmal love/loss that is represented in this unexpected gift.

In her novel *Deluge* (1992) Cixous gives the child who is writing a name – Isaac.[104] The name of a child who springs from the desert and from laughter. The most beloved who also ruptures relations (Sarah/Hagar, Sarah/Abraham,[105] Abraham/God). This splitting apart is a 'great threat ... it engenders all sorts of forms of death, of denial, of repression, of flight, of anguish' (Cixous and Gruber, 1997: 94) in human relationships. Writing again appears as the child that destroys faith as well as being the fulfilment of faith's covenant.

Writing as daughter

But perhaps the most compelling name of all for the strange child, 'writing', is daughter. For Cixous in the mother/daughter relationship which is 'the most intense relationship, the closest as far as the body is concerned – unheard-of things can occur that can never exist in everyday life, which are the very secret of our lives' (1993: 89). The mother-daughter relation, which Irigaray has argued is made invisible by patriarchy (see Walker, 1998: 159–175), is here presented as the most sacred and most mysterious analogy for writing. It is not because the mother and daughter are fused, lacking identity (as is taken to be the case in some schools of psychoanalysis), but rather because they are surprising strangers to each other that the relationship is so significant.

I do not recognize her, my child even, I do not recognize her. The benediction is to be able to say to the beloved ... Faithfully from the first minute I haven't ceased not understanding you with amazement. (1998b: 80)[106]

Like the daughter, writing is the familiar strange beloved and also, like the daughter, writing represents life and death in one mysterious form. A rediscovery of the work of Hannah Arendt has led to the concept of natality being celebrated in the work of contemporary religious feminists. This stands as a very welcome contradiction to the focus upon mortality which, it is argued, has dominated Western theology (see Jantzen, 1998: 128–155). Cixous, however, always

---

104 'I love "Isaac": it is the name I have given my love, so he can have a name. Because if I say simply, "I love to write", that's not it. It is such a mystery. I's the other. It is not I' (Cixous, in Cixous and Gruber, 1997: 92).

105 According to many traditional interpretations of the story of Isaac, Sarah never forgave her husband's willingness to slay her son.

106 There are many interesting correspondences and differences between Cixous' understanding of the mother/daughter relation and Levinas' meditations on the relationship of the father and the son. Unfortunately a discussion of these themes lies beyond the scope of this text.

emphasises that there is no birth that is not also death. This is not primarily because we are brought close to our own mortality when giving birth but rather because we are forced to contemplate the mortality of the beloved child: 'as soon as I love death is there, it camps right out in the middle of my body, getting mixed up with my food' (1998b: 86). Referring to Lispector, who was conceived in the mistaken belief that a pregnancy might cure her dying mother, Cixous reflects that there is always 'a tied and nonuntiable relation of birth and death between mother and daughter ... It is enough for us to have a child to know the link with life and death' (1993: 72). However, this is a joyful as well as a tragic fact. Bound together as they are, mother and daughter continually engender each other as they pass through the waters of life and death.

We are familiar with the fact that mother-daughter relations have been neglected or sentimentalised and that the mother-son relation is often regarded as a site of dangerous intensity. However, Cixous' reflections on the passions of the mother for her daughter open up a world of loving and losing according to a different economy. It is not absence and lack which issue in language here but the vitality of difference which issues in love, 'that love is dreadful. As dreadful and desirable as God' (Cixous, in Cixous and Gruber, 1997: 113). Writing as daughter is the incarnation of this dreadful love.

Not a person — not a home

Through the many maternal images in her later work, Cixous defamiliarises us with writing and presents it back to us as a wild child, the body's treasure and the token of mortality.

This development does not represent a betrayal of her former concerns, but is an intensely condensed symbol of her passion for writing. This passion is a dangerous one. We are not to imagine ourselves safe in the world of writing. Quoting Kafka, Cixous states that a book should be like an axe to the frozen sea inside us (1993: 17). It should shatter our everyday assumptions and present us with a terrifying epiphany:

The unveiling, the staggering vision of the construction we are, the tiny and great lies, the small nontruths we must have incessantly woven to be able to prepare our brother's dinner and cook for our children. An unveiling that only happens by surprise, by accident, and with a brutality that shatters: under the blow of the truth, the eggshell we are breaks. (1993: 63)

Literature in this frame is not good bedtime reading. It does not imprint a friendly human face on hostile circumstances. Nor is it a place of shelter from the tragic events of history. 'A book does not have a head and feet. It does not have a front door' (1998b: 145), Cixous tells us. She thus encourages the feminist religious reader to espouse a less conventional relation to women's writing than has been customary in the past. We are not to settle down here and live comfortable, orderly lives. She requires us to love literature not for the stability and succour it brings but for the yearning it creates for the other.

Cixous' work is vivid, intense and passionate. The brightness of her writing, however, should not blind us to a number of troubling questions which lie at the heart of her writing project and which are serious enough to disturb even the most sympathetic reader. Does Cixous faithfully represent the other in her writing? Does the desire she has to be attentive to the particularity of the other actually result in work which preserves the integrity of her subjects? How are we to judge the authenticity of the voice that she gives to the silenced? Does she even present the testimony of her own witnesses with fidelity?

Hillesum, Celan and others are called upon to confirm Cixous' faith in poesis as a witness to human suffering. However, their own views on this subject were deeply ambivalent.[107] Furthermore, Cixous is a theoretically sophisticated and deeply metaphorical writer. Her work is difficult to read. Is the cruel suffering of those who do not speak to be entrusted to writing that some of her critics would describe as obscure, indulgent and inaccessible? The very literary form that Cixous employs demonstrates how the author must mutate her subjects, and does this process render their 'being in themselves' irretrievable to the reader?

In Cixous' defence, these are questions which she herself voices at many points throughout her work. In similar forms they haunt all creative, critical and theoretical writing. There is no innocence here for any of us. Rather than innocence, Cixous affirms faith. Faith in writing, in literature, as a divine force that transforms the political into the holy and discerns within human suffering the mysteries that beat in the heart of the world.

107 Celan was particularly concerned about the morality of creating beauty out of horror and Hillesum's diary is a testament to doubt and despair as well as hope and faith.

CHAPTER 8

An open conclusion

And if literature is still a girl ...

This book began by interrogating the relations between literature and theology as they are presented in contemporary theological thinking. I demonstrated that this interdisciplinary encounter has been constructed as a gendered relationship in which literature has functioned as the subordinated feminine term. I then argued that if 'literature is a girl' this no longer implies a continuing hierarchical relationship between the disciplines. Both feminist politics and poststructuralist theory have alerted us to the disruptive potential of the repressed feminine partner within the binary system which characterises Western culture. There is now instability in the coupling of literature and theology, which reflects a changing social and symbolic order.

Religious feminists have been quick to recognise that women's literature can be strategically placed in opposition to the paternal authority of religious, tradition, and this creative move has been of decisive significance in the development of feminist theology – as my readings of Christ, Ostriker, Cannon and Sands make clear. Yet there has remained a reluctance to engage with poststructuralist theory when reading women's literature and I believe that this has prevented religious feminists from discerning the radical role that literature can play in relation to the continuing development of feminist theology.

Those theologians (usually male theologians)[108] who have welcomed the new dimensions that poststructuralism brings to the encounter between literature and theology have argued that traditional characterisations of the relations between the disciplines have bound the energies of literature to the service of theology. They have asserted that this has conservative religious and social consequences. Instead of the theological critique or annexation of literature, they advocate a new practice 'religious reading'. This takes place beyond the influence of magisterial authority, on the liminal boundaries of the theological tradition. Through

---

108 For men have less to lose than women when concepts of authorship, interpretation and identity are contested by poststructuralist thought (see chapter 4).

religious reading theology is provoked and challenged by an encounter with an other which it is unable to discipline or assimilate.

These theologians have not been reluctant to follow the conventions of post-structuralism in casually ascribing a feminine identity to those forces which dispute logocentric authority. However, there has been little in their work that explores the significance of gender further and I have noted the conspicuous failure to engage with the important work of women poststructuralist theorists. My own close readings of the work of Kristeva, Irigaray and Cixous have demonstrated that these women point towards ways in which the traditionally gendered relationship between literature and theology can be reinscribed and re-visioned. From their work we can begin to construct an agenda for feminist religious reading that takes us beyond the conventions that now regulate the uses of literature in feminist theology and into a wilder and more dangerous place.

Literature at last

For feminist religious reading begins when the dangerous power of literature is recognised and affirmed.

We are now moving beyond a lamp-lit scene in which story books are innocently taken down from the shelves and inspiring passages diligently inscribed within our theological texts. Through reading Kristeva, Irigaray and Cixous we learn to see 'feminine' literature as black fire, molten lava, the 'incandescence of imaginary space ... challeng[ing] the place of the sacred' (Kristeva, 1995: 187). Literature is presented here as having the potential to overwhelm the conventional world and its good, old God. Literature, in this frame, refers beyond itself to all that the symbolic order is unable to regulate and control. However, it assumes this role because it is the clearest manifestation of, to quote again from Kristeva, an 'embodied imagination: that is to say ... a space where words and their dark, unconscious manifestations contribute to the weaving of the world's unbroken flesh' (1993b: 5). These powerful words affirm the deep connection between literature and the unspeakable, often tragic, mysteries of existence which achieve their incarnation through metaphoric utterance.

To view literature in this way is unfamiliar to English-speaking feminists, and yet women authors have long asserted their sense that writing is a very risky activity and that the creation of literature entails the destruction of the everyday world. The poet H.D. vividly describes how human beings wish to live safe in the small houses they have built for warmth and shelter.

Each comfortable little home shelters a comfortable little soul – and the wall at the back shuts out any communication with the world beyond.
Man's (sic) chief concern is keeping his little house warm and making his little wall strong ...
Outside is a great vineyard and grapes and rioting and madness and dangers. It is very dangerous. (1988: 96)

To create literature is to abandon these dwellings. Cixous expresses similar sentiments when she forcefully reminds us that a book is not a refuge, is not a home: 'a book does not have a front door' (1998b: 145).

Similar views of literature can be found in the work of male writers. In particular, Paul Ricoeur has drawn attention to literature as the dangerous space in which new worlds are imagined and the world as it is stands confronted by the world as it might become. But the particular force with which literature is opposed to the logocentric disciplines of theology and philosophy in the work of women theorists owes much to the way they have redeployed the gendered terms conventionally used to describe the relationship between literature and theology in new and powerfully evocative ways.

Kristeva, Irigaray and Cixous are not content to show that the logocentric disciplines exalt the abstract, rational and universal masculine above the embodied, located and contingent feminine. They also name theology and philosophy as sites where the feminine is feared, abjected and annihilated. In differing ways they expose the extreme gynophobia of the symbolic system and make clear that what presents itself as a question of custom and convention, i.e. language use, also in fact represents the continuing power men exercise over women.

Having shown how theology excludes the feminine they all then present the active power of the female imaginary contending against this exclusion. Both Kristeva and Cixous explicitly name literature as the site of feminine revolt. Although this is a heuristic device it also signifies the potential that literary and artistic works do possess to affect political change and challenge our understanding of the sacred. In my estimation Cixous is the theorist who most deeply and persuasively expresses the challenge that literature/writing poses to logocentric authority. In her work we initially see literature characterised as a feisty and excessive female force that is mounting a sexual challenge to the powers that be. In her later writing literature becomes a sacred embodiment of unbearable beauty and extreme pain. It becomes the power of remembrance and the guardian of hope: 'religious writing'.

The way we read now

It is tempting to stop writing at this point, because if there is one thing I wish this book to accomplish it is to challenge religious feminists to admit the importance of literature and allow its dangerous power to infect feminist theological thinking. I want us to leave home and walk around in the wild places exploring all that can be experienced there. I want us to read more widely, all sorts of books, including those we have previously dismissed as indulgent, difficult or strange. I also want us to read books written by men. I have no desire to present certain texts or authors as more valuable than others, or to lay out a new set of rules that govern the way feminist religious readers approach the books that fascinate and inspire them. However, I do believe that bringing the insights of Kristeva, Irigaray and Cixous to bear on the way in which we read literature will result in certain shifts in focus and perspective that will provoke changes in the way we read now. And some of these are significant enough to merit re-empha-sising here.

To begin with, the strong attachment of contemporary theologians (including feminist theologians) to realist literature should now be called into question. We may wish to apply our 'hermeneutics of suspicion' to the fact that contempo-rary theology (including feminist theology) shows a strong preference for this particular genre. Feminist religious readers will wish to ask whether there is an implicit understanding of God and the world that lies behind this literary prefer-ence and, if so, is this one which we would wish to buy into? We may also wish to question the dominant, if unstated, assumption that the apparent veracity of realism represents the only way of writing literature that is sufficiently trust-worthy to carry the precious burden of women's pain and women's aspirations.

Kristeva has encouraged us to see realism as perhaps the literary form *least* able to embody revolution within language. Irigaray has demonstrated that the 'real world' is in fact the world of the male imaginary and that the female imaginary breaking into signification will sound strange, or even 'unreal', in the beginning. Cixous has repeatedly asserted that realism holds together a world built upon the denial and the forgetting of lost things. For her poesis, putting the metaphor in the place of suffering, is the means through which literature fulfils its sacred function, and she regards it as a political necessity to write in ways that are at odds with the realist conventions that sustain our common-sense world.

It is unlikely, however, that these objections to realism will result in religious feminists setting aside their favourite books, embroidered around the everyday lives of women, and turning instead to slim volumes of experimental poetry. Nor should they, of course. What is at stake, rather, is the recognition that realism is a literary genre – a way of writing fiction. This we might begin to affirm while contesting the tendency within poststructuralism to regard this form of writing as inherently conservative. Indeed, when we recognise that realism invites us to inhabit a fictional world, we may discover that some of our most well-known and well-loved realist novels are haunted by uncanny presences we have previously discounted or ignored. We may also begin to feel less suspicious of other literary genres and concede that they are able to embody and express important concerns relating to women that cannot be accommodated in this particular literary form. Moving beyond realism does not only entail reading complex books without decent plots. Romance, gothic horror and detective fiction are forms of writing that women have made particularly their own. It should be enjoyable as well as creative to bring these neglected texts into relationship with feminist theology.

Another significant challenge raised by reading the work of Kristeva, Irigaray

and Cixous is: do we dare to allow our overriding interest in the content of literary texts to be modified by an equal concern for form? Instead of always asking 'What is this woman saying?', we might begin by asking instead 'Why is this being said in this way?' We have already discussed the importance of genre, but form also relates to language use, symbolism, metaphors, literary tropes and devices, intertextual references, rhythm, rhyme, fragmentation of the text, adherence to or rejection of grammatical conventions, neologisms etc. Together these make up the body of the text, and they matter. For example, religious feminists might find there is more of theological interest in the fact that P.L. Travers used the very familiar devices of children's literature to create a counter-world of domestic female magical power during the depression and war years than in an analysis of the characters and actions of Mary Poppins and Mr Banks. Or they might discover that the poet H.D.'s autobiography *The Gift* (1984), written during the London Blitz, is theologically significant, not principally because of the life events it records but rather because it experiments with the intertextual use of ancient myths and Mennonite traditions. It is unusual and valuable because it incorporates mystical visions within the autobiographical form and uses an authorial voice that brings the child's perspectives to the centre of the adult world.

Of course male authors use similar devices to women to create works of literature, and Kristeva has argued that when they write in ways that disrupt normal signifying patterns they can also be seen as opposing the power of the paternal symbolic order. This is a point that some feminists would wish to contest – although personally I think that religious feminists would find much of theological value in engaging with literature written by men as well as women. What is more to the point here is that there are some ways that we can identify in which women do shape their texts using stylistic and symbolic devices that are less frequently found in the work of men, and these will be of particular interest to the feminist religious reader.

One of these (which has been an important feature of feminist literary studies since the pioneering days of gynocriticsm) is the way that women writers understands authorship. Because it has not proved straightforward for women to assume the role of author (see pp. 37–38, 50–51 and 88–90) they developed many creative strategies to turn their 'anxiety of authorship' to literary advantage. And each of the women theorists we have studied has also made her own specific contribution to deconstructing the authorial role. Kristeva's early work on Bakhtin contributed greatly to the development of thinking upon intertextuality – a way of understanding the nature of literary texts that displaces the author's authority. Some of Irigaray's most powerful writing consists of actively deauthorising canonical texts. Cixous, in particular, has actively sought ways of writing in which she places the woman writer in an accountable relationship with her characters and readers. Feminist religious readers will be sensitive to the theological significance of these experiments with authorship. They have direct

171

implications for the way we understand divine creativity and point towards ways of understanding the world, not as a book written by God but rather as something more like the sacred palimpsest to which H.D. repeatedly refers in her writing or even the 'unwritten book' which she places in the hands of the divine lady in *Trilogy* (1983: 57).[109]

As well as a different approach to authorship, we might expect to find in women's writing an alternative range of symbols and metaphors drawn from their particular way of being in the world. Once again this issue is something which has been of interest to feminist literary critics for many years – as my discussion of Ostriker's creative work on this theme demonstrates. However, the women poststructuralist theorists go beyond suggesting that female bodily experience will give rise to embodied imagery that will resource their writing. As we have seen Kristeva, Irigaray assert that the cultural order is a system of representations based upon the male body and that cultural change is bound up with women finding their own body, home and place within language – although each would have different ideas about how this transformation might be achieved. The revolutionary power that they accord to the female body coming into language is based on their analysis of the immense effort that supports her current exclusion. Irigaray is perhaps the most utopian in her thinking on this issue. She offers an alternative morphology drawn from the female body and claims that when this body comes into language women will not only transform culture but approach the threshold of the divine.

So feminist religious readers will be sensitive to the way in which women writers employ imagery drawn from female embodiment in their writing – according this a great deal more significance than it was formerly accorded. And yet, like Patricia Yaeger, they will probably wish to argue that Kristeva, Irigaray and Cixous are not pointing to a world that is to come. Women writers have been developing a sublime aesthetic based upon the female body for many years. Although she is a sympathetic reader of 'French feminism' Yaeger writes

The French feminist writers whose utopian projects I have outlined make a similar mistake. In omitting the practices of real historical women from their analyses of women's writing they remain blind to what has actually happened in women's texts[110] – to the seriously playful emancipatory strategies that women writers have invented to challenge and change the tradition. (1988: 20)

Feminist religious readers will be likely to concur with her argument that in order to anticipate the changes that may be wrought through the writing of the future 'we must be permitted to see its features in the writing of the past' (1988: 16). They may welcome the new political and theological focus that

109 She carries a book but it is not the tome of the ancient wisdom 'the pages, I imagine, are the blank pages / of the unwritten volume of the new ...'
110 Although this charge could more reasonably be sustained against Irigaray and Kristeva than Cixous.

poststructuralism has undoubtedly brought to the analysis of the importance of female morphology in women's writing. However, they will wish to return to beloved texts and explore these in the light of the new insights they have gained (see Stockton, 1994).

And so to bed ... with a good book!

I have highlighted a number of issues that I believe will characterise feminist religious reading. The most important of these is a re-evaluation of the significance of literary texts and their power to challenge theological thinking. I have also mentioned some shifts in attention that will affect our literary perspective. I have envisioned a new willingness to engage with many different genres, including not only the 'difficult' works of clever men but also the feminised genres of romance, gothic horror and detective fiction. The importance of form as well as content has been stressed and the need to understand, in particular, the significance of the way in which female authorship is portrayed and the importance of gendered morphology in women's creative writing. This is my list of particular concerns. No doubt other feminist religious readers would wish to add their own points to this checklist. I hope this book will serve as an open invitation for other women to bring many differing perspectives to their theological engagements with literature.

The last thing to say is that all I have written about the relations between literature and theology springs from a deep concern for both disciplines. Although in this work I have contended on behalf of literature as a feminine voice I do not imagine literature and theology in perpetual conflict. I cherish the vision of a threshold of love and desire where the two disciplines meet and embrace, where they come to themselves through the other. This threshold is not some distant point out there, or yet to be discovered. We make this place of meeting ourselves. We can arrive at that holy place of 'cosmic and aesthetic generation' (Irigaray 1993a: 150) each time we open a book and read.

Reading Elizabeth Smart

Returning to the beginning

This has been a book full of long words and complicated arguments. It has been helpful, I hope, in clarifying some issues and demonstrating that literary theory itself can sometimes be evocative, beautiful and fascinating. But! I have travelled a long way from the point where Christ and Plaskow passionately proclaimed a new relationship between women's literature and feminist theology;[111] when they fell in love with the writing of Doris Lessing.

This sense of being in love with women authors and their writing has continued within feminist theology to the present day. Despite the criticisms and frustrations that I have expressed in this work concerning the current uses of literature within feminist theology it is this passion that has kept the relationship alive. Whatever forms of feminist religious reading develop in the future I trust that they will continue to be marked by pleasure and desire. With this hope, and as a sign of my conviction that whatever theoretical paths we follow they should always lead us back to literature again, I offer at the close of this book my own 'religious reading' of the work of Elizabeth Smart – an author with whom I have been in love for many years.

I am playing in this space. I do not intend what follows to serve as a pattern or template that other religious feminists should follow. There should never be a 'correct' way of reading literature – just lots of good and interesting ones. Nevertheless, I would claim that the new agenda for reading that I have set out in this book frees me to bring the work of Smart into dialogue with feminist theology. For it must be admitted that she is a very unsuitable author for a feminist to fall in love with. Delicious as her writing is, she has certainly not produced a body literature that appears compatible with the feminist project. Both the content and the style of her writing are problematic. The topics addressed in her texts seem intensely personal and apolitical, and her privileged social status cannot provide her with the credentials that would justify the interest of feminist readers eager

111 See pages 42–43.

to reclaim marginalised women's voices. She explores traditional feminine roles and relations, writing as a mistress, a mother and a daughter. She writes about situations of ambiguity and constraint and is not free from personal fears or social prejudices. She does not provide in herself, or in those she writes about, role models for women to follow into a more liberated future. Furthermore, Smart writes in a fragmented and non-realist style and agonises over the work of writing rather than using writing in the service of some cause or project. The metaphors through which she explores the divine cannot easily or comfortably be judged, according to the dominant criteria of feminist theology, as supporting the project of women's emancipation. So Smart is my disreputable love. An author whose work I am reading with an imagination schooled through an encounter with feminist poststructuralism and in the conviction that her work has a great deal to contribute to feminist theology.

Smart's writing life

Because Elizabeth Smart constructed most of her work from material first written in her journals it will be helpful to present a brief chronological account of her life as an aid to understanding her texts. She also had an interesting life which, in itself, represents a story worth telling.

Smart was born in Ottawa in 1913. Her family was wealthy, widely travelled and interested in the arts. Smart's mother, Louie, was a powerful and attractive woman who suffered from extreme passions. Her 'hysteria' threw the life of the household into frequent turmoil. From childhood Smart had an intense preoccupation with babies and children, and in a fantasy life centred upon her own maternity sought to deal with the traumas which had swept across her early years.

Smart was a very beautiful woman and enjoyed all the pleasures of her social position. In painful tension with this enjoyment was her determination to be creative and to pursue achievements requiring personal mortification and intense self-discipline. Initially she strove to become a professional musician she then travelled the world as companion to a 'lady reformer'. She eventually turned to writing and to motherhood as occupations demanding complete dedication and a high degree of sacrifice.

In her early twenties, as Smart divided her time between studies in music and literature and social life in London and Canada, she came to know significant political actors. But, although she was friendly with public figures engaged in left-wing politics (e.g. Sir Stafford Cripps, Barbara Castle and Michael Foot), she never felt attracted to their activist solutions to social problems – or their preference for the useful over the beautiful.

In the years immediately preceding the Second World War, Smart became emotionally distant from her Canadian family and sought the company of artists

175

and writers in Europe and America. She was intimate with a community of surre-alist painters and poets – becoming the lover of the artist Jean Varda. In Mexico (where she lived just in the period leading up to the surrealist exhibition) she had a brief but wild affair with Alice Paalen, a poet and the wife of the artist Wolfgang Paalen. When war broke out her Bohemian circle became tortured by feelings of responsibility about the conflict in Europe. Smart distrusted these sentiments and was disgusted with the jingoism of her Canadian family and distanced herself from their influence.

In the early 1940s Smart became involved in a love affair with the English poet George Barker. Smart's fascination with Barker had begun several years earlier when, upon reading a volume of his poetry and checking the brief biographical data on the back cover, she had decided that he was the one she would marry and raise children with. She was shocked to discover later that Barker already had a wife, but still believed that there had to be an intense relationship of some kind between herself and the man whose use of language so well represented her poetic ideal.

Barker's status as a British non-combatant resident in the United States made him the target of official surveillance. His marriage to Jessica brought the adul-terous couple into conflict with statutes designed to prevent immorality. Despite his involvement with Smart, Barker continued to spend time with Jessica and did not leave his wife when Smart gave birth to their child. In 1943, pregnant once more, Smart decided to leave Barker and travelled to England. He followed her shortly afterwards.

The years that followed saw no resolution of the relationship with Barker. Reflections on this turbulent love affair provide the loose narrative structure of Smart's most famous work, By Grand Central Station I Sat Down and Wept. This was published in 1945 just before the birth of her third child. The couple were even-tually to have four children and Smart shouldered the responsibility for their upbringing alone. She had to work extremely hard to maintain her family and her journalistic career (Homes and Gardens not The New Statesman) and this led to difficult periods of separation from her children.

The 1950s and 1960s were years of juggling with many demands and coping with feelings of exhaustion. She did not find an easy balance between mothering and writing and had to cope with the intense frustration at never being able adequately to focus upon one area of her life. Her journals are full of painful reflections about her sense of having gifts that could not be used and love that has been wasted.

In 1970 Smart retired to the country hoping to take up her writing career once more. However, her youngest daughter, Rose, was now seriously addicted to drugs and Smart had to take frequent responsibility for caring for her grand-children. She achieved some recognition and fame at last with the republication of By Grand Central Station. In 1977 a small book of her poetry appeared in print. In

1978 her second prose work, *The Assumption of the Rogues and Rascals*, was published. This draws upon material composed in the difficult years during which her passion for Barker ebbed and she struggled to provide for her children.

In 1982 Smart's daughter, Rose, died from paracetamol poisoning. This event overshadowed the last and most difficult period of Smart's writing life in which she struggled to give form to what she called the 'mother book'. This project first germinated out of her intense relationship with Alice Paalen in 1939. However, she had never been able to distil her initial writings on this theme into a coherent text and the effort to do so after the death of Rose became unbearable. Eventually Smart abandoned her hopes for the 'mother book'.

In 1984, with the help of Canadian academic Alice Van Wart, Smart published *In the Meantime*. This combines 1940s fragments of 'the mother book' (titled 'Let Us Dig a Grave and Bury our Mother'), some unpublished poems and her later reflections on struggles with the mother theme and the work of writing. Smart died in London in 1986 and two selections from her journals, *Necessary Secrets* (1992b) and *On the Side of the Angels* (1994), planned by Smart and edited by Van Wart, were published posthumously. Her poems were issued in one volume in 1992.

Writing from a small room

Because feminist theological readings of women's writing have tended to focus upon narrative content I will concentrate in my reading of Smart's work largely upon the relatively neglected questions of form and begin by exploring the textual construction of her three major works *By Grand Central Station* (1992a [1945]), *The Assumption of the Rogues and Rascals* (1991 [1978]), and *In the Meantime* (1984).

Smart began writing as a child and sought advice from a number of authors as to the best way to develop her talents. She was advised to keep a journal and took this advice very seriously. She kept a writer's diary from her teenage years to the end of her life. In adolescence she enjoyed the indulgence of a private space in which to express hopes, fears and yearnings. In her early twenties the journals became a site of more experimental writing; they contain reflections upon her reading and the minute details of her everyday life. Despite the scope they offered her to 'try out' different styles and voices she regards her journalling as second-order writing. The journals provided opportunity to practise writing in the same way as she routinely practised the piano. They did not fulfil her literary ambitions.

Each bit could be so much better, if I sat and thought and turned it over before I wrote. But it is a diary.
It is preparation.
I feel I could do so much better. I feel I am not doing my best. (1992b: 177)

Smart's sense of dissatisfaction grew as she struggled to find a medium through which to express herself. The panoramic plots associated with nineteenth-century novels were rejected. Poems and short fragments seemed best suited to the intensity she wished to convey; but even these were founded upon conventions she found frustrating. Smart had yet to discover a form in which to express herself.

I do not want, I am irritated with the devious method and hidden indirectness of the novel, for instance, or even the short story or a play. Poems, notes, diaries, letters, or prose such as *House of Incest*, in *The Black Book*, only meet my need.

Yet would I not be happy to make a book like *Green Mansions* or *Wuthering Heights*, *The Waves*, or *Tess of the D'Urbervilles*? Well, yes. But when I think of things I want to say, I cannot think of that way of saying them. The fierce impart things, drawn over this huge irrelevant skeleton. But what form? Infinite pains for a poem. But I need a new form even for a poem. I have used up my ones. Tricks begin to slouch about. Each word must rip virgin ground. No past effort must ease the new birth. Rather than that, the haphazard note, the unborn child, the bottled embryo. (1992b: 217)

Eventually it was the journals she had disparaged which provided the key to attaining the intense yet varied form she desired. In their pages she was able to move between genres and speak in a variety of voices. Passages from her voluminous notes were re-assembled and reconfigured into what Smart referred to as her 'prose works', choosing this general epithet in order to distinguish them from more easily categorised forms of literature.

Critical writing on Smart has tended to see the creation of a distinctive form, the novel-journal, as one of her most significant achievements. Dee Horne, for example, writes: 'Smart creates an experimental novel – a novel-journal – which bears some resemblance to established forms ... but is a powerful and unique artistic vision' (1991: 143). The journal-novel is applauded as a form of writing true to women's lives and bearing the imprint of the social, historical and material conditions of its production (see, for example, Nancy Wright, 1992/93: 15).

What such critical appraisals overlook, however, is that Smart did not simply edit her work and rearrange it. It is rather that she compressed her many pages of notes into small spaces, very slim books indeed, in order to achieve the force she required from her writing. It is this sense of compression and constraint that gives her texts their power (she used the metaphor of the black hole towards the end of her life to describe the nature of creative energy, 1984: 140). For Smart the physical symbol of writing compressed into a small space complements the verbal images she employs to describe the conditions under which her prose works are produced.

In *By Grand Central Station* the narrator makes a distinction between the space she enjoyed before meeting her lover (the Californian Big Sur; long, lazy, empty days; the Canadian wilderness) and the conditions of her life after she begins her love affair. The most powerful image of her loss of freedom is found in a passage in which the narrator is imprisoned on immorality charges. It contains the evocative line: 'I sat in a little room with barred windows while they typed' (1992a: 47). While she is locked up the men outside produce pages and pages, copy after copy, of the details of her sexual life. In contrast to these her cell is adorned by tiny marks, etchings made on the stone wall by a prisoner writing with a pin (1992a: 48). I find this one of the most powerful evocations of the constraints experienced by women writers. Other metaphors of the small compressed space from which she writes complement this image. The prison room recalls the hotel rooms where she endlessly awaits her lover (1992a: 81). It evokes the parental home where she returns as a prodigal daughter and a court-house where her morals are placed on trial (1992a: 61). It is significant that the title she chooses for her work recalls Psalm 137, the famous psalm of exile in which captives sing songs out of their bondage.

Smart employed a similar compressed form of writing in her second prose work, The Assumption of the Rogues and Rascals (1991). Against the advice of critics, who suggested that if she wanted to succeed as a writer she should broaden her vision, she insisted upon focusing intently upon her own condition of confine-ment and presenting it in a form appropriate to its effect upon her. Notes written by Smart during the preparation of her work show how she sought to distil her writing into a powerful essence.

It is false and ridiculous to listen to fools advising me to think of other people and their positions, to invent characters and imaginary towns and situations for them. I don't want the scope of the world laid out like the largest newspaper, no, but squeezed dry and com-pressed and reduced to its minimum but most potent. (in Sullivan, 1992: 330)

Once again the compressed textual form works together with the metaphors employed in the text. Powerful images in this work are 'confinement' in the labour ward and the corresponding confinement of the 'labourer' in the endless drudgery of housework/office work/caring work – the many activities which prevent a space being found for writing. Instead of being a grand adventure, human life is pictured as a desperate scramble to send a small 'precious package through the post' (1994: 73). The package is a baby, a book, or even the body of the narrator travelling between its birth and death, tightly wrapped and bound.

Smart's final work is In the Meantime (1984). It is a larger book than these others but it is made up of small and broken pieces. Although connections between the fragments of the text must be made by the reader, underlying the symbolics is a connection between the place of birth and the place of death. The work begins with Smart's attempts to explore the relationship with her mother, to bring her mother into her womb (1984: 92). It ends after she has entombed her own daughter (1984: 111–12). The 'little space' in this text is both the womb and the grave. It is also the bounded space of growth and decay that is a garden: the Garden. The narrator mourns the Rose she has returned to the earth and considers how she has raked up her own life to make a seedbed (1984: 15). Her final verdict upon her own achievement recalls the poppy, the flower of death and dreaming which lifts the senses to heaven.

Better get in touch with Heaven, again …
Little drops – of blood?
Think of the opium poppy, wounded, scratched, oozing its white then black blood, scraped off in tiny harvests. (1984: 158)

In a similar manner to Cixous she affirms the courage of the woman writer who has struggled to attain the power to focus upon the source of knowledge: 'Gazing on one tree, one apple' (1984: 155).

Smart's choice of distinctive shape for her work represents in textual form the situation of constraint in which she finds herself as a woman and a writer. Working together with imagery in her texts it produces writing of penetrating effect:

Sometimes a shaft of pain comes out of a tree for no reason at all. Sharp, diagonal, sudden out of a landscape, it finds the vulnerable bit to pierce into. (1991: 112)

Of particular interest for the feminist religious reader is how it also generates a distinctive form of sublime discourse. When narratives of everyday life are presented in Smart's work they are crushed into crystal. Yaeger (1989: 191–212) explores the way the sublime is used in women's writing and talks about a prosody of transcendence produced in a different key (1989: 199). The key Smart plays upon is a life which is both confined and creative. It could be described as a 'domestic sublime':

And Henry Vaughan, that dear beauteous jewel says: 'Keep clean, bear fruit and wait.'
This seems to cover housework, childbirth and sainthood. (1991: 21)

It gathers up all the commonplace matters of existence and irradiates it with energy:

All the paraphernalia of existence, all my sad companions of these last twenty years, the pots and pans in Mrs Wurtle's kitchen, ribbons of streets, wilted geraniums, thin children's legs, all the world solicits me with joy, leaps at me electrically, claiming its birth at last. (1992a: 40)

The sublimation process retains the directly referential language of realist fiction, for example 'wilted geraniums' and 'pots and pans', but transforms the objects referred to into strange and holy shapes. Again, like Cixous, Smart believes that when the world is met with attention to the particularity of its forms it emits the faint scent of transcendence:

Cut down the wild prickly roses little by little.
The pathos of the silver teapot.
If I could show – *explain*; what? The good, the glory, the splendour, the greatness, the beauty, the beneficence.

The essence. (A tinge of vanilla here, all the words are dusty, cobwebby, unworthy. A bird's song never has this outworn air, is never liable to misinterpretation – provokes no malice.) *Keep small. Keep the perfect drop in mind.* (1984: 158, my emphasis)

The author's voices

As I stated earlier, her journals gave Smart the opportunity to employ different genres and voices. Within them she is able to move easily between light descriptive passages and pages dense with symbolism. They provide her with the opportunity to become dialogical with herself and allow her to converse with the texts of other writers.

All these features are carried over into her prose works. The narrators in these texts are able to express contradictory emotions and present differing accounts of the same events. This is a very effective rhetorical device. For example, the ending of By Grand Central Station moves easily between tragic and ironically humorous prose. This prevents tragedy from having quite the last word and raises the faint hope that love will wake again. Similarly, in The Assumption of the Rogues and Rascals, Smart alternately pictures her state as wretched and beatified without choosing either state as a true description. Her strategy is similar to Irigaray's in that she is able to assume differing positions without giving one priority over the rest. She shows a similar awareness to Kristeva of the many voices in dialogue within the divided subject.

Smart also carries into her prose works the conversations with other writers. It is a sad fact that Smart's beauty and her lifestyle have lead her to be frequently cast as the 'dumb blonde' of the literary world. It is astounding that most of Smart's critics (and even some of her close friends, see David Gascoyne, 1992: 9–17) viewed her prose works as simple love stories fashioned out of her own experience. As Brigid Brophy points out in her 'Introduction' to the Paladin edition of By Grand Central Station (1992: 7–13), this tendency ignores the fact that the work draws upon an immense variety of literary sources which are deeply integrated into the text. It is Smart's skill that her highly intertextual writing deepens the account of a woman's love of life itself – what we are presented with is far from a simple woman's account of her grand passion.

Although Smart adopts various voices and genres her texts do not read as bricolages of discordant effects. They are made coherent by the adoption of a particular narrative stance within each work. An authorial position is chosen and this determines which voices and genres are called into play. The authorial positions Smart experiments with are ones that are uncommon – even in women's writing.

In By Grand Central Station the authorial position is that of the 'woman lover'. This is, as Irigaray points out (1993a: 193), quite different from that of the female beloved. The prose work contains some of the most powerful accounts of 181 female desire to be found in literature. Smart offers vivid descriptions of what the untranslatable word 'jouissance' is used to convey:

I am over-run, jungled in my bed, I am invested with a menagerie of desires; my heart is eaten by a dove, a cat scrambles in my sex ...
I am shot through with wounds which have eyes that see a world all sorrow, always to be, panoramic and unhealable, and mouths that hang unspeakable in the sky of blood. (1992a: 23)

The woman lover speaks with a number of voices within the text. For example, when Smart evokes Psalm 137 it is as a means of suggesting that she sings her song out of bondage. The end of the same psalm, however, also refers to the 'daughter of Babylon' who will see her babies dashed upon the rocks. Smart uses both of these positions in her discourse. The narrator is both the suffering victim of those who deny love and the adulterous maternal whore of Babylon engulfed in devastation.

The Song of Songs is also an important intertextual reference within this work. Its dialogical love lyrics structure the central portion of the text. It is a feature of this biblical love song that the voices within the text, and particularly those of the male and female lover, are difficult to distinguish. I have argued elsewhere that the Song of Songs offers images of the disintegration of the subject and the binary categories of gender definition:

The lovers frequently eat each other, pass into each other and an illustration of this is the fact that scholars have disagreed over which lover is speaking when. It is hard to identify the point at which one voice stops and another takes up the same theme in echo, reminiscence and submersion. (Walton, 1994: 34)

Smart makes a similar assault upon these psychological and sexual conventions in her narrative. The confusion and disintegration of identities she envisages are described in this important passage where the narrator meditates upon her own many different faces and the reflection of her image in her lover:

The mirror is the best breeder. On lucky nights it returned me my face as if it were bestowing a proud honour: this is the face that launched a thousand nights of love ...
But sometimes, alone, it caught my eyes like two butterflies on pins ... The sight of that mad face in the half-lit room drove me to prayers and loud noise. Your own shadow meeting you announces the end ...
But again and again when I peer in the mirror to find a distortion of my own image which would make my pain into a bearable legend, that form bends over me in embrace forever. (1992a: 81–82)

In *The Assumption of the Rogues and Rascals* Smart also assumes another unusual authorial stance for a woman – that of witness. The work is written as a *testimony* or a *testament*. It is a testimony to those things not normally regarded as significant. It is a testament in the sense of a balancing of the accounts, an assessment of what endures from the labours of a lifetime. Such memorials and calculations have rarely been made of women's lives. As Irigaray has argued, what has been assumed to be important is the ground they provide for the generation and nurturing of others. They have rarely risen from this imminence to become visible to themselves or to each other by inscribing their own monuments (1993a: 66). Engulfed in bitter depression as her dreams of love with Barker faded, Smart recorded in her journal:

I have children but I have ceased to care about anything. I have no personal ambition … Nor do I have use for sensation. Nor do I care. Cessation. It is a technical circling, encir-cling cycle of giving the body to be burned, but having no charity. (1994: 15)

Yet although there no longer seemed any chance of escaping from this vegetative state and fulfilling her literary ambitions there remained the obligation to testify to her blank, aching life:

And yet I must put it down because of all the other drowning women to whom no one has ever thought it worthwhile to speak, or to whom no one would speak. (1994: 17)

Shoshona Felman argues that 'texts that testify do not simply record facts but, in different ways, encounter – and make us encounter – strangeness' (1992: 7). This is why literature can often communicate agonies that are unreportable without symbolic mediation. It is also necessary to make strange, rather than report real-istically, happenings which appear too commonplace to merit their own memo-rials. The poet Sylvia Plath 'makes strange' her own depression at confinement through the use of holocaust imagery (see, for example, 1981: 244–247). Smart continues to use her 'domestic sublime' to testify to her predicament. In contrast to Plath she assumes neither a heroic nor martyred stance:

I am, after all, just a woman in a fish queue with her bit of wrapping paper waiting for her turn. (1991: 10)

I am a woman of 31½ with lice in her hair and a faithless lover. (1991: 33)

Despite her unglamorous position she testifies to the painful epiphanies she has witnessed, to everyday 'Assumptions'.

All right. I accept. The price of life is pain, since the price of comfort is death and damna-tion. Histrionics are not necessary. Nothing specific is necessary. Not even one rogue with any particular name. Not one rascal.
Now, on the train, returning, the rogue with bleary eyes has a halo because he says, 'Have a brandy. Here is my address'. A sunburnt family offers me apples from their bundles. I am poor. I am rich. The bare bone is sweet.
Victoria Station is golden and anonymous. Angels cavort in the rafters. Loiterers lean like a Botticelli chorus by the ham-roll counter with their tea. (1991: 43)

Smart intersects her narrator's voice with those of other women who live common, blasted but glorious lives. These resonances heighten the effect of her testimony. From among the babbling chorus of women whose words bleed away like miscarriages or after births she is driven to turn her blood into writing, 'Driven to drivel, driven to dribble ... signs of parturition' (1991: 102). Her voice rises above the rest:

But where, woman, wailing above your station, is it you want to go to, get to, accomplish, communicate? Can't you be satisfied with such pain, such babies, such balancing?
No, No. There is the blood flecked urge to go even a step further.
Above the laughter, above the miseries, above the clatter of glasses and the cries of children, I hear a voice saying: Isn't there some statement you would like to make?... Is it all to be wasted? All blasted? What about that pricey pain? (1991: 57)

It would seem strange to argue that such a deeply wounded and broken text as In the Meantime also has a distinctive authorial position. What, however, joins the fragments in this text is attention to the voice of that which lies beyond the threshold of speech. The narrator tries to hear, and to speak, the underwater world, the dream world, the world of hallucination and womb talk. This is the world of the dead and the unborn, and it is also particularly the world of women.

The work begins:

I am 63, the happiest person in the world.
But I still cry out at night heard through the house, through several walls, still wrestling with infantile anguishes and anxieties.
'Mother! Mother! Mother!'
It makes a rude intrusion into the pleasant sleep of the dinner guests; it jolts the nerves of the deeply sleeping drinkers: an involuntary inhospitality.
'Mother! Mother! Mother!'
Desolate. Eery. Desperate. (1984: 7)

In the pages that follow Smart makes many attempts to describe her experience of a bodily mystery that is almost beyond words.

The moon forces my mouth open and enters me as I lay shaking in the brittle beige grass. Like a baby forcing the womb open, its electric globe forces open my mouth. It is in me. Then I notice how each single star in that enormous wideness has pinned me here and there so my blood is gathered in points. So I am strung on a clothes line sagging where there are no stars ...
I am hiding something. Did you know? Why am I hiding it? It is not shame nor even a sacred secretiveness. It is something only the body's language can say, oiled by the source-less tides of mysterious passion. The mind's surveys, measurements, calculations never know anything. (1984: 70–71)

Smart's writing in passages such as these carries many resemblances to Cixous' attempts to write the body. It also recalls Kristeva's fascination with the semiotic and the place of terror and ecstasy beyond language. Like Kristeva, Smart expresses the conviction that it is through art that these inexpressible places are given a form. Poetic language is a special medium of communication, 'a meaningful scream/between folded womb and grave' (1984: 28).

The final part of *In the Meantime* is entitled 'Diary of a Blockage'. It not only records Smart's personal struggles to write her 'mother book', it also makes this the metaphor for the journey writers must make to 'a terrible place' (1984: 132) in order to bring back some knowledge of its mystery. 'Art, for a little while, gives it a shape, celebrates its beauty, articulates its pain, puts its tears to use' (1984: 152). However this voyage is extremely difficult to make: 'no! no! I can't, don't make me! I'm frightened! It hurts' (1984: 153). Smart offers her narrator as a very unlikely traveller to this underworld. In her idiosyncratic domestic sublime she describes a grandmother, a raunchy old woman ('legs in Air/Never a care', 1984: 149), taking little pills and frequent drinks to help her on her 'trip' into the dark world where she attains her mystic's vision.

> If only one could always be a sharp vibrating, functioning instrument! But even *domestic energy* goes wrong, trips out, and this is much more complicated. (1984: 148, my emphasis)

In this section I have attempted to show how Smart adopts various authorial locations in order to explore themes rarely expressed in male-centred culture. These authorial positions are never monological. The conversational style of her journalling is intensified in her prose works. The use of a variety of authorial positions in seeking a woman's writing voice is similar to the strategies employed by both Cixous and Irigaray. Her concern to communicate that which strains to be articulated from the just-beyond of language draws her very close to Kristeva.

What is particularly important for the feminist religious reader is that, in making these authorial experiments, Smart makes her personal experience 'strange' in order to communicate, and penetratingly intense rather generally applicable. It is by performing these gestures that she achieves a vision that becomes significant for others. It is Smart's concentrated particularity that is the key to her spirituality. Her writing is intensely personal but not, for that reason to be seen as immature, irrelevant or individualistic. Her own life is offered as a threshold for others to perceive the possibility of making similar journeys.

> Am I really old? Am I really going to die soon?
> Can these things be?
> Have I said I was Here?
> Did you know I loved you? and you? and you? ...
>
> Poor people.
> Still, there's nothing to tell except what this breathing (still) nugget, this going-on person can tell you. What's the use of pretending you know what's going on in other nuggets of life? (1984: 151)

Reading her work encourages sensitivity to a domestic strangeness. It is a writing that polishes commonplace objects so that they shine out with a particularity and vivid intensity. It brings transcendence within the housewife's reach.

185

The body of the poet

The Mexican artist Frida Kahlo made many artistic representations of her own body. It became the instrument through which she registered not only her painful personal history but also the struggles of her colonised country and the repressed memories of its spiritual traditions. Paula Cooey writes that Kahlo,

saw her pain and pleasure, represented by multiple projections of her body, as metaphor for her country in relation to an oppressive neighbour ... Her body projected came to represent many cultural voices in tension with her, holding in common only a detouring of any religious and political tendencies to dematerialise human values. Her images became no longer simulation but flesh itself groaning with value. (1994: 128)

Smart lived in Mexico, among a circle of artists and writers, during the period leading up to the first international exhibition of surrealist art – which was organised by her host Wolfgang Paalen. It would be a massive decontextualisation of Smart's work not to remark upon the close connection she enjoyed over a number of years with surrealist artists and poets. The work of these artists included dislocating and disfiguring conventional images of the body in order to challenge the values associated with these representations.

In a similar manner to Kahlo, Smart presents multiple projections of the female body in all her writings. These are used in symbolic contradiction to the norms of the culture in which she writes. Like the surrealists she makes the body strange. Brigid Brophy describes *By Grand Central Station* as a legend of metamorphoses: 'a metaphor of the very process of metaphor – of, that is, the very process of literary art' (1992: 11). Smart takes her body, with its passions, pregnancies and wounds of abandonment, and uses it as a way of describing what she believes can be achieved through writing in a world that lives according to calculation rather than a passion for mystery. The challenge represented by these 'metamorphoses' is particularly evident in *By Grand Central Station* and the poems Smart wrote during the Second World War.

In a letter written to her daughter during the conflict, Smart's mother, Louie, asked: 'Do you consider your writing is sufficient contribution to a troubled and war torn world? Is there still a reading public for abstract ideas? If so I'm afraid I don't know them' (in Sullivan, 1992: 151–152). Smart's conviction was precisely the opposite of her mother's. She regarded the contribution that writing could make as being particularly important when the bombs were falling. She symbolises this conviction through contrasting the erotic passion of the narrator with the events taking place in the world around her. The fact that a cataclysm is approaching cannot obscure the simple hope she clings to: 'Why should even ten centuries of the world's woe lessen the fact that I love?' (1992a: 80).

Because she 'loves', the narrator believes a chance remains that the world might be healed. In a very similar way to Cixous, Smart takes female jouissance as the symbolic counterforce to the powers of death.

When I saw a horde of cats gathering at a railway terminus to feed on a fish-head thrown near the tracks, I felt, it is the lavishness of my feelings that feeds even the waifs and strays. There are not too many bereaved or wounded but I can comfort them, and those 5,000,000 who never stop dragging their feet around Europe, are not too many or too benighted for me to say, Here's a word of hope, I can spare a whole world for each and every one ...
Set me as a seal upon your heart, as a seal upon thine arm for love is as strong as death. (1992a: 43–44)

Her 'loving' gives the female narrator the power to seek out what she desires even when it lies 'under the Romanian dead' (1992a: 25). Through its power she is able to 'smear corpses with seeds of daffodils' (1992c: 33) Pressing her bodily metaphor further Smart insists that she is pregnant from her loving.

> Hope and Europe die behind your head.
> But I still holding you hold a world
> Ripe with unwritten history, to be beguiled
> And even now big with child. (1992c: 26)

It is important to stress that many of the important passages concerning erotic love and pregnancy in By Grand Central Station were written before Smart even met Barker and many months prior to the conception of her first child. The narrative of a love affair provides the framework for their articulation. It was not the love affair that produced these images. They are metaphorical reflections upon the necessity of keeping another world in view through writing. This is illustrated in the 'pre-Barker' journal passage below – which is one that was later adapted for the prose work. It is a typical example of Smart's reflections upon the coming war and her commitment to cherish an artistic vision despite the approaching cataclysm:

I insist on looking the other way, like the last pregnant woman in a desolated world. It is the vital thing to keep your eyes on the sun, to grow calm, to hang to that hope, to cherish with every ounce of love to be squeezed from the universe, the seed, the frail seed ...
(Cradle the seed, cradle the seed, even in the volcano's mouth.) (1992b: 215)

Smart takes as her motto in By Grand Central Station the phrase from the Song of Songs 'love is as strong as death'. It is her repeatedly sung refrain. What the narrator conceives and carries has the possibility to confound the horrors that surround her.

I can bring forth new worlds in underground shelters while the bombs are dropping above ... and, O, when I do it quietly in the lobby while the conference is going on, a lot of statesmen will emerge twirling their moustaches and see the birth-blood and know they have been foiled.
Love is as strong as death. (1992a: 65–66)

However, despite being a record of faith in 'love', by Grand Central Station is also a tragic text. The narrator perceives that the hope represented by her 'loving' will not be accepted. Her lover cannot be reached by her words, refuses her body. He has swallowed, and now chokes upon, 'the ball of the world spiked where Europe is' (1992a: 107). In his sleep he sees the bird of catastrophe flying: 'Both its wings are lined with the daily paper. Five million other voices are shrieking too. How shall I be heard?' (1992a: 111). Just as the narrator is rejected, so the world emerging from the chaos of war will turn away from the life that might renew it. This does not prevent Smart from continuing to call for re-awakening.

Look at the idiot boy you begot with that night. He is all the world that is left. He is America and better than love. He is civilisation's heir, O you mob, whose actions brought him into being ...
I myself prefer Boulder Dam to Chartres Cathedral. I prefer dogs to children. I prefer corncobs to the genitals of the male. Everything's hotsy-totsy, dandy, everything's OK. It's in the bag. It can't miss.
My dear, my darling, do you hear me where you sleep? (1992a: 112)

It is very hard to read Smart's reflections upon the relationship between politics and art. They appear immoral to post-war sensibilities. The scandal is even greater for the feminist reader because Smart has metamorphosed her convictions into a love story and expressed artistic vision as female sexual desire. There is always something scandalous about making love in a war. The scandal becomes even greater since Smart makes no attempt to excuse or justify her chosen path. She expresses no shame or doubt in her conviction that she possesses the one means to restore to the world what has been violated.

Smart's vision is very similar to Cixous'. It is the mystical notion that the world cannot be renewed unless poetry is able to offer a rose to the dying (see chapter 6). It is the conviction that unless the poet/writer/prophet retains a vision at variance to what is happening in the world then we are all condemned. In Smart's work this variant vision is represented through a woman's body.

> In the Cathedral calm and cold
> Kneel the erroneous-memoried old.
> But in the womb's cathedral calm
> The walls collapse in a birth psalm ...
> And over all the angels dart
> Like squadrons in a war apart
> Dropping parachutes of bliss
> On everything that is. (1992c: 41)

The body of god

In this final section of my reading of Smart's work I shall explore the images of the divine to be discerned through her use of female bodily symbolics.

As a young woman Smart found that her sensual nature was a powerful distraction from her vocation as a writer. She saw writing as a spiritual task, an attempt to form an image, in words, of the Word. This gently ironic poem illustrates her dilemma:

> I'm going to be poet, I said
> But even as I said it I felt the round softness of my breasts ...
> My brain was to be
> A mirror reflecting things cut in eternal rightness
> But before I could chisel the first word of a concrete poem
> My breast fell voluptuously into my hand
> And I remembered I was a woman. (1992b: 70)

In order to fulfil her calling, Smart armed herself to fight against the 'powerful, the irresistible, the compelling monster sex' (1992b: 62). She failed. However, her affairs with Varda and Paalen generated a different understanding of her sexual energy. Through her body she had discovered a new instrument to play on in her writing (1992b: 252). The distinction that she had formerly made between a spiritual world to which the poet seeks admission and the intoxicating world of the flesh fell away: 'it is God. It is sex' (1992b: 183). She no longer asserted the superiority of things 'less inextricably woven with the undiluted flesh' (1992b: 280), but rather sought to achieve a style through which her new understanding of the relation of the body to spirituality might be expressed:

Entering daily and nightly into the body of God, yet unable to do other than suggest -

And now – upwards to that staggering vision. Will I have the courage to raise my eyes? Can I face the things I laboriously flee? (1992b: 187)

Having attained her own vision of a sensible transcendental, a God known in the body, Smart employs this important new understanding in her work. In By Grand Central Station religions of spiritual purity and innocence prove irrelevant to the passion she experiences, 'for now Jesus Christ walks the waters of another planet, bleeding only history from his old wounds' (1992a: 33). The ambiguous, fleshly and bloody, nature of creativity can be embraced. The narrator shrugs of the idea that there has ever been a process of generation without fault or pain. 'Don't think I haven't seen chipmunks' tails abandoned on logs to save their lives, nor gnawed rabbit paws in traps mixed up with the steel' (1992a: 68).

The figures in the love affair confirm this difficult truth. The narrator's rival is innocent but sterile, 'why are her arms so empty' (1992a: 24). The narrator's passion, while described as guilty and even murderous, is also fruitful. Like Eve, the narrator has taken her own apple and abandons Eden for a world of labour and birth pains. As with Eve's action there was never any choice associated with the decision. The desire that impelled the act was overwhelming:

IT is coming. The magnet of its imminent finger draws each hair of my body, the shudder of its approach disintegrates kisses, loses wishes on the disjointed air. The wet hands of the castor-tree at night brush me and I shriek, thinking that at last I am caught up with. The clouds move across the sky heavy and tubular. They gather and I am terror-struck to see them form a long black rainbow out of the mountain and disappear across the sea. The Thing is at hand. There is nothing to do but crouch and receive God's wrath. (1992a: 27)

It is interesting to note that Smart writes in a similar way of being overwhelmed by desire and being compelled to write:

I know I've *heard* the poem. I've felt the WORD
And above all I am aware of the inconvenient gift trapped in my lap. NOT to be ignored.
A sacred duty is not too strong a way to put it. (1994: 107–108)

The relation between the body, writing and God is explored further in *The Assumption of the Rogues and Rascals*. The later work takes the rising and the falling of generations rather than eros as its central theme:

Erotics are far from those parts that now strain like Hercules in labours almost more than they can bear. They are at work. THIS IS WORK. Serious, gigantic, absolute. All other occupations seem flibbertigibbet by comparison with the act of birth …
But celebrate! Celebrate! Celebrate!
It is not too much to bear a womb. (1991: 28–29)

A God beyond the body is irrelevant to this work. He stands by 'like a husband at a birth' and a 'rough woman' commands this birthing process (1991: 28). In passages such as these Smart is reaching towards some way of articulating an understanding of the divine in a female form. In observing this process, a spiritual journey which she made largely alone, the reasons for Smart's adoption of a 'domestic sublime' begin to become much clearer.

It initially appears strange that, as a sensual young woman whose privileged and Bohemian background kept her far from household chores, Smart used imagery connected with this limited female sphere of life to explore the divine. Even in early texts she is 'strung on a clothes line' (1984: 70) by mystery and witnesses an epiphany among 'pots and pans' (1992a: 40). In *The Assumption of the Rogues and Rascals*, as she is beginning to explore the umbilical threads that still tie her to her mother, she presents a strange dream sequence which defies straightforward interpretation but points towards a poetic elision between the domestic world and an ambivalent maternal presence that dwells within it:

A strange dream happens, and keeps happening when times are worse.
There was a small domestic castle, brushed over with pale orange plaster inside, with small unsteady spiral staircases of stone leading down to cellars that were happy, but full of lonely anguish …
I tried to hurry down the worn steps to the cellar to rescue that lost child, sobbing forsakenly, but the cry came from an unidentifiable spot.
A weak quiet light started through the small top windows, sunken in the massive walls: a peaceful promise from the contented past, like a wild rose in a disused lane.
O Mother, this body is your house, inconsolable, anguished, dark, mysterious and happy.
If I can bear this onrush, this excruciating pain and ecstatic fear, it will be a castle I can

hold. Would I dare then, in the face of a naked mystery, to sweep those stairs and put up gingham curtains. Knit bootees to avoid awe. (1991: 87–88)

It seems that passages such as this hold the key to Smart's preferred mode of sublime discourse. Her sublime is 'domestic' because her vision of the divine is maternal.

Smart devoted the last years of her literary career to exploring the maternal connection: 'my mother – this mystery that pursues me' (1984: 52). As a young writer Smart believed she had come to some reconciliation with the mixture of horror and attraction her mother represented for her through her relationship with Alice Paalen (named Ruth in In the Meantime). In embracing another woman, whose misery and need recalled Louie's, Smart thought she had put the intense emotions of her childhood behind her.

Ruth, Ruth. I will be your mother. And with consoling kisses receive again my mother from your lips. Not to her womb again but she into mine. I am hiding the thing that haunts me in my womb. But my womb is as large and as forgiving as the world. I walk complete and free, the giver of life. (1984: 92)

In later years Smart recognised that while her mother might be 'in her womb' this meant that the same destructive and creative forces known in her child-hood continued to be imprinted on her own relationships. As she now was both mother and daughter and knew there could be no escape from the 'messy, living, terrible, excruciating reality' (1994: 101) of being forever umbilically bound and forever abandoned. The wailing of an old woman for her mother in dreams becomes a pathetic night-time echo of Smart's daylight mourning for her daughter. Smart wrestles to write about the dark uncomfortable, too close and too distant force of the maternal. Towards the end of her life Smart pictures this as a terrible power that condenses the relationship between the generations into one cry of love/loss and compels them into history:

Oh but we were so. We were all-in-all to each other. A total understanding.
'Mum? Mum?' I heard the young woman cry out in her sleep.
Forty years later the cry is worse, more agonised, bereft ...
Collapsed in on themselves (but is collapsed the word?) and condensed to a millionth fraction of their former selves; but powerful, drawing in with overwhelming suction, and able to give out HOLY energy? (1994: 133)

Smart never managed to express her meditations on the mother theme in a way that she found adequate. In the end what was published in In the Meantime was a record of her failure to write this mystery. However, I see her creation of intensely compressed prose works, her domestic sublime and even the jouissance of By Grand Central Station as evidence of the influence throughout her work of this sacred relation. The 'rough woman' who forms the writer's body as 'the perish-able instrument through which all work and visions have to trickle' (1991: 90) is a compelling image of God. This God is both intimate and absent, tenderly

191

loving and destructive. Although God may be far removed she is never further away than the threshold. Smart places God at the opening of the womb.

Love as strong as death

My reading of Smart has shown how works of literature which are very different from those normally read by feminist theologians can yield significant and challenging insights. Smart shows women grappling with powerful constraints and achieving some moments of triumph and many of pain. She causes us to question whether it is possible, or even desirable, to escape from the cultural conditions through which identity is formed. Instead of encouraging us with visions of a transformed horizon she points us towards what Butler describes as the 'difficult labor of forging a future from resources inevitably impure' (1993: 24). We are offered an alternative image of emancipation, one which Yaeger describes as 'an explosive protest brought about by a split subject who simultaneously gives into and resists the burden' (1988: 252).

Smart also presents forms of sublime discourse and images of the divine which are troubling for feminist theologians. While the jouissance of *By Grand Central Station* may be applauded as a vivid expression of female power, the use of a 'domestic sublime' and an ambivalent maternal divine are less easy to accommodate. Smart's writing confronts the reader with the 'messy, living, terrible, excruciating reality' of God. Many religious feminists have taken maternal images of the divine as an affirmation of female identity and 'connectedness' to spiritual power. Smart, like Kristeva, emphasises the mystery and discomfort that lurks within the maternal relation. For them it is a site of bliss *and* terror; the threshold of the Other that can never adequately be spoken. Such a divine could never be co-opted into the service of a particular cause or project but is capable of generating the constant challenge and energy of alterity which resists totalising systems and keeps faith emerging in new forms.

Smart's 'perishable instrument' for exploring transcendent realms is her own body. In her later work this body is generally rooted in the domestic home and garden. Just as Irigaray enjoys playing the philosopher's wife, Smart seems to find pleasure in portraying a harassed mother who is also the interpreter of life's mysteries. It is clear that Smart does not wish to escape from the material realities of living to some disembodied spiritual place. It is rather that through attention to the body, love/death/birth, an ambivalent future is kept open. The next generation are emerging through this threshold to play in the beautiful garden/graveyard:

And what will the rose and the briar tell my sister's children playing near the grave? It pricks my hand, the pretty flower. Of a rose is all my song.
But what did they kill each other for? How should I know my little Wilhelmine? It is the language of love which nobody understands. It is the first cry of my never-to-be-born child. Go into the garden, for your apples are ripe. (1992a: 112)

It would be foolish to argue that Smart has a concealed political agenda within her work. What can be said is that she takes human pain and social injustice with the greatest seriousness but believes that solutions cannot be found to end the cycle of violence through conventional means. Smart pursues an alternative artistic/mystical vision. As a writer, she was not alone in choosing this path. Other women, like H.D. (1983) and Virginia Woolf (1990 [1941]), were exploring similar concerns in the midst of war. They too make a symbolic contradiction between a specifically feminine alternative vision and the conflict in which they are engulfed. These writers anticipate the work of radical feminists and feminist poststructuralists who have used the symbol of sexual difference as a means to envisage a radically different cultural order (see Walton, 2002). Feminist theology has much to gain from taking the opportunity to explore the potential of such thinking in greater depth through cultivating renewed interest in the work of visionary women writers.

In a short war-time verse entitled 'Political Poem', Smart imagines Engels and Christ attempting to span a bridge over chaos to prove 'there is remedy in recipe and design'. Their efforts are watched by the dead, whose pains defy this attempt at healing. Two lines are particularly significant:

But the wound, the wound mocks louder and the germ's why
Rises to encourage the cradle to become the tomb. (1992c: 40)

In Smart's symbolic world the wound refers simultaneously to the marks of war, the umbilical wounds and also the wound of her sex. The germ is both that which destroys the flesh and the seed of life. Smart conveys how the cradle and the grave are metamorphosed one to the other. While the chaos cannot be spanned without mocking the dead we are nevertheless led to consider that a secret life might be concealed even in the wound/the germ, something strangely resilient that the designers are unable to engineer.

My reading of the work of Elizabeth Smart does not lead me to believe that feminist theologians should turn away from political visions, but rather to affirm that these are always held in tension with what Smart refers to as an 'unresolvement' beyond our control. If we lose this sense of an awkward and demanding alterity we are in danger of replicating the totalising politics we struggle against. Our political designs must remain provisional in the face of life's tragedies. We must remember that we construct our solutions in the presence of the dead. There will be times when we must admit our helpless inadequacy in the face of the suffering we encounter. Instead of blind political optimism, alternative resources must be sought. We will need the vision of those who have tended other gardens to sustain us.

Smart stands at the threshold of the garden and seduces us with a 'vivid, unforgettable, leaping, hope' (1994: 148).

References

Abrams, Meyer Howard, Adams, Robert and Daiches, David (eds) (1974) *The Norton Anthology of English Literature.* New York: W.W. Norton.

Adams, Richard (1974) *Watership Down.* Harmondsworth: Penguin.

Albrecht, Gloria (1995) *The Character of Our Communities.* Nashville: Abingdon Press.

Allison, Dorothy (1992) *Bastard out of Carolina.* New York: Penguin Books.

Altizer, Thomas (1990) *Genesis and Apocalypse: A Theological Voyage toward Authentic Christianity.* Louisville, Ky: Westminster/John Knox Press.

Anderson, Pamela Sue (1996) 'Wrestling with Strangers: Julia Kristeva and Paul Ricoeur on the Other', in A. Jasper and A. G. Hunter (eds), *Talking It Over: Perspectives on Women and Religion.* Glasgow: St Mungo Press, pp. 129–149.

—— (1997) 'Julia Kristeva (b.1930): Introduction', in G. Ward (ed.), *The Postmodern God: A Theological Reader.* Oxford: Blackwell, pp. 215–223.

—— (1998) *A Feminist Philosophy of Religion.* Oxford: Blackwell.

Antze, Paul and Lambek, Michael (eds) (1996a) *Tense Past: Cultural Essays in Trauma and Memory.* London: Routledge.

Antze, Paul and Lambek, Michael (1996b) 'Introduction: Forecasting Memory', in P. Antze and M. Lambeck (eds), *Tense Past: Cultural Essays in Trauma and Memory,* London: Routledge, pp. xi–xxxviii.

Arnold, Matthew (1974 [1853]) 'Dover Beach', in M.H. Abrams, R. Adams and D. Daiches (eds), *The Norton Anthology of English Literature.* New York: W.W. Norton, pp. 1355–1356.

Atwood, Margaret (1972) *Surfacing.* Toronto: McClelland and Stewart.

Auerbach, Erich (1953) *Mimesis: The Representation of Reality in Western Literature.* Princeton: Princeton University Press.

Bal, Mieke (1985) 'Sexuality, Sin and Sorrow', *Poetics Today,* 6, pp. 21–42.

—— (1987) *Lethal Love: Feminist Literary Readings of Biblical Love Stories.* Bloomington: Indiana University Press.

—— (1989) *Anti-Covenant – Counter Reading Women's Lives in the Hebrew Bible.* Columbia/Sheffield: Almond.

—— (1991) *Reading Rembrandt.* Cambridge: Cambridge University Press.

Barth, Karl (1977) *The Epistle to the Romans,* tr. E. Hoskyns. Oxford: Oxford University Press.

Barthes, Roland (1977 [1968]) 'The Death of the Author', in R. Barthes, *Image, Music, Text.* London: Fontana, pp. 142–149.

Bataille, Georges (1985) *Literature and Evil.* New York: Marion Boyars.

Battersby, Christine (1989) *Gender and Genius.* London: The Women's Press.

194

Bauer, Dale and McKinstry, Susan (1991) *Feminism, Bakhtin and the Dialogic.* Albany: State University of New York Press.

Bell, Roseann, *et al.* (eds) (1979) *Sturdy Black Bridges.* New York: Anchor Books.

Belsey, Catherine (1994) *Desire: Love Stories in Western Culture.* Oxford: Blackwell.

Belsey, Catherine and Moore, Jane (eds) (1989) *The Feminist Reader.* London: Macmillan.

Benedict, Ruth (1935) *Patterns of Culture.* London: Routledge Kegan Paul.

Benjamin, Walter (1973 [1940]) *Illuminations,* ed. H. Arendt. London: Fontana/Collins, pp. 255–266.

Berry, Phillipa and Wernick, Andrew (eds) (1992) *Shadow of Spirit: Postmodernism and Religion.* London: Routledge.

Blanchot, Maurice (1995) *The Writing of the Disaster,* tr. A. Smock. Lincoln: University of Nebraska Press.

Bloom, Harold (1973) *The Anxiety of Influence.* Oxford: Oxford University Press.

Bons-Storm, Riet (1996) *The Invisible Woman: Listening to Women's Silences in Pastoral Care and Counselling.* Nashville: Abingdon Press.

Boyce Davies, Caroline (1994) *Black Women, Writing and Identity.* London: Routledge.

Braidotti, Rosi (1991) *Patterns of Dissonance: A Study of Women in Contemporary Philosophy.* Cambridge: Polity.

—— (1994) *Nomadic Subjects: Embodiment and Sexual Difference in Contemporary Feminist Thought.* New York: Columbia University Press.

Bronfen, Elizabeth (1992) *Over Her Dead Body: Death, Femininity and the Aesthetic.* Manchester: Manchester University Press.

Brophy, Brigid (1992) 'Foreword', in E. Smart, *By Grand Central Station I Sat Down and Wept.* London: Flamingo, pp. 7–13.

Bruce, Gregory (1994) 'Textuality and Community: Giving Beyond Death', in D. Jasper and M. Ledbetter (eds), *In Good Company: Essays in Honour of Robert Detweiler.* Atlanta: Scholars Press, pp. 93–119.

Budick, Sanford and Iser, Wolfgang (1989) *Languages of the Unsayable: The Play of Negativity in Literature and Literary Theory.* New York: Columbia University Press.

Burgher, Mary (1979) 'Images of Self and Race in the Autobiographies of Black Women', in R. Bell, *et al.* (eds), *Sturdy Black Bridges.* New York: Anchor Books, pp. 111–123.

Burke, Caroline, Schor, Naomi and Whitford, Margaret (eds) (1994) *Engaging with Irigaray: Feminist Philosophy and Modern European Thought.* New York: Columbia University Press.

Butler, Judith (1990) *Gender Trouble and the Subversion of Identity.* London: Routledge.

—— (1993) *Bodies that Matter: On the Discursive Limits of Sex.* London: Routledge.

Cameron, Deborah (ed.) (1990) *The Feminist Critique of Language: A Reader.* London: Routledge.

Cannon, Katie (1988) *Black Womanist Ethics.* Atlanta: Scholars Press.

—— (1989) 'Moral Wisdom in the Black Women's Literary Tradition', in C. Christ and J. Plaskow, *Weaving the Visions: New Patterns in Feminist Spirituality.* New York: Harper Collins, pp. 281–292.

Caputo, John (1993) *Against Ethics.* Bloomington: Indiana University Press.

Cargas, Henry J. (1976) *Henry James Cargas in Conversation with Elie Wiesel.* New York: Paulist Press.

Carpentier, Martha (1998) *Ritual, Myth and the Modernist Text.* Amsterdam: Gordon and Breach.

Cavarero, Adriana (2000) *Relating Narratives: Storytelling and Selfhood.* London: Routledge.

Celan, Paul (1978 [1960]) 'The Meridian', *The Chicago Review,* 29: 3, pp. 29–40.

Chanter, Tina (1993) 'Kristeva's Politics of Change: Tracking Essentialism with the Help of a Sex/Gender Map', in K. Oliver (ed.), *Ethics Politics and Difference in Julia Kristeva's Writing*. London: Routledge, pp. 179–195.

—— (1995) *Ethics of Eros: Irigaray's Rewriting of the Philosophers*. London: Routledge.

Chopin, Kate (1972 [1899]) *The Awakening*. New York: Avo Books.

Chopp, Rebecca (1989) *The Power to Speak: Feminism, Language, God*. New York: Crossroad.

—— (1993) 'From Patriarchy into Freedom', in S. M. Simonaitiz, S. St. Ville and M. Kim (eds), *Transfigurations: Theology and the French Feminists*. Minneapolis: Fortress Press, pp. 31–48.

—— (1995) *Saving Work: Feminist Practices of Theological Education*. Louisville, Ky: Westminster/John Knox Press.

Christ, Carol (1979a [1975]) 'Spiritual Quest and Women's Experience', in C. Christ, and J. Plaskow (eds), *Womanspirit Rising: A Feminist Reader in Religion*. San Francisco: Harper & Row, pp. 228–245.

—— (1979b) 'Why Women Need the Goddess', in C. Christ, and J. Plaskow (eds), *Womanspirit Rising: A Feminist Reader in Religion*. San Francisco: Harper & Row, pp. 273–284.

—— (1980), *Diving Deep and Surfacing: Women Writers on the Spiritual Quest*. Boston: Beacon Press.

Christ, Carol and Plaskow, Judith (eds) (1979a) *Womanspirit Rising: A Feminist Reader in Religion*. San Francisco: Harper & Row.

—— (1979b) 'Preface', in C. Christ and J. Plaskow (eds), *Womanspirit Rising: A Feminist Reader in Religion*. San Francisco: Harper & Row, pp. ix–xi.

—— (1979c) 'Introduction', in C. Christ and J. Plaskow (eds), *Womanspirit Rising: A Feminist Reader in Religion*. San Francisco: Harper & Row, pp. 1–18.

—— (1989) 'Introduction', in C. Christ and J. Plaskow (eds), *Weaving the Visions: New Patterns in Feminist Spirituality*. New York: Harper Collins, pp. 1–14.

Christian, Barbara (1980) *Black Women Novelists: The Development of a Tradition*. Westport, CT: Greenwood Press.

Cixous, Hélène (1979) *Vivre l'Orange/To Live the Orange*. Paris: des femmes.

—— (1981) *(With) Ou l'Art de l'innocence*. Paris: des femmes.

—— (1982) *Limonade tout etait si infini*. Paris: des femmes.

—— (1987) 'Her Presence through Writing', tr. D. Carpenter, *Literary Review*, 30, pp. 445–453.

—— (1988) 'Extreme Fidelity', tr. A. Liddle and S. Sellers, in S. Sellers (ed.), *Writing Differences: Readings from the Seminar of Hélène Cixous*. Milton Keynes: Open University Press, pp. 9–35.

—— (1989a [1975]) 'Sorties: Out and Out: Attacks/Ways Out/Forays', tr. A. Liddle, in C. Belsey and J. Moore (eds), *The Feminist Reader*. London: Macmillan, pp. 101–116.

—— (1989b) 'From the Scene of the Unconscious to the Scene of History', tr. D. Carpenter, in R. Cohen (ed.), *The Future of Literary Theory*. London: Routledge, pp. 1–18.

—— (1990a [1975]) 'The Laugh of the Medusa', in D. Walder (ed.), *Literature in the Modern World*. Oxford: Oxford University Press, pp. 318–326.

—— (1990b) *Reading with Clarice Lispector*, ed. and tr. V. Andermatt Conley. Hemel Hempstead: Harvester Wheatsheaf.

—— (1990c) 'Difficult Joys', in H. Wilcox, K. McWatters, A. Thompson and L.R. Williams (eds), *The Body and the Text: Hélène Cixous, Reading and Teaching*. Hemel Hempstead: Harvester Wheatsheaf, pp. 5–30.

—— (1991) *The Book of Promethea*, tr. B. Wing. London: University of Nebraska Press.

—— (1993) *Three Steps on the Ladder of Writing*. tr. S. Cornell and S. Sellers. New York: Columbia University Press.

—— (1994a) *Manna to the Mandelstams to the Mandelas*, tr. C. MacGillivray. Minneapolis: University of Minnesota Press.

—— (1994b [1974]) 'First Names of No One', in S. Sellers (ed.), *The Hélène Cixous Reader*. London: Routledge, pp. 27–33.

—— (1998a) *Firstdays of the Year*. Minneapolis: University of Minnesota Press.

—— (1998b) *Stigmata: Escaping Texts*. London: Routledge.

Cixous, Hélène with Clément, Catherine (1986) *The Newly Born Woman*, tr. B. Wing. Minneapolis: University of Minnesota Press.

Cixous, Hélène and Gruber, Mirielle (1997) *Hélène Cixous Rootprints: Memory and Life Writing*. London: Routledge.

Clément, Catherine and Kristeva, Julia (2001) *The Feminine and the Sacred*. New York: Columbia University Press.

Coakley, Sarah (1996) 'Kenosis and Subversion', in D. Hampson (ed.) *Swallowing a Fishbone: Feminist Theologians Debate Christianity*. London: SPCK, pp. 82–111.

Cohen, Ralph (ed.) (1989) *The Future of Literary Theory*. London: Routledge.

Conley, Vera A. (1991) *Helene Cixous: Writing the Feminine*. London: University of Nebraska Press.

Cone, James (1991) *The Spiritual and the Blues: An Interpretation*. New York: Orbis.

Cooey, Paula (1994) *Religious Imagination and the Body*. Oxford: Oxford University Press.

Crites, Stephen (1989 [1971]) 'The Narrative Quality of Experience', in S. Hauerwas and L. Gregory Jones (eds), *Why Narrative? Readings in Narrative Theology*. Eugene, Or: Wipf and Stock Publishers, pp. 65–88.

Crownfield, David (ed.) (1992a) *Body/Text in Julia Kristeva: Religion, Women and Psychoanalysis*. Albany: State University of New York Press.

—— (1992b) 'Pre-Text', in D. Crownfield (ed.), *Body/Text in Julia Kristeva: Religion, Women and Psychoanalysis*. Albany: State University of New York Press, pp. ix–xx.

—— (1992c) 'The Sublimation of Narcissism in Christian Love', in D. Crownfield (ed.), *Body/Text in Julia Kristeva: Religion, Women and Psychoanalysis*. Albany: State University of New York Press, pp. 57–63.

Culler, Jonathan (1984) 'A Critic against the Christians', *Times Literary Supplement* (23rd November 1984), pp. 1327–1328.

Cupitt, Don (1991) *What Is a Story?* London: SCM Press.

Curti, Linda (1998) *Female Stories, Female Bodies*. Basingstoke: Macmillan.

Daly, Mary (1986 [1973]) *Beyond God the Father*. London: The Women's Press.

Dawson, David (1995) *Literary Theory*. Minneapolis: Fortress Press.

Daggers, Jenny (2000) 'The Rehabilitation of Eve': British 'Christian Women's Theology 1972–1990, in S. Parsons (ed.) *Challenging Women's Orthodoxies in the Context of Faith*. Aldershot: Ashgate.

de Beauvoir, Simone (1972 [1949]) *The Second Sex*, tr. H.M. Parshley. London: Pan Books.

de Certeau, Michel (1992) *The Mystic Fable: Volume 1, the Sixteenth and Seventeenth Centuries*. Chicago: University of Chicago Press.

de Concini, Barbara (1994) 'Unspeakable Hungers and the Stratagems of Sacrifice', in D. Jasper and M. Ledbetter (eds), *In Good Company: Essays in Honour of Robert Detweiler*. Atlanta: Scholars Press, pp. 199–220.

de Lauretis, Teresa (1987) *Technologies of Gender: Essays on Theory, Film and Fiction.* London: Macmillan.

Derrida, Jacques (1978) *Writing and Difference.* London: Routledge, Kegan & Paul.

—— (1989) 'How to Avoid Speaking', in S. Budick and W. Iser (eds), *Languages of the Unsayable: The Play of Negativity in Literature and Literary Theory.* New York: Columbia University Press, pp. 3–70.

Detweiler, Robert (1985) 'What Is a Sacred Text?', *Semeia*, 31, pp. 213–230.

—— (1989) *Breaking the Fall: Religious Readings of Contemporary Fiction.* London: Macmillan.

—— (1990) 'Introduction', in R. Detweiler and W. Doty (eds), *The Daemonic Imagination.* Atlanta: Scholars Press.

Detweiler, Robert and Doty, William (eds) (1990) *The Daemonic Imagination.* Atlanta: Scholars Press.

Douglas, Mary (1966) *Purity and Danger: An Analysis of the Concepts of Pollution and Taboo.* London: Routledge.

Du Plessis, Rachel B. (1990) *The Pink Guitar: Writing as Feminist Practice.* London: Routledge.

Eaglestone, Robert (1997) *Ethical Criticism: Reading after Levinas.* Edinburgh: Edinburgh University Press.

Eagleton, Mary (ed.) (1991) *Feminist Literary Criticism.* London: Longman.

Eckardt, R. (1978) 'The Recantation of the Covenant', in A. H. Rosenfield and I. Greenberg (eds), *Confronting the Holocaust: The Impact of Elie Wiesel.* Bloomington: Indiana University Press.

Edelstein, Marilyn (1992) 'Metaphor, Meta-Narrative and Mater-Narrative in Kristeva's "Stabat Mater"', in D. Crownfield (ed.), *Body/Text in Julia Kristeva: Religion, Women and Psychoanalysis.* Albany: State University of New York Press, pp. 27–52.

—— (1993) 'Toward a Feminist Postmodern Polethique: Kristeva on Ethics and Politics', in K. Oliver (ed.), *Ethics, Politics and Difference in Julia Kristeva's Writing.* London: Routledge, pp. 196–214.

Edrich, Louise (1993) *Love Medicine.* New York: Harper Collins.

Elam, Diane (1994) *Feminism and Deconstruction.* London: Routledge.

Eliot, T.S. (1933) *The Use of Poetry and the Use of Criticism.* London: Faber & Faber.

—— (1939) *The Idea of a Christian Society.* London: Faber & Faber.

—— (1951 [1935]), 'Religion and Literature', in *Selected Essays.* London: Faber & Faber, pp. 388–401.

—— (1975) *Selected Prose of T.S. Eliot*, ed. F. Kermode. London: Faber & Faber.

Exum, Cheryl (1992) *Tragedy and Biblical Narrative: Arrows of the Almighty.* Cambridge: Cambridge University Press.

—— (1996) *Plotted, Shot and Painted: Cultural Representations of Biblical Women.* Sheffield: Sheffield Academic Press.

Farley, Wendy (1990) *Tragic Vision and Divine Compassion: A Contemporary Theodicy.* Louisville, Ky: Westminster/John Knox Press.

Felman, Shoshana (1992a) 'Education and Crisis, or the Vicissitudes of Teaching', in S. Felman and D. Laub, *Testimony: Crises of Witnessing in Literature, Psychoanalysis and History.* London: Routledge, pp. 1–56.

—— (1992b) 'After the Apocalypse: Paul de Man and the Fall to Silence', in S. Felman and D. Laub, *Testimony: Crises of Witnessing in Literature, Psychoanalysis and History.* London: Routledge, pp. 120–164.

Felski, Rita (1989) *Beyond Feminist Aesthetics: Feminist Literature and Social Change.* Cambridge, Ma:

Harvard University Press.

Feuerbach, Ludwig (1957 [1854]) *The Essence of Christianity*, tr. G. Eliot. New York: Harper & Row.

Fiddles, Paul S. (1991) *Freedom and Limit: A Dialogue between Literature and Christian Doctrine*. Houndmills: Macmillan.

Fish, Stanley (1994 [1980]) *Is there a Text in this Class? The Authority of Interpretive Communities*. Cambridge, Ma: Harvard University Press.

Ford, David (1981) *Barth and God's Story*. Frankfurt: Peter Lang.

Foucault, Michel (1965) *Madness and Civilisation: A History of Insanity in the Age of Reason*, tr. R. Howard. London: Routledge.

—— (1979 [1969]) 'What Is an Author?', tr. J.V. Harari, in J. Harari (ed.), *Textual Strategies: Perspectives in Post-Structuralist Criticism*. Ithaca, Ny: Cornell University Press.

—— (1981) *The History of Sexuality:Volume 1*. Harmondsworth: Penguin.

—— (1991) *Discipline and Punish*. Harmondsworth: Penguin.

Frei, Hans W. (1974) *The Eclipse of Biblical Narrative: A Study in Eighteenth and Nineteenth Century Hermeneutics*. New Haven:Yale University Press.

—— (1993) *Theology and Narrative: Selected Essays*, ed. G. Hunsinger and W.C. Placher. New York and Oxford: Oxford University Press.

Friedman, Susan S. and Du Plessis, Rachel B. (eds) (1993), *Signets: Reading H.D.* Madison: University of Wisconsin Press.

Fulkerson, Mary M. (1994) *Changing the Subject:Women's Discourses and Feminist Theology*. Minneapolis: Fortress Press.

Fuss, Diana (1989) *Essentially Speaking: Feminism, Nature and Difference*. London: Routledge.

Gallop, Jane (1988) *Thinking through the Body*. New York: Columbia University Press.

Gascoyne, David (1992) 'Introduction', in E. Smart, *The Collected Poems*. London: Paladin, pp. 4–17.

Georgaca, Eugenie (1995) 'Things Beyond Language? Lacan and Kristeva', unpublished research paper, postgraduate seminar series, Manchester Metropolitan University Discourse Unit.

Gilbert, Sandra and Gubar, Susan (1979) *The Madwoman in the Attic: The Woman Writer and the Nineteenth Century Literary Imagination*. New Haven:Yale University Press.

Goldberg, Michael (1991) *Theology and Narrative: A Critical Introduction*. Philadelphia: Trinity Press International.

Graff, Gerald (1992) *Beyond the Culture Wars: How Teaching the Conflicts Can Revitalize American Education*. London and New York: W.W. Norton.

Graham, Elaine (1995) *Making the Difference: Gender, Personhood and Theology*. London: Mowbray.

—— (1996) *Transforming Practice: Pastoral Theology in an Age of Uncertainty*. London: Mowbray.

—— (1997) '"Only Bodies Suffer": Embodiment, Representation and the Practice of Ethics', unpublished paper presented to John Rylands Research Institute, 1st October 1997.

Graham, Elaine and Walton, Heather (1991) 'A Walk on the Wild Side: A Critique of the Gospel and Our Culture', *Modern Churchman*, xxxiii:1, pp. 1–7.

Grant, Jacqueline (1989) *White Woman's Christ and Black Woman's Jesus: Feminist Christology and Womanist Responses*. Atlanta: Scholars Press.

Greene, Gayle (1991) *Changing the Story: Feminist Fiction and the Tradition*. Chicago: University of Chicago Press.

Grosz, Elizabeth (1989) *Sexual Subversions:Three French Feminists*. London: Allen & Unwin.

—— (1995) *Space, Time and Perversion: Essays on the Politics of Bodies.* London: Routledge.

Guberman, Ross (ed.) (1996) *Julia Kristeva: Interviews.* New York: Columbia University Press.

Gunew, Sneja (ed.) (1990) *Feminist Knowledge: Critique and Construct.* London: Routledge.

H.D. (1961 [1948]) *Helen in Egypt.* New York: New Directions.

—— (1983 [1944–46]) 'Trilogy', in *The Collected Poems, 1912–1944.* New York: New Directions, pp. 505–612.

—— (1984) *The Gift.* London: Virago.

—— (1988) 'Notes on Thought and Vision', in B. Kime Scott (ed.), *The Gender of Modernism.* Bloomington: Indiana University Press, pp. 93–109.

Hampson, Daphne (ed.) (1996) *Swallowing a Fishbone: Feminist Theologians Debate Christianity.* London: SPCK.

Handleman, Susan (1982) *The Slayers of Moses: The Emergence of Rabbinic Interpretation in Modern Literary Theory.* Albany: State University of New York Press.

Haraway, Donna (1991) 'A Cyborg Manifesto: Science, Technology and Socialist Feminism in the Late 20th Century', in D. Haraway, *Simeons, Cyborgs and Women: The Reinvention of Nature.* London: Free Association Books, pp. 149–182.

—— (1992 [1989]) *Primate Visions: Gender, Race and Nature in the World of Modern Science.* London: Verso.

Hartman, Geoffrey (1980) *Criticism in the Wilderness.* New Haven: Yale University Press.

Hauerwas, Stanley (1974) *Vision and Virtue.* Indiana: Fides Publishers.

—— (1981) *A Community of Character: Toward a Constructive Christian Ethic.* Notre Dame, In: University of Notre Dame Press.

—— (1994) *Dispatches from the Front: Theological Engagements with the Secular.* Durham, NC and London: Duke University Press.

—— (2001) *The Hauerwas Reader.* Durham, NC and London: Duke University Press.

Hauerwas, Stanley and L. Gregory Jones (eds) (1989) *Why Narrative? Readings in Narrative Theology.* Eugene, Or: Wipf and Stock Publishers.

Heaps, Denise A. (1994) 'The Inscription of "Feminine Jouissance" in Elizabeth Smart's *By Grand Central Station I Sat Down and Wept*', *Studies in Canadian Literature,* 19: 1, pp. 142–155.

Hermann, Alice (1989) *The Dialogic and Difference: 'An/Other Woman' in Virginia Woolf and Christa Wolf.* New York: Columbia University Press.

Hillesum, Etty (1999) *An Interrupted Life: The Diaries and Letters of Etty Hillesum 1941–43,* tr. A. Pomerans. London: Persephone Books.

Hodgson, Peter (2001) *Theology in the Fiction of George Eliot.* London: SCM Press.

Hogan, Linda (1995) *From Women's Experience to Feminist Theology.* Sheffield: Sheffield Academic Press.

Holloway, Karla (1992) *Moorings and Metaphors: Figures of Culture and Gender in Black Women's Literature.* New Brunswick: Rutgers University Press.

Hollywood, Amy (1993) 'Violence and Subjectivity: *Wuthering Heights*, Julia Kristeva and Feminist Theology', in S. M. Simonaitiz, S. St Ville and M. Kim (eds), *Transfigurations: Theology and the French Feminists.* Minneapolis: Fortress Press, pp. 81–108.

hooks, bel (1991) *Yearning: Race, Gender and Cultural Politics.* London: Turnaround.

Horne, Dee (1991) 'Elizabeth Smart's Novel-Journal', *Studies in Canadian Literature* 16: 2, pp. 128–146.

Humm, Maggie (1994) *A Readers Guide to Contemporary Feminist Literary Criticism.* London: Harvester Wheatsheaf.

Hurston, Zora Neale (1971 [1934]) *Jonah's Gourd Vine*. New York: Lippincot.

—— (1978 [1937]) *Their Eyes Were Watching God*. Urbana: University of Illinois Press.

Irigaray, Luce (1985a [1974]) *Speculum of the Other Woman*, tr. G. Gill. Ithaca: Cornell University Press.

—— (1985b [1977]) *This Sex Which Is Not One*, tr. C. Porter. Ithaca: Cornell University Press.

—— (1990) 'Women's Exile', in Deborah Cameron (ed.), *The Feminist Critique of Language: A Reader*. London: Routledge, pp. 80–96.

—— (1991a) *Marine Lover of Friedrich Nietzsche*, tr. G. Gill. New York: Columbia University Press.

—— (1991b) 'Questions to Emmanuel Levinas', in Margaret Whitford (ed.), *The Irigaray Reader*. Oxford: Blackwell, pp. 178–189.

—— (1992) *Elemental Passions*, tr. J. Collie and J. Still. London: Athlone Press.

—— (1993a [1984]) *An Ethics of Sexual Difference*, tr. C. Burke and G. Gill. London: The Athlone Press.

—— (1993b [1987]) *Sexes and Genealogies*, tr. G. Gill. New York: Columbia University Press.

—— (1993c [1990]) *je, tu, nous: Toward a Culture of Difference*. tr. A. Martin. London: Routledge.

—— (1996) *i love to you. Sketch for a Felicity Within History*. tr. A. Martin. London: Routledge.

Jantzen, Grace (1996) 'Sources of Religious Knowledge', *Literature and Theology*, 10:2, pp. 91–111.

Jantzen, Grace (1998) *Becoming Divine: Towards a Feminist Philosophy of Religion*. Manchester: Manchester University Press.

Jardine, Alice (1985) *Gynesis: Configurations of Women and Modernity*. Ithaca and London: Cornell University Press.

Jasper, Alison and Hunter, Alistair G. (eds) (1996) *Talking it Over: Perspectives on Women and Religion*. Glasgow: St Mungo Press.

Jasper, David (1992) 'The Study of Literature and Theology: Five Years On', *Literature and Theology*, 6: 1, pp. 1–10.

—— (ed.) (1993a) *Postmodernism, Literature and the Future of Theology*. Basingstoke: Macmillan.

—— (1993b) 'Introduction', in D. Jasper (ed.) *Postmodernism, Literature and the Future of Theology*. Basingstoke: Macmillan.

—— (1993c) *Rhetoric, Power and Community: An Exercise in Reserve*. London: Macmillan.

—— (1995) 'What Then, Is Reading the Bible', discussion paper, Liverpool, Engaging the Curriculum Programme.

—— (1996) 'The Death and Rebirth of Religious Language', *Religion and Literature*. 28: 1, pp. 5–17.

—— (1997) 'Theology and Postmodernity: Poetry, Apocalypse and the Future of God', in *Svensk teologisk Kvartalskrift*, vol. 73, pp. 97–103.

Jasper, David and Ledbetter, Mark (eds) (1994a) *In Good Company: Essays in Honour of Robert Detweiler*. Atlanta: Scholars Press.

Jasper, David and Ledbetter, Mark (1994b) 'Introduction', in D. Jasper and M. Ledbetter (eds), *In Good Company: Essays in Honour of Robert Detweiler*, Atlanta: Scholars Press, pp. 1–5.

Jonte-Pace, Diane (1992) 'Situating Kristeva Differently: Psychoanalytic Readings of Women and Religion', in D. Crownfield (ed.) (1992) *Body/Text in Julia Kristeva: Religion, Women and Psychoanalysis*. New York: State University of New York Press, pp. 1–22.

Kirmayer, Laurence (1996) 'Landscapes of Memory: Trauma, Narrative and Disassociation', in P. Antze and M. Lambek (eds), *Tense Past: Cultural Essays in Trauma and Memory.* London: Routledge, pp. 173–198.

Kime Scott, B. (ed.) (1988) *The Gender of Modernism.* Bloomington: Indiana University Press.

King, Nicola (2000) *Memory, Narrative, Identity: Remembering the Self.* Edinburgh: Edinburgh University Press.

Kojecky, Roger (1971) *T.S. Eliot's Social Criticism.* London: Faber & Faber.

Kristeva, Julia (1980) *Desire in Language: A Semiotic Approach to Literature and Art,* tr. L. Roudiez. Oxford: Blackwell.

—— (1982) *Powers of Horror: An Essay on Abjection,* tr. L. Roudiez. New York: Columbia University Press.

—— (1984) *Revolution in Poetic Language,* tr. M. Waller. New York: Columbia University Press.

—— (1986a [1974]) 'About Chinese Women', in T. Moi (ed.), *The Kristeva Reader.* Oxford: Blackwell, pp. 139–159.

—— (1986b [1977]) 'A New Type of Intellectual: The Dissident', in T. Moi (ed.), *The Kristeva Reader.* Oxford: Blackwell, pp. 292–302.

—— (1987a) *In the Beginning Was Love: Faith and Psychoanalysis,* tr. A. Goldhammer. New York: Columbia University Press.

—— (1987b) *Tales of Love,* tr. L. Roudiez. New York: Columbia University Press.

—— (1989) *Black Sun: Depression and Melancholia,* tr. L. Roudiez. New York : Columbia University Press.

—— (1991) *Strangers to Ourselves,* tr. L. Roudiez. New York: Columbia University Press.

—— (1993a) *The Old Man and the Wolves,* tr. B. Bray. New York: Columbia University Press.

—— (1993b) *Proust and the Sense of Time,* tr. S. Bann. London: Faber & Faber.

—— (1995) *New Maladies of the Soul,* tr. R. Guberman. New York: Columbia University Press.

—— (1996a [1985]) 'Psychoanalysis and Politics', interview with E. Kurtzwell, in R, Guberman (ed.), *Julia Kristeva: Interviews.* New York: Columbia University Press, pp. 146–161.

—— (1996b [1985]) 'A Conversation with Julia Kristeva', interview with I. Lipkovitz and A. Loselle, in R. Guberman (ed.), *Julia Kristeva: Interviews.* New York: Columbia University Press, pp. 18–34.

—— (1996c [1988]) 'Julia Kristeva in Person', France-Culture Broadcast', in R. Guberman (ed.), *Julia Kristeva: Interviews.* New York: Columbia University Press, pp. 3–11.

—— (1996d [1989]) 'Cultural Strangeness and the Subject in Crisis', interview with S. Clark and K. Hulley, in R. Guberman (ed.), *Julia Kristeva: Interviews.* New York: Columbia University Press, pp. 35–60.

—— (1996e [1990]) 'On the Samurai', in R. Guberman (ed.), *Julia Kristeva: Interviews.* New York: Columbia University Press, pp. 242–253.

—— (1996f [1993]) 'New Maladies of the Soul', interview with C. Franco, in R. Guberman (ed.), *Julia Kristeva: Interviews.* New York: Columbia University Press, pp. 85–91.

—— (1996g [1994]) 'Proust: A Search for Our Time', interview with A. Nicholas, in R. Guberman (ed.), *Julia Kristeva: Interviews.* New York: Columbia University Press, pp. 235–241.

—— (1996h) 'Julia Kristeva Speaks Out', interview with R. Guberman, in R. Guberman (ed.), *Julia Kristeva: Interviews.* New York: Columbia University Press, pp. 257–270.

—— (2000) *The Sense and Non-sense of Revolt,* tr. J. Herman. New York: Colombia University Press.

——— (2004) *Colette*, tr. J. Todd. New York: Colombia University Press.

Lacan, Jacques (1973 [1966]) *Écrits. A Selection*, tr. A. Sheriden. London: Tavistock Press.

Lauret, Maria (1994) *Liberating Literature: Feminist Fiction in America*. London, Routledge.

Lechte, John (1990) *Julia Kristeva*. London: Routledge.

Ledbetter, Mark (1997) 'Centre Shouts and Peripheral Echoes', in K. Tsuchiya (ed.) *Dissent and Marginality: Essays on the Border of Literature and Religion*. Basingstoke: Macmillan, pp. 115–125.

Le Doeuff (2002 [1980]) *The Philosophical Imaginary*, tr. C. Gordon. London and New York: Continuum.

Lessing, Doris (1990a) *Martha Quest*. London: Paladin.

——— (1990b) *A Proper Marriage*. London: Paladin.

——— (1990c) *A Ripple from the Storm*. London: Paladin.

——— (1990d) *Land Locked*. London: Paladin.

——— (1990e) *The Four-Gated City*. London Paladin.

Leonard, Diana and Adkins, Lisa (1996) *Sex in Question: French Materialist Feminisms*. London: Taylor and Francis.

Levinas, Emmanuel (1979) *Totality and Infinity: An Essay on Exteriority*, tr. A. Lingis. The Hague: Martinus Nijhoff.

——— (1985) *Ethics and Infinity: Conversations with Phillipe Nemo*. Pittsburgh: Duquesne University Press.

——— (1987) *Time and the Other*, tr. R. Cohen. Pittsburgh: Duquesne University Press.

Lindbeck, George (1984) *The Nature of Doctrine: Religion and Theology in a Postliberal Age*. Philadelphia: Westminster Press.

Lobdell, David (1990) 'Eros in the Age of Anxiety: Elizabeth Smart and Louise Maheux-Forcier', *Essays on Canadian Writing*, 40, pp. 57–79.

Lorde, Audre (1984) *Sister Outsider: Essays and Speeches by Audre Lorde*. New York: The Crossing Press.

Loughlin, Gerard (1996) *Telling God's Story: Bible, Church and Narrative Theology*. Cambridge: Cambridge University Press.

Lowe, Walter (1993) *Theology and Difference: The Wound of Reason*. Bloomington: Indiana University Press.

Lucy, Sean (1960) *T.S. Eliot and the Idea of Tradition*. London: Cohen and West.

McAfee, Noelle (1993) 'Abject Strangers: Towards an Ethic of Respect', in K. Oliver (ed.), *Ethics Politics and Difference in Julia Kristeva's Writing*. London: Routledge, pp. 116–134.

MacGillivray, Catherine (1994) 'Introduction: The Political Is – (and the) Poetical', in H. Cixous, *Manna to the Mandelstams to the Mandelas*, tr. C. MacGillivray. Minneapolis: University of Minnesota Press, pp. vii-ix.

MacIntyre, Alasdair (1981) *After Virtue: A Study in Moral Theory*, London: Duckworth.

Mc Nelly Kearns, Cleo (1993) 'Kristeva and Feminist Theology', in S. M. Simonaitiz, S. St Ville and M. Kim (eds) *Transfigurations: Theology and the French Feminists*. Minneapolis: Fortress Press, pp. 49–79.

Madsen, C., *et al* (1989) round table discussion: 'If God is God, She is Not Nice', *Journal of Feminist Studies in Religion* 5: 1, pp. 103–117.

Marks, Elaine and de Courtivron, Isobel (eds) (1980) *New French Feminisms: An Anthology*. Amherst: University of Massachusetts Press.

Martin, Alison (2000) *Luce Irigaray and the Question of the Divine*. Leeds: Maney Publishing.

May, Melanie (1995) *A Body Knows: A Theopoetics of Death and Resurrection*. New York: Continuum.

Mead, Margaret (1977 [1949]) *Male and Female: A Study of the Sexes in a Changing World*. Westport, Ct: Greenwood Press.

References

Miller, Nancy (1991) 'The Text's Heroine: A Feminist Critic and Her Fictions', in Mary Eagleton (ed.), *Feminist Literary Criticism*. London: Longman, pp. 61–69.

Mitchell, Juliet and Rose, Jillian (eds) (1982) *Feminine Sexuality*. Basingstoke: Macmillan.

Moi, Toril (1985) *Sexual/Textual Politics: Feminist Literary Theory*. London: Methuen.

—— (ed.) (1986) *The Kristeva Reader*. Oxford: Blackwell.

—— (ed.) (1987) *French Feminist Thought: A Reader*. Oxford: Blackwell.

-(1989) 'Feminist, Female, Feminine', in C. Belsey and J. Moore (eds), *The Feminist Reader*. London: Macmillan, pp. 117–132.

—— (1990) 'Feminism and Postmodernism: Recent Feminist Criticism in the United States', in T. Lovell (ed.), *British Feminist Thought*. Oxford: Blackwell, pp. 367–379.

Moltmann, Jürgen, *The Crucified God: The Cross of Christ as the Foundation and Criticism of Christian Theology*. London: SCM Press.

Moore, Stephen (1996) *God's Gym: Divine Male Bodies in the Bible*. London: Routledge.

Morrison, Toni (1970) *The Bluest Eye*. New York: Holst Rinehart and Winston.

—— (1987) *Beloved*. London: Chatto & Windus

Noddings, Nel (1989) *Women and Evil*. Berkeley: University of California Press.

Novak, Michael (1970) *The Experience of Nothingness*. New York: Harper & Row.

Nussbaum, Martha (1986) *The Fragility of Goodness: Luck and Ethics in Greek Tragedy*. Cambridge: Cambridge University Press.

—— (1990) *Loves Knowledge: Essays on Philosophy and Literature*. Oxford: Oxford University Press.

—— (1997) 'Narrative Emotions: Beckett's Genealogy of Love', in S. Hauerwas and L. Jones (eds), *Why Narrative, Or Readings in Narrative Theology*, Eugene, Or: Wipf and Stock Publishers, pp. 216–250.

Oliver, Kelly (ed.) (1993a) *Ethics, Politics and Difference in Julia Kristeva's Writing*. London: Routledge.

Oliver, Kelly (1993b) 'Introduction: Julia Kristeva's Outlaw Ethics', in K. Oliver (ed.), *Ethics Politics and Difference in Julia Kristeva's Writing*. London: Routledge, pp. 1–22.

—— (1993c) *Reading Kristeva: Unravelling the Double-Bind*. Bloomington: Indiana University Press.

Ostriker, Alicia (1965) *Vision and Verse in William Blake*. Madison: University of Wisconsin Press.

—— (1987) *Stealing the Language: The Emergence of Women's Poetry in America*. London: The Women's Press.

—— (1989) 'Entering the Tents', *Feminist Studies*, 15, pp. 541–548.

—— (1990a) 'No Rule of Procedure: H.D. and Open Poetics', in S. Stanford Friedman and R. Blau Du Plessis (eds), *Signets: Reading H.D.* Madison: University of Wisconsin Press, pp. 336–351.

—— (1990b) 'The Road of Excess: My William Blake', in G. W. Ruoff (ed.), *The Romantics and Us: Essays on Romantic and Modern Culture*. New Brunswick: Rutgers University Press, pp. 67–88.

—— (1993) *Feminist Revision and the Bible*. Oxford: Blackwell.

—— (1997) *The Nakedness of the Fathers: Biblical Visions and Revisions*. New Brunswick: Rutgers University Press.

Pacini, David (1994) 'Symbol Then and Now: Remembering and Connecting', in D. Jasper and M. Ledbetter (eds), *In Good Company: Essays in Honour of Robert Detweiler*. Atlanta: Scholars Press, pp. 121–150.

Parsons, Susan (ed.) (2002) *The Cambridge Companion to Feminist Theology*. Cambridge: Cambridge University Press.

Plaskow, Judith (1980), *Sex, Sin and Grace: Women's Experience and the Theologies of Reinhold Niebuhr and Paul Tillich*. Washington: University Press of America.

Plath, Sylvia (1981) 'Lady Lazarus', in *Sylvia Plath: Collected Poems*. London: Faber & Faber, pp. 244–247.

Ramazanoglu, Caroline and Holland, Janet (2000) 'Still Telling It Like It Is? Problems of Feminist Truth Claims', in S. Ahmed *et al*. (eds), *Transformations: Thinking Through Feminism*. London: Routledge.

Raphael, Melissa (1996) *Thealogy and Embodiment: The Post-Patriarchal Reconstruction of Female Sociality*. Sheffield: Sheffield Academic Press.

Raschke, Carl (1988) *Theological Thinking: An Inquiry*. Atlanta: Scholars Press.

Raschke, Carl (1992) 'Fire and Roses: Or the Problem of Postmodern Religious Thinking', in P. Berry and A. Wernick (eds), *Shadow of Spirit: Postmodernism and Religion*. London: Routledge, pp. 93–109.

Rich, Adrienne (1973) *Diving into the Wreck: Poems 1971–1972*. New York: W.W. Norton.

—— (1978a) *The Dream of a Common Language: Poems 1974–1977*. New York: W.W. Norton.

—— (1978b) 'When We Dead Awaken: Writing as Revision', in Adrienne Rich, *On Lies, Secrets and Silences: Selected Prose 1966–1978*. New York: W.W. Norton.

Ricoeur, Paul (1985) *Time and Narrative, Volume 2*. Chicago: University of Chicago Press.

(1991) *A Ricoeur Reader: Reflection and Imagination*, ed. M. Valde, Hemel Hempstead: Harvester Wheatsheaf.

Riley, Denise (1988) *Am I that Name? Feminism and the Category of Woman in History*. London: Macmillan.

Robinson, Marilynne (1991 [1980]) *Housekeeping*. London: Faber & Faber.

Roemer, Michael (1995) *Postmodernism and the Invalidation of Traditional Narrative*. Maryland: Rowman and Littlefield.

Rose, Jacqueline (1982) 'Introduction', in J. Mitchell and J. Rose (eds), *Feminine Sexuality*. Basingstoke: Macmillan, pp. 27–57.

Roudiez, Leon (1980) 'Introduction', in J. Kristeva, *Desire in Language: A Semiotic Approach to Literature and Art*, tr. L. Roudiez. Oxford: Blackwell.

Rowley, Hazel and Grosz, Elizabeth (1990) 'Psychoanalysis and Feminism', in S. Gunew (ed.), *Feminist Knowledge: Critique and Construct*. London: Routledge.

Ruether, Rosemary (1983) *Sexism and God Talk: Towards a Feminist Theology*. London: SCM Press.

Ruoff, Gene W. (ed.) (1990) *The Romantics and Us: Essays on Romantic and Modern Culture*. New Brunswick: Rutgers University Press.

Saiving, Valerie (1979 [1960]) 'The Human Situation: A Feminine View', in C. Christ and J. Plaskow (eds), *Womanspirit Rising: A Feminist Reading in Religion*. San Francisco: Harper & Row, pp. 25–42.

Salesne, Pierre (1988) 'Hélène Cixous' *Ou l'art de l'innocence*: The Path to You', in S. Sellers (ed.), *Writing Differences: Readings from the Seminar of Hélène Cixous*. Milton Keynes: Open University Press, pp. 113–126.

Sands, Kathleen (1994) *Escape from Paradise: Evil and Tragedy in Feminist Theology*. Minneapolis: Fortress Press.

Sellers, Susan (ed.) (1988) *Writing Differences: Readings from the Seminar of Hélène Cixous*. Milton Keynes: Open University Press, pp. 113–126

—— (ed.) (1994) *The Hélène Cixous Reader*. London: Routledge.

Shange, Ntozake (1986) *For colored girls who have considered suicide/when the rainbow is enuf*. New York: Bantam Books.

Shiach, Morag (1991) Hélène Cixous: A Politics of Writing. London: Routledge.

Showalter, Elaine (1977) A Literature of Their Own: From Charlotte Bronte to Doris Lessing, London: The Women's Press.

—— (1986) 'Feminist Criticism in the Wilderness', in E. Showalter (ed.) The New Feminist Criticism: Essays on Women, Literature and Theory. London: Virago, pp. 243–270.

Simonaitiz, S. M., St Ville, S. and Kim, M. (eds) (1993) Transfigurations: Theology and the French Feminists. Minneapolis: Fortress Press.

Smart, Elizabeth (1984) In the Meantime. Ottawa: Deneau Publishers.

—— (1991 [1978]) The Assumption of the Rogues and Rascals. London: Paladin.

—— (1992a [1945]) By Grand Central Station I Sat Down and Wept. London: Flamingo.

—— (1992b [1991]) Necessary Secrets, ed. Alice Van Wart. London: Paladin.

—— (1992c) The Collected Poems. London: Paladin.

—— (1994) On the Side of the Angels, ed. Alice Van Wart. London: Harper Collins.

Smith, Anna (1996) Julia Kristeva: Readings of Exile and Estrangement. London: Macmillan.

Soskice, Janet M. (1996) 'Turning the Symbols', in D. Hampson (ed.), Swallowing a Fishbone? Feminist Theologians Debate Christianity. London: SPCK, pp. 17–32.

Spender, Dale (1986) Mothers of the Novel: 100 Good Women Writers Before Jane Austen. London: Pandora.

Spivak, Gayatri (1987) In Other Worlds: Essays in Cultural Politics. London: Routledge.

Stanton, Donna (1986) 'A Critique of the Maternal Metaphor in Cixous, Irigaray and Kristeva', in N. Miller (ed.), Poetics of Gender. New York: Colombia University Press, pp. 157–182.

Steiner, George (1961) The Death of Tragedy. London: Faber & Faber.

Stockton, Katherine (1994) God between their Lips: Desire between Women in Irigaray, Bronte and Eliot. Stanford: Stanford University Press.

Sullivan, Rosemary (1992) By Heart: The Life of Elizabeth Smart. London: Flamingo.

Surin, Kenneth (1986) Theology and the Problem of Evil. Oxford: Blackwell.

Sykes, Stephen (1983) 'Theology', in A. Richardson and J. Bowden (eds), A New Dictionary of Christian Theology. London: SCM Press, pp. 566–567

Thistlethwaite, Susan (1989) Sex, Race and God: Christian Feminism in Black and White. London: Geoffrey Chapman.

van Heijst, Annelies (1995) Longing for the Fall. Kampen: Kok Pharos Publishing House.

Van Wart, Alice (1986) 'By Grand Central Station I Sat Down and Wept: The Novel as a Poem', Studies in Canadian Literature, 1:1, pp. 38–51.

Walder, D. (ed.) (1990) Literature in the Modern World. Oxford: Oxford University Press.

Walker, Alice (1976) Meridian. London: The Women's Press.

—— (1983) The Color Purple. London: The Women's Press.

—— (1984) In Search of Our Mother's Gardens: Womanist Prose. London: The Women's Press.

—— (1994) 'In the Name of the Father and of the Mother', Literature and Theology, 8:3, pp. 311–327.

Walker, Michelle B. (1998) Philosophy and the Maternal Body: Reading Silence. London: Routledge.

Walton, Heather (1994) 'Theology of Desire', Theology & Sexuality, 1 (September, 1994), pp. 31–41.

—— (2002) 'Extreme Faith in the Work of Elizabeth Smart and Luce Irigaray, Literature and Theology, 16:1, pp. 40–50.

Ward, Graham (1995) Barth, Derrida and the Language of Theology. Cambridge: Cambridge University Press.

—— (1996) *Theology and Contemporary Critical Theory*. London: Macmillan.

—— (ed.) (1997a) *The Postmodern God: A Theological Reader*. Oxford: Blackwell.

—— (1997b) 'Introduction, or, A Guide to Theological Thinking in Cyberspace', in G. Ward, *The Postmodern God: A Theological Reader*. Oxford: Blackwell, pp. xv–xlvii.

Waugh, Patricia (1989) *Feminine Fictions: Revisiting the Postmodern*. London: Routledge.

Weed, Elizabeth (1994) 'The Question of Style', in C. Burke, N. Schor and M. Whitford (eds) (1994) *Engaging with Irigaray: Feminist Philosophy and Modern European Thought*. New York: Columbia University Press, pp. 79–110.

Weedon, Chris (1987) *Feminist Practice and Poststructuralist Theory*. Oxford: Blackwell.

Weir, Alice (1993) 'Identification with the Divided Mother: Kristeva's Ambivalence' in K. Oliver (ed.), *Ethics Politics and Difference in Julia Kristeva's Writing*. London: Routledge, pp. 79–91.

Weisel, Elie (1960 [1958]) *Night*, tr. S. Radway. Harmondsworth: Penguin

Welch, Sharon (1985) *Communities of Resistance and Solidarity*. New York: Orbis.

—— (1990) *A Feminist Ethic of Risk*. Minneapolis: Fortress Press.

Whitford, Margaret (1991a) *Luce Irigaray: Philosophy in the Feminine*. London: Routledge.

—— (ed.) (1991b) *The Irigaray Reader*. Oxford: Blackwell.

—— (1994a) 'Reading Irigaray in the Nineties', in C. Burke, N. Schor and M. Whitford (eds) (1994) *Engaging with Irigaray: Feminist Philosophy and Modern European Thought*. New York: Columbia University Press, pp. 15–36.

—— (1994b) 'Irigaray, Utopia and the Death Drive', in C. Burke, N. Schor and M. Whitford (eds) (1994) *Engaging with Irigaray: Feminist Philosophy and Modern European Thought*. New York: Columbia University Press, pp. 379–400.

Wilcox, Helen, McWalters, K., Thompson, A. and Williams, L.R. (eds) (1990) *The Body and the Text: Hélène Cixous Reading and Teaching*. Hemel Hempstead: Harvester Wheatsheaf.

Williams, Simon and Bendelow, Gillian (1998) *The Lived Body: Sociological Themes: Embodied Issues*. London: Routledge.

Winquist, Charles (1986) *Epiphanies of Darkness: Deconstruction in Theology*. Philadelphia: Fortress Press.

—— (1989) 'Lacan and Theological Discourse', in E. Wyshograd, D. Crownfield and C. Raschke (eds), *Lacan and Theological Discourse*. New York: State University of New York Press, pp. 26–33.

—— (1995) *Desiring Theology*. Chicago: University of Chicago Press

Woodhead, Linda (1997) 'Spiritualising the Sacred: A Critique of Feminist Theology', *Modern Theology*, 13:2, pp. 191–212.

Woolf, Virginia (1971 [1931]) *The Waves*. Harmondsworth: Penguin.

—— (1976 [1925]) *Mrs Dalloway*. Harmondsworth: Penguin.

—— (1990 [1941]) *Between the Acts*. London: Grafton.

—— (1995 [1942]) 'Professions for Women', in *Killing the Angel in the House*. Harmondsworth: Penguin, pp. 1–9.

Wright, Nancy E. (1992/93) 'The Proper Lady and the Second World War in Elizabeth Smart's Narratives', *Essays on Canadian Writing* 48, pp. 1–19.

Wright, Terence (1988) *Theology and Literature*. Oxford: Blackwell.

Wyshograd, Edith, Crownfield, David. and Raschke, Carl (eds) (1989) *Lacan and Theological Discourse*. New York: State University of New York Press.

Yaeger, Patricia (1988) *Honey-Mad Women: Emancipatory Strategies in Women's Writing*. New York: Columbia University Press.

—— (1989) 'Toward a Female Sublime', in L. Kauffman (ed.), *Gender and Theory: Dialogues on Feminist Criticism*. Oxford: Blackwell, pp. 191–212.

Yorke, Liz (1991) *Impertinent Voices: Subversive Strategies in Contemporary Women's Poetry*. London: Routledge.

Young, James (1988) *Writing and Re-Writing the Holocaust*. Bloomington: Indiana University Press.

Young, Pamela D. (1990) *Feminist Theology/Christian Theology: In Search of a Method*. Minneapolis: Augsburg Fortress.

Ziarek, Ewa (1993) 'Kristeva and Levinas: Mourning, Ethics and the Feminine', in K. Oliver (ed.), *Ethics Politics and Difference in Julia Kristeva's Writing*. London: Routledge, pp. 62–78.

Index

Note: 'n.' after a page number indicates the number of a note on that page.

abjection 107–9, 112
Adams, R. 23
Adkins, L. 144
Adorno, T. 33
Akhmatova, A. 160
Albrecht, G. 23–4
Allende, I. 38
Allison, D. 73
alterity 5, 31, 34, 77, 105, 193
Anderson, P. S. 6, 53, 134, 144
Antze, P. 32
Aristotle 15
Arnold, M. 56
Atwood, M. 38, 45–6
Auden, W.H. 14
Auerbach, E. 20–3
Augustine 69
authorship 88–90, 106, 164, 171, 181–5

Bakhtin, M. 97, 105
Bal, M. 56–7
Barker, G. 176, 187
Barth, K. 20–1, 23, 69
Barthes, R. 88–9, 129
Battersby, C. 88
Bendelow, G. 86–7
Benjamin, W. 30
biblical narrative 20–2, 24
black women's writing 46, 61–7
Blake, W. 49, 53
Blanchot, M. 7, 33, 146
Bloom, H. 50

Boas, F. 63
body 35–6, 121, 138–40, 188
    see also poststructuralist theory; writing
    the body
Bons-Storm, R. 81
Braidotti, R. 19, 82–4, 137
Brophy, B. 181, 186
Bruce, G. 92
Burgher, M. 64
Butler, J. 83, 85–6, 88, 192

Calle-Gruber, M. 145
Cannon, K. 5, 59–68, 167
Caputo, J. 35
Cargas, H.J. 32
Carpentier, M. 37
Castle, B. 175
Cavarero, A. 29–30
Celan, P. 33–4, 82, 146, 160
Chanter, T. 127, 132, 140
Chopin, K. 43, 44
Chopp, R. 29, 78
Christ, C. 4, 11, 13, 29, 37, 39–47, 51,
    58, 60, 69, 80, 90, 167, 174, 193
    see also spiritual quest; women's
    experience
Christian, B. 65
Cixous, H. 7, 77, 82, 93, 144–66,
    168–72, 180, 184–5, 188
    see also writing the body
Clément, C. 121
Coakley, S. 44

Conley, V. A. 148
Cooey, P. 186
Cripps, Sir S. 175
Crites, S. 25–8, 30
Crownfield, D. 99
Cupitt, D. 3, 15, 27–8
Curti, L. 39, 79, 83, 85

Daggers, J. 2
Daly, M. 43, 44
Davies, C.B. 62
de Beauvoir, S. 10, 40, 42, 85
deconstruction 131
    feminine writing 148–9
de Courtivron, I. 77
de Lauretis, T. 84
Derrida, J. 18, 29, 34, 89, 104, 127, 129,
    131, 139, 147–8
Detweiler, R. 90–3
difference 67
differences between women 46, 60
domestic sublime 180, 183, 190–1
Douglas, M. 108, 135
Duras, M. 115

Eaglestone, R. 18
Eagleton, M. 79, 89
Edelstein, M. 109
Eliot, G. 28
Eliot, T.S. 15–16, 18
    view of women 16
Engels, F. 193
Erdrich, L. 73
ethics 23, 64–5

Felman, S. 32, 183
female divine 5, 34, 38, 56, 123
female sublime 38, 180, 192
    see also domestic sublime
feminine language 132
feminist religious reading 6, 93
Feuerbach, L. 138
Fiddes, P. 17–18
Foot, M. 175
Ford, D. 20
Foucault, M. 6, 70, 75–6, 88–9
Frei, H. 20–3, 25, 48
Freud, S. 54, 110, 127–8

Gascoyne, D. 181
Gatens, M. 87
Georgaca, E. 99–100, 104
Gilbert, S. 37, 50–2
goddess 38, 54
    see also female divine
Goldberg, M. 27
Graff, G. 81
Graham, E. 15, 80
Greene, G. 42
Greenspan, H. 32
Grosz, E. 39, 78
Gruber, M. 164–5
Gubar, S. 37, 50–2
gynocriticism 50, 51, 89

H.D. 37–8, 53–4, 57, 168, 171–2, 193
Hartman, G. 78
Hauerwas, S. 17, 23–5, 48
Heidegger, M. 139, 155
Hillesum, E. 82, 146, 160, 166
Hodgson, P. 28
Hogan, L. 83
Holbein, H. 114–15
Holland, J. 4, 80
Holocaust, the 30–4, 159–60, 162, 183
hooks, b. 61, 63
Horne, D. 178
Hugo, V. 120
Humm, M. 107
Hurston, Z. N. 5, 61, 63–5, 67

identity 26, 90
    black women's 62
    female 85–6
    Jewish 55, 152
imaginary 98–100, 133–6, 143, 145, 168
    see also mirror stage
interdisciplinary study 11–18
Irigaray, L. 6–7, 77, 93, 125–46, 168–73,
    181, 183–5
    see also imaginary; sensible transcen-
    dental

Jantzen, G. 6, 80, 126, 134–5, 144, 164
Jardine, A. 19, 77, 81–2, 84
Jasper, D. 35, 56, 76, 92–3
Jones, L. G. 17

Jonte-Pace, D. 100
Joyce, J. 147

Kafka, F. 165
Kahlo, F. 186
Kant, I. 69
Kelsey, D. 20
Kime Scott, B. 107
King, M. L. Jr 64
King, N. 81
Kirmayer, L. 32
Kojecky, R. 15–16
Kollontai, A. 10
Kristeva, J. 6–7, 77, 81–2, 93, 96–126,
    144–6, 168–72, 184–5, 192
  see also poetic language; semiotic; thetic
    break
Kundera, M. 25

Lacan, J. 81, 98–102, 109–10, 115, 128,
    134–5, 149–50
Lambek, M. 32
Laurence, D. H. 54
Lechte, J. 104, 110
Ledbetter, M. 34, 92–3
Le Doeff, M. 134
Leonard, D. 144
lesbian 73, 157
literature
  avant-garde 58, 104
  challenge to theology 122
  complementarity of literature and
    theology 16–18, 49, 142
  as dialogical 97–8, 181
  gendering of 19, 31, 33, 60, 121
  journals 178–9
  literary form 14, 122–3, 171, 177
  realism 21–2, 25, 48, 90, 170
  see also poetic language; tragedy
Lessing, D. 42–3, 45, 174
Levinas, E. 81, 129, 140
Lindbeck, G. 20–1, 23
Lispector, C. 146, 153–6, 159, 165
logocentrism 36
Lorde, A. 61
Loughlin, G. 21
Lowe, W. 81
Lyotard, J.-F. 81, 92

MacGillivray, C. 158, 161
MacIntyre, A. 13, 23
Maitland, S. 38
male authors 8
Mandela, N. 158–9
Mandela, Z. 158–9
Mandelstam, N. 158–9
Mandelstam, O. 158–9
Maritain, J. 16
Marks, E. 33, 77
Martin, A. 77
Mead, M. 40–2
Midrash 55
Mill, J.S. 50
Miller, N. 88
mirror stage 99
Mitchell, J. 100
Moi, T. 77, 84, 144
Moore, S. 136
morphology 87, 135–6, 172
Morrison, T. 38, 61, 66, 72

narrative 20–30
  biblical 20–2, 24
  identity 28–30
narrativity 29
Nietzsche, F. 129
Nin, A. 51
Novak, M. 43
Nussbaum, M. 17–18

Oliver, K. 101, 104
Ostriker, A. 4, 39, 48–56, 58, 60, 77, 167,
    172

Paalen, A. 176–7, 191
Paalen, W. 176, 186
Pacini, D. 34
palimpsest 54, 57
Parsons, S. 13
phallus 7
philosophy 129–31
  relation with literature 17–18, 31n.31
  relation with theology 3, 15, 28, 31,
    169
Plaskow, J. 11, 13, 40–2, 44, 46–7, 80,
    174
Plath, S. 183

Plato 15, 127–8, 138
poesis 35, 81
poetic language 103–4
poststructuralist theory 5
    body as construct 86–8
    death of the author 88–90
    feminist critique 67–8, 77–90
    politics 83–6
    woman as metaphor 19, 84
Pound, E. 53–4
Proust, M. 119–20

racism 61, 66
Ramazanoglu, C. 4, 80
Raphael, M. 87
Raschke, C. 34
religious reading 92–3
revision 51–7
Rich, A. 45, 51–2, 54, 56–7
Ricoeur, P. 24, 28, 169
Riley, D. 79
Roberts, M. 38
Robinson, M. 73
Roemer, M. 18, 25, 31
Rose, J. 100
Rowley, H. 39, 78
Ruether, R. 69, 80, 91, 141

sacred texts 90–3
Saiving, V. 4, 41–2, 80
Salesne, P. 156
Sands, K. 5, 47–8, 59, 67–76, 167
semiotic 100–1, 103, 123–5
sensible transcendental 137–42
Shange, N. 46
Showalter, E. 50, 52, 78
Smart, E. 8, 38, 174–93
Smith, A. 123
Soskice, J. M. 13
Spender, D. 14
spiritual quest 43–6
Spivak, G. 89, 148
Stockton, K. 134, 136–7, 173
surrealism 186
Sykes, S.W. 12
symbolic order 98–102, 131

Tan, A. 38
testimony 31–4, 82
theology
    canonical narrative 3, 20–5
    constructive narrative 3, 25–30
    definition 13
thetic break 102–3, 105
Thistlethwaite, S. 66–8, 87
Thurman, H. 64
Tillich, P. 69
tragedy 69–71, 75–6
Travers, P. L. 37
Trollope, H. 23–4

van Heijst, A. 46, 48, 83, 91
Van Wart, A. 177
Varda, J. 176, 189
Virgin Mary 54, 111–13

Walker, A. 11, 61, 63, 65–6
Walker, M. B. 145, 162, 164
Walton, H. 136, 182, 193
Ward, G. 145
Weed, E. 129
Weedon, C. 89–90
Weir, A. 110, 112
Weisel, E. 32
Welch, S. 70
Whitford, M. 129, 131, 136
Williams, S. 61, 86–7
Winterson, J. 38
Wollstonecraft, M. 10
womanism 61–2
Womanspirit Rising 40, 47
women's experience 41–2, 46, 60, 79–83
Woodhead, L. 80
Woolf, V. 10, 37, 85, 123, 134, 193
Wright, N. 178
Wright, T. 13–14, 16, 18
writing the body 148–51, 184

Yaeger, P. 38, 134, 172, 180, 192
Yorke, L. 33, 55
Young, P. 80

Ziarek, E. 116